222
Si 3  Silver, Daniel Jeremy.
        Images of Moses.

# Images of Moses

# IMAGES OF
# MOSES

Daniel Jeremy Silver

Basic Books, Inc., Publishers

NEW YORK

Library of Congress Cataloging in Publication Data

Silver, Daniel Jeremy.
  Images of Moses.

  Includes index.
  1. Moses (Biblical leader)   2. Bible.   O.T. Penta-
teuch)—Criticism, interpretation, etc.—History
I.   Title.
BS580.M6S483   1982        222'.10924        82-72386
ISBN 0-465-03201-X

DESIGNED BY VINCENT TORRE
10 9 8 7 6 5 4 3 2 1

To

Jonathan, Michael, and Sarah,

who have taught me

that each generation

should see the world

with its own eyes

# Contents

# Introduction

I HAVE LONG BEEN of the opinion that the continuities within any religious tradition are formal and institutional rather than doctrinal. Words are empty vessels into which successive generations of believers pour the wine of their convictions. It has long been recognized that distinguishable cultural traditions—the Chinese, the Indian, the Mesopotamian, the Greek—exist and that within each tradition significant political, social, and attitudinal changes have occurred. We live with change and accept that all that is alive changes, with one exception—religion. If the religious tradition of a culture has died—Greek paganism, for example—we acknowledge its organic nature, but if it has survived, as have Judaism and Christianity, we tend to see it as a cultural constant. This is particularly true in the West where the major religions claim authority on the basis of revelation and base themselves on a scripture which imposes forms of worship, thought, and language on the community. Believers forget that though they read from an old scripture and feel bound to its instructions, they inevitably read into it their feelings and needs and shape its instructions to fit current perceptions of what is right and proper. Religious traditions testify to the same process of dynamic adaptation and organic change that affects other elements in the culture of which they are a part and for the same reasons.

The tendency to deny change derives from a basic need for reassurance. Life is brief. Our experiences are confusing. Much of what constitutes religion satisfies the human need to create a sense of order and stability in the midst of flux. If we are not conscious at the moment of this need, evidence of its power is all about us. The land is full of men and women whose fear of change is so great that they have politicized the need for stability and are working to force the schools to promote and validate their view that the Bible is literally true. Such emotional needs are understandable, but it would be disastrous for our society to surrender its critical spirit.

This essay is a modest attempt to point up the changes which have taken place within one religious tradition—Judaism—as they relate to one figure—Moses—who is central to it. As the title, *Images of Moses*, suggests, I have tried to sketch the various portraits of Moses which were etched in the hearts and minds of those who formed the Jewish community during the several cultural epochs Jews have lived through and to show why these images are significantly different from each other.

My aim throughout has been to be synthetic and analytic rather than encyclopedic. Those who wish to know more of the details of Moses' many lives can consult such magisterial compendia as Louis Ginsberg's *Legends of the Jews*. Arguments can be made against my admittedly arbitrary choice of material and selection of cultural milieus. I could have made other choices, but they would not have changed my basic argument: that the religious heroes of the past, like the concepts and ceremonies consecrated in Scripture, become vessels into which a tradition pours new values and ideas as they come to seem appropriate.

I chose Moses as the focus of this essay for a number of reasons. Because the Torah describes him as the prophet-messenger of the revelation, the religious leadership always had to handle the image of Moses with care. I was not likely to find myself dealing with images which were purely fanciful. Then, too, since the Torah has been read publicly each week in the synagogue for two thousand years, and since four-fifths of the Torah deals with narratives in which Moses is involved or with Instructions which he mediated, I would be dealing with a figure who had been familiar to all Jews at all times.

The place of heroes and hero worship has long intrigued me. As an educator I am conscious of the universal need for patterning figures. Children think literally long before they are able to think conceptually. They recognize Moses before they understand the Ten Commandments. It was inevitable that parents and teachers present Moses as a hero, and their stories, classes, and sermons reveal a good bit of their image(s) of heroes. It was also inevitable that others would disapprove of the use of Moses as a model. The rabbinic tradition denies perfection to any human being. God alone is to be the model for the development of ethical attributes.

In working out the problem I set for myself, I discovered how greatly preconceptions of Moses as liberator, lawgiver, and leader had skewed my understanding of the Torah. I had looked for and found an imposing and vital man. Learning to read the Torah for what it says rather than for what I expected it to say was an exciting task and one full of surprises. I expected a larger-than-life Moses, but I discovered that, contrary to the usual pattern of legendary embellishment, the editors of the Torah had, out of religious commitment, deliberately diminished Moses' role.

The Torah is not a contemporary account of the original Moses but an account in which the events and personalities described are shaped by the later and special interests of Israelite society and religious leaders. Its image of Moses is particularly arresting because it reduces rather than enlarges the role of the community's revered founder and so challenges the popular theory that such narratives grow by a process of accretion as legends and stories embellish an original event.

During the last presidential campaign, while preparing a lecture on the American political system, I reread Theodore White's several books on the subject, each titled *The Making of the President*. Probably because I was also working on an article analyzing a Hellenistic story about Moses as commander-in-chief of Egypt's armed forces, I began to think about the art of image making and how it was practiced in ages past, particularly how it had affected the image of Moses.

Like most readers, I had tended to accept the numerous stories and legends which surround a classic figure like Moses as individual pieces, more or less interesting as examples of an individual storyteller's imagination or a preacher's concerns and skill. Now I began to wonder if broader patterns could be discovered within this scattered and diffuse material, whether in fact one could distill from the stories created at particular times and places images of Moses which would accurately reflect each particular community's values and preconceptions. Several years and much reading and thinking later, I am convinced that this is possible.

I am also convinced the analogy with political hucksters must not be pressed too far; they practice a manipulative art, their aim to make a candidate's words conform to what is perceived as the general will and his presence conform to patterns which the public generally approves. The various images of Moses were shaped disingenuously. Moses was not consciously made over in an image which would deliberately serve a particular interest group. Each new Moses came into being as a new cultural period expressed in its stories and sermons another version of the leader, the Moses, it was prepared to see. Experience and conventional wisdom, the psychological mechanisms we call conditioning and projection, played a major role in the making of each portrait. In each age the pious instinctively assumed that the man and his message affirmed their way of life and theology.

New images for presidential candidates must be contrived every four years. New images of Moses are not only uncontrived but appear far less frequently or regularly. They appear when Jewish life undergoes a period of cultural transformation, and each new image reveals what is special about that period's understanding of the Jewish tradition and of itself.

I found myself embarked on what proved to be a fascinating journey, one I hope you will enjoy taking with me. Although along the way I came across many unexpected and intriguing Moses stories, I focused on the composite image of the founder-prophet which underlies the stories of a particular age rather than on the individual narratives. My attempt to define changes and to evaluate differences be-

# Introduction

tween the several presentations of Moses was helped im-
measurably by the centrality of the Torah in Jewish life.
Each generation of Jews, at least for the last twenty-three or
twenty-four hundred years, has studied the same Torah and
been thoroughly conversant with its text. Each generation
has not only absorbed its predecessors' various traditions but
could and did go back to a fixed sacred text and read into it,
and out of it, its own preconceptions. Thus each cultural period had to shape its portrait around the same incidents and
narratives, and the Moses story never became unrecogniz-
able.

I am grateful to the Oxford Centre for Postgraduate Hebrew Studies for an appointment as a resident fellow during
the Michaelmas term, 1979, which allowed me to put aside
the pressures of congregational life and work on this study
without interruption. Dr. David Patterson and his staff were
generous of their time and facilities. The Leo Baeck College
in London gave me the opportunity to discuss many of these
ideas with a group of rabbinical students in an exciting sem-
inar; these discussions helped to sharpen my own thinking
and shape my work. The Temple in Cleveland has always
been understanding of a rabbi who spends a considerable
amount of time in the library and has provided the secretar-
ial help this work required. Several preparatory studies were
published in the *Jewish Quarterly Review* and *The Journal
of Jewish Law,* and though the material has been completely
revised, the chance to publish those articles and to receive
comments from friends and colleagues has been of immea-
surable assistance.

Some people think only with pen in hand. I think best
with a typewritten sheet before me, so I am grateful to
Marie Pluth and Lillian Abramovitz for their long hours de-

# Introduction

ciphering my scrawl and preparing for me the clean copy which I would again fill with more illegible scrawl. The idea for this work was first discussed with my wife, Adele, during long walks in the English countryside. She has been throughout not only a helpmate but my chief editor and critic. The work would have been more delayed than it was, had it not been for her encouragement, effort, and love.

I know that the basic thesis of this book will ruffle many feathers, but I hope that even those who disagree with my basic thesis will find the images of Moses presented here worth looking at afresh.

DANIEL JEREMY SILVER

CHAPTER

**1**

# The
# Diminished Hero

**F**OR MORE THAN two centuries, ever since many Jews and Christians began to realize that the Bible could not be accepted as a factual history on its own authority, researchers have been seeking evidence which would enable us to judge the accuracy of the Biblical narrative. The results, so far, are mixed. We have gained a new appreciation of the fidelity with which oral traditions were passed from generation to generation. Many details of the patriarchal periods and later can now be substantiated. But no event described in the Torah and no persons named there have been specifically identified. Aside from the Biblical manuscript itself, there is no contemporary or near-contemporary reference to Moses or to an escape of Hebrew slaves from Egypt. There is a good deal of archeological evidence of Israelite penetration into Canaan beginning in the thirteenth century B.C.E.; many cities were destroyed and crudely rebuilt about that time. But the Biblical report of the conquest of Canaan by Joshua and his successors cannot be confirmed.

We have learned that the Biblical account of Moses' life and activities is set and furnished appropriately for events described as happening in West Asia and Egypt during the fourteenth and thirteenth centuries B.C.E. We now know that other peoples of that time and general area told of a future leader who came to them as a child, borne on a sacred river. We know that many of the laws of Israel's neighbors were similar in intent, and even in form, to the Torah's regulations. We know that during the period of Hyksos domination of Egypt (ca. 1750–1550 B.C.E.), these alien lords recruited for their bureaucracy talented West Asians of other nations whose descendants were killed or enslaved when the Hyksos pharaohs were overthrown by a native dynasty. We know that Ramesses II was a Napoleonic builder who dotted Egypt with palaces, temples, and cities bearing his name and that he conscripted massive drafts of Asian and African slaves to build them. But—and this is the heart of the matter—the gap remains, as great as ever, between what the Bible reports of Moses and what we can corroborate on the basis of outside information. No one can write with absolute confidence any sentence that begins, "Moses did this," or "Moses taught that."

Any biography of Moses, however learned, remains an imaginative exercise which reveals more of the writer's conceptions than of the actual life history of Israel's most famous hero. In 1924 Rudolf Kittel of Leipzig University, a giant among Bible scholars, enjoyed popular success with his book, *Great Men and Movements in Israel*, in which he summarized for a general audience the course of Biblical history as it appeared after a century of critical research.

# The Diminished Hero

Kittel wrote with the authority of academic scholarship, so a reader is surprised to come across, in the course of his presentation of Moses, a physical and psychological description of a man whose very existence cannot be proved:

> ... the tall and beautiful frame, the well-poised head, the sharp penetrating eye of the leader, of the victor over man and obstacles, the firm hand of the ruler ever alert and faithful to his duty ... the keen insight of the man who found God and dwelt in Him, the insight which penetrated even the divine being and saw deeply into the heart of man, we may still recognize, despite the faded colors and retouching of the ages [Kittel 19–20].

This description is pure invention. It goes far beyond the Biblical report which does not contain a single line of physical description. The Torah does not indicate whether Moses was short or tall, thin or fat, dark-skinned or fair, whether he had what might be considered a commanding presence. Kittel ascribes to Moses his preconceptions of what a hero should look like; and his imagined hero, hence the Moses he imagines, is the noble and superior leader whom he and many other Germans of the time prayed would arise to redeem the fatherland from what they considered the disgrace of Versailles and the democratic sickness of the Weimar Republic.

The same imaginative process is at work in illustrated books of Bible stories which doting grandparents give to unsuspecting six-year-olds and in the Hollywood films that portray Moses as tall, white, well muscled, handsome. I have yet to see any children's book or any popular movie depict Moses as a small, dark, hollow-chested man, though, given his stock and background, Moses would most likely have inherited such a body type. Sunday School teachers, casting directors, certainly grandparents, can be forgiven; scholars should know better.

The Bible provides scant description of any of its major figures. The twentieth century has a highly developed sense of self, perhaps an overdeveloped one. The Hebrews and most peoples of the second millennium B.C.E. did not. Most surviving statues are not portraits but highly stylized versions of what a person of a particular rank or position should ideally look like. Had Moses been sculpted by a contemporary—perhaps by Bezalel, the master craftsman whom, the Bible tells us, Moses commissioned to prepare the sacred instruments of the shrine—the resulting piece would in all probability have been an idealized presentation of a leader, not unlike statues of some Old Kingdom pharaohs or nobles of Lagash, Sumer, and Akkad which can be seen today in art museums. Bezalel's Moses would carry the accepted signs of rank and authority, but the face would bear no distinguishing individual character; only if the statue were inscribed would we know that it represented Moses rather than some other West Asian leader.

Though the second millennium B.C.E. was a time when noblemen were eager to commemorate themselves in their palaces, shrines, and mausoleums, so far as we know no Israelite drew or carved an image of Moses. The leaders of ancient Israel, even Israel's most worldly kings, seem not to have sought their immortality through images, even idealized ones. Scripture rarely describes a person's physical attributes unless a particular feature plays a significant role in a Biblical episode: for example, Goliath's size or Bathsheba's beauty. The Israelite eye and spirit were relatively indifferent to all those marks of individuality of which we are so conscious. Because the survival of any seminomadic clan depends on every member's unconditional loyalty to the group and complete obedience to the decisions of the tribal chief, individuality is a danger rather than a mark of distinction to be prized. A rebel, an individualist, is a stray, a danger to himself and to others.

Modern man leaves home to make his fortune. Biblical man's fortune depended on staying with his own. We travel easily. He traveled only if accompanied by a strong and trusted retinue. Certainly there were wanderers. Jacob fled Beer-sheba after he tricked Esau. Moses fled Egypt after he killed the Egyptian overseer. But the operative word here is *fled*. These were not carefree journeys but dangerous ones, taken under duress; and the wanderer quickly seeks new ties, Jacob with an uncle in Syria, Moses by adoption into Jethro's tribe. From birth an Israelite lived within a formalized network of blood ties and tribal obligations which determined his rank, his work, his responsibilities, his faith, and his fate. In life, as in death, it was important that one be "gathered to his fathers."

This cast of mind is evident in the Torah law that denounces the rebellious son who disobeys a parent and permits such a rebel, with or without a cause, to be put to death if he persists in his defiance (Deut. 21:18). The law, which can be paralleled in other ancient West Asian law codes, describes the action of an adult son who is a mature married man whose disobedience is a deliberate challenge to the authority of parent and clan because it threatens to remove from that authority not only himself but also his wives, children, cattle, and slaves. In a society where each clan had to be self-sufficient, such an act so endangered the ability of the rest to survive that it was treated as a capital offense.

The point here is that the Bible tells us just what it be-

lieves we need to know about Moses: his geneology. Were I
to write a biography of Winston Churchill I doubt that my
opening sentence would read, "A certain Englishman married a certain American woman." Yet, that is precisely the
way the Torah opens the Moses story: "A certain man of the
house of Levi went and married a Levite woman" (Exod.
2:1). The Bible tells us nothing of Moses' personal characteristics, but it tells us that his father's name was Amram;
that his grandfather was Kohath who was a son of Jacob's
son Levi (Exod. 6:16–19; 1 Chron. 4:1–3); that his mother's
name was Jochebed; that Aaron and Miriam were his natural brother and sister; that he married both a Cushite
woman and a certain Zipporah, daughter of Jethro, a priest
of Midian who subsequently adopted him into his tribe
(Exod. 3:1). Moses' features are veiled but his geneology
and connections are clear and exact.

An Israelite listener did not really care whether Moses
was heavy footed or lithe, tall or black-haired; such details
did not play as significant a role in anyone's fate as did his
place in his society. The matter of consequence was that
Moses belonged to the tribe of Levi. Tribesmen had special
duties to each other, and the future of each member depended on the tribe's collective strength. It was the Levites
who rallied to Moses' side when the camp got out of control
and danced wildly before the infamous Golden Calf (Exod.
32:25 ff). Because tribal loyalties and duties were so crucial,
no feud was more bitter than one between tribesmen es-
tranged over a question of precedence or possession. Israelite
listeners would have nodded knowingly when they learned
that the severest challenge to Moses' authority came from a
fellow Levite, Korah, and that the precipitating issue was a
question of precedence—which Levite, Korah or Aaron,

Moses' brother, should be appointed to the priesthood (Num. 16). Understanding that the family of a disgraced man shared his fate, they would have felt no surprise at the Biblical report that the wives and children of the Levites who rebelled against Moses were put to death along with the conspirators. They would also have understood that Moses married Zipporah not for love but for the privilege of being adopted into Jethro's tribe; only in this way could he have remained in Midian. In Biblical times geneology determined social place, political fate, and vocation; so, not surprisingly, these are the identifications which were carefully presented. No feature of Scripture more swiftly tires modern readers than the seemingly endless geneologies, but few features of Scripture meant more to the original audience.

The brief comment that Moses' mother saw "how beautiful he was" (Exod. 2:2) does not invalidate my observation of the Bible's pervasive indifference to the physical details of Moses' person. The comment conveys no factual information. What mother would not praise her child? Nor does the well-known "fact" that Moses suffered from a speech impediment upset my argument. It is no fact at all. The image of a tongue-tied or stammering Moses, though it appears frequently in Jewish folklore, is a creation of interpreters who turned a text to their own purposes by reading more into it than is actually there.

The text in question appears in the Exodus report of God's conversation with Moses at the Burning Bush. God informs Moses of His decision to send him to Egypt. Moses pleads that he is unworthy of the assignment: "Who am I that I should go to Pharaoh . . ." (Exod. 3:11). In so declaring his inadequacy, Moses is the quintessential Near Eastern courtier who, as a matter of good form, makes exaggerated formal expressions of unworthiness when asked to assume an office in order to insure that the king recognize his humility and loyalty and appropriately reward him. Moses elaborates his courtesies and demurrers with typical Oriental exaggeration and elegance: "Please, O Lord, I have never been a man of words, either in times past or now. . . . I am slow of speech and slow of tongue" (Exod. 4:10). It is possible, but not wise, to take this language literally and declare Moses a stammerer or tongue-tied, but in context the statements indicate only that Moses lacked experience as a diplomat or public orator. God's response makes the meaning clear. God does not say, "I will heal your infirmity" but "I will be with you as you speak and will instruct you what to say" (Exod. 4:11).

God did not choose a tongue-tied prophet to be His spokesman and mediator of His revelation. Aside from these entirely conventional expressions of unworthiness, the narratives about Moses assume that he was a consummate orator. The Torah repeatedly describes Moses speaking easily and effectively to Pharaoh, to the Hebrew chiefs, and to the entire nation. Time and again God commands Moses, "Tell the Israelites," or "Thus shall you say to the Israelites," with full confidence that Moses will repeat the law so clearly that everyone will hear and understand. The notion of a speech impediment might never have been conceived had not an editor appended to the commissioning scene a sentence in which God "angrily" tells Moses that his brother Aaron, a skilled diplomat, would act as his spokesman (Exod. 4:14). But that is not what happens. Except for one occasion before the tribal council, Moses acts as his own spokesman (Exod. 4:30). Modern commentators have recognized both references as priestly interpolations, designed to enhance the rank and reputation of Aaron, the first priest, father to them all.

The Torah veils more than Moses' physical attributes. It is equally silent about his motives. It is important to notice what we are not told about Moses. We are told nothing of his childhood or adolescence, his education, his role in the palace hierarchy, or, indeed, if he lived in the palace. From his young manhood there is one episode—we are told that he killed an Egyptian taskmaster, but we are not told why. Was he enraged by the official's brutal beating of a Hebrew slave? Did he suddenly feel the tug of kinship? Are we to interpret this episode as an act of identification with his people? Did Moses simply act on impulse?

We are told nothing of the nature or quality of Moses' relationships with his parents, Pharaoh's daughter, his wives, or his sons. We are not privy to any of Moses' feelings when he descends from Mount Sinai after forty days and nights. Was he exalted, spent, transformed? We are offered only a description of the afterglow of the experience, "the skin of his face was radiant" (Exod. 34:29), something that could be noticed by others. Growth, illness, accident, age, and the ordinary changes of life are not part of Moses' story. He is a three-month-old infant in one sentence and a full-grown adult in the next. At the end of his life, we are told, "Moses was a hundred and twenty years old when he died, his eyes were undimmed and his vigor unabated" (Deut. 34:7). I have always felt that one of the reasons that the Torah continues to fascinate is that the absence of detail and explanation allows the reader's imagination relatively free rein. The stories are never cramped. As so often, here is a situation where less is better.

The Torah editors seem even to have lost, or to have deliberately cut off, most of Moses' name. Though we call him Moses and capitalize the *M*, Moses is not a proper name but a conventional Egyptian name element. The Torah indicates that the princess who found the child floating on the Nile in his watertight cradle named him. Having, in effect, given him life she was entitled by ancient custom to give the baby the name that would suggest his destiny. According to the text she called the child Moses, explaining, "I drew him out of the water" (Exod. 2:10). The etymology behind this explanation is a rough identity of sound between the Hebrew verb *mashah*, which means "to draw out," and *Moshe*, which suggests the miracle of Moses' early escape, his special relationship to God, and God's redemptive power.

To examine Moses' name more cautiously is to recognize that however attractive this derivation, it cannot be defended. First, an Egyptian princess would not have known enough Hebrew, then a little-known West Asian dialect, one among many, to make such a subtle play on words. Furthermore, the suggested etymology will not bear critical examination. There is no transition in Hebrew from *mashah* to *moshe* because the language is not constructed that way. About a century ago, linguists recognized that, despite the Torah's explanation, Moses' name is not of Hebrew derivation at all but is a transliteration into Hebrew of a formal Egyptian name element which means "son of" or "born of," as in the royal names Thutmose (son of Thoth) and Ramesses (son of Ra). Moses, then, is a nonspecific name element, cut away from precisely the kind of theophoric name that an Egyptian princess would have given to her foundling. Who performed this surgery? Conservative interpreters suggest that Moses himself eliminated the reference to an Egyptian God when YHVH came into his life. It is more likely that Moses' original name was chopped off by Israel's early religious leaders who thought it best to bury the fact that Israel's founder and foremost prophet had originally been known by a name reflecting a special relationship with an Egyptian god.

The Torah presents the biography of a hero without a proper name or definable physical characteristics. It is as if the text had been deliberately fashioned to signal to its audience that there is something radically different about this man. There is. He is the only classic hero who is not his own man. He is, as the Torah specifically calls him, *ish-elohim*, God's man (Deut. 34:5). Moses' significance lies entirely in his usefulness to another, Who also has no name.

To return to Kittel for a moment. It seems grotesque this side of the Holocaust to find Moses recast as one of Wagner's Teutonic heroes, as the prototype of the Fuehrer who would lift the Reich to glory from what Kittel considered the bourgeois Jewish disaster of Weimar; but I have not resurrected Kittel for shock effect or for the pleasure of criticizing his racist assumption that heroes come packaged in six-foot frames with blue eyes and blond hair. He simply provides us with a telling example of a widely held assumption that the Torah presents Moses as a man of tremendous drive, energy, and accomplishment. The image of Moses as Siegfried shocks everyone, but the image of Moses as a vital, dynamic man, an effective leader, does not. It underlies almost every sermonic or written description of Moses I have ever heard or read. Most readers bring to the Torah narrative a conviction that no other kind of man could have liberated a group of slaves from a powerful tyrant and successfully led them under difficult conditions for almost a lifetime until they not only reached their destination but coalesced

into a nation bound to a demanding religious covenant—
and take away the assumption that this is the kind of man
the Torah seeks to present. It is this approach which Kittel
adopts as he attributes to Moses the larger-than-life accomplishments of a Great Man:

From earliest times in Israel, generation after generation has told
the story of the great man who, even before the Israelites could be
called a nation, led them from Egypt, the house of bondage, into
freedom and a new life. He broke the Egyptian yoke, led his hosts
into the desert where he gave them the code of laws of their God,
and finally led them through the desert to the land which they
had learned to look upon as their own. Through all the ages
Moses has been honored as the helper in need, the leader, the
founder of the nation, but most revered as the messenger of the
new God and His laws [Kittel 19].

Though common sense seems to require the assumption
that Moses must have been a great leader, literature is other
than life, and the Torah was written as a special kind of literature, not as ordinary history. It does not tell of a Great
Man who rallied a slave community, led them from Egypt,
gave them their God and their code of laws, and finally led
them to the Promised Land. This is precisely *not* the thrust
of the Biblical narrative. It tells the story of the Great God
Who redeemed a motley of slaves from Egypt, revealed to
them His name, gave them their laws, provisioned them in
the empty wilderness, and led them to the Land that He
had promised them.

To understand the afterlives of Moses, we must recognize
that in his first life, the life given him by the Torah, he is not
described as a hero in the usual sense of a man of great courage and initiative, the chief character of a saga or chronicle.
God is the hero of the Biblical saga and its chief character.

# The Diminished Hero

Moses is God's principal and most obedient servant. His courage is not the physical bravery of Odysseus or Prometheus' fearless disobedience of the gods, but the courage of submission, the special courage of a shaman or holy man. Moses is not a victor over overwhelming obstacles or a leader of imposing wisdom and accomplishment or a soldier of physical daring and tactical initiative. Moses is God's agent whose faith enables him to confront a mob and face it down armed only with the confidence that God will protect him.

Anyone who tries to turn the Bible into recognizable history, history defined as the record of human accomplishment, has little choice but to adopt some version of Kittel's it-must-have-been approach. Common sense rejects as illogical any conclusion that denies to Moses a decisive leadership role in the great events that shaped the beginnings of the people of Israel. In our experience there are always leaders. How else could the Exodus have taken place unless Moses or someone like him led the escape?

This conclusion also runs counter to an observation that has proved useful in studies of ancient sagas, that such epics develop from a personal experience or a kernel of historical fact and grow as generations of storytellers and priests add drama and piety to the original story. By reversing the process and first identifying and then peeling away the successive layers of legend, students of ancient literature feel they eventually recover the actual event and the hero's role in it. Whatever the usefulness of this approach in other situations, it is not helpful when applied to the Torah narrative.

The historically minded can transform every Torah episode into the way it must have been: in real life the sea does not part, manna does not fall from heaven, water does not gush from barren rock; instead there may have been a well-timed tidal wave or someone discovered that certain desert plants were edible or the tribes chanced on an unexpected spring. Children of a secular age, we automatically treat the Torah's suggestion that God's almighty and outstretched hand achieved the exodus as a metaphor expressing the slaves' amazement and awe at an unexpected stroke of good fortune. Since we would mistrust anyone who claimed to have heard God speak, it seems to us reasonable that the covenant must have been established by an actual lawgiver, Moses or someone like him.

I want to suggest that we ought at least consider the possibility that our passion for fact is itself a form of gullibility. What logic allows us to assume that what seems reasonable must be the real story? "Reasonable" reconstructions are based on a premise that cannot be substantiated, that the Torah account presents a many-layered embellishment of an actual event. It is equally plausible that the Torah account represents the embellishment of a myth or folk tale which has no historical basis or that it appropriates events which happened to an entirely different group at another time or that political events of which the Hebrews were unaware made possible an escape from Egypt which they ascribed to God's outstretched hand.

I believe there was a Moses, that he played a central role in the life of the tribes who escaped from Egypt, and that his major achievement was not so much getting them out but the far more difficult task of welding a disparate group of tribes, a motley riffraff by the Torah's own account, into a community over the course of a long, punishing wilderness trek—one that, symbolically and in the event remarkably, resembles Mao Zedung's Long March. I believe this in part

16

because I have been conditioned to believe it and, in part because, as I'll try to show, a close reading of the Torah text reveals that the editors have consciously phrased the narrative to withdraw from Moses responsibility for all that happens to Israel while he is Israel's acknowledged leader. Successive editions seem to have struggled against Moses' reputation rather than to have elaborated it.

First, the conditioning. Though I am a graduate of the critical academic tradition, I was nurtured by a Jewish tradition which I love and in which I feel very much at home, a tradition in which Moses and the Torah are inextricably paired. In every synagogue there is an ark, in every ark there are parchment scrolls, Torah scrolls, which contain the Hebrew text of Genesis, Exodus, Leviticus, Numbers, and Deuteronomy. Each scroll is written by hand to conform precisely to a venerable scribal tradition. Every Sabbath a prescribed portion of these five books is read in the synagogue. At this steady weekly pace, every year the whole Torah is read through or, rather, chanted, and each portion commented on. The last four of these five books record events in which Moses plays a central role or list the laws of God which Moses mediates to the community. The portion that is read is generally translated from the Hebrew into the congregation's vernacular. If the service includes a sermon, it will customarily be based on the text.

A hundred generations of teachers have commented and preached on these texts, and in every generation Jews have celebrated the holidays which memorialize these events until the events and the themes they celebrate have become part of the Jew's unconscious. To Jews the Torah scroll is *Torat Moshe*, the Torah of Moses, and the identification is so complete that when the Torah is taken from the ark to be read, even in theologically liberal congregations which take for granted that the scroll contains a variety of materials from different times and sources, the reader will recite, "This is the Torah that Moses placed before the people of Israel to fulfill the word of God" (*Gates* 419). The match is so perfect that it takes an act of will for a Jew to imagine the one without the other. Since the Torah is unquestionably there, Moses must stand somewhere close behind it.

Yet, Judaism is not Mosaism. I have never been asked to revere Moses or to pray to him. If I ever try to imagine Moses I do not see him in the classic pose chosen by Michelangelo, a vigorous, philosopher-king modeled after Zeus, but as one of the straight-backed and bearded Semites, skirted and helmeted, portrayed in Egyptian tomb paintings or as one among the ranks of bearded West Asians cut in bas relief on an Assyrian emperor's stele. I cannot tell which of those men he is. I was taught what he said, not how he looked; his was the resounding prophetic voice rather than the heroic physique. Yet even as I try to imagine his voice I am reminded that I have no feeling about its timbre or range. It is neither his stature nor his voice but the words of Instruction which he mediated, the Torah, that establish his power over my soul.

Judaism is woven out of the themes and commandments contained in the Five Books of Moses: the Exodus is freedom, God's Will to save me, Israel, and all mankind from spiritual and political tyranny, a historical event which is at the same time a redemptive promise. Sinai represents the fact of revelation and a particular revelation. There is a definite way, clear mandates. The community is bound to God's way. The forty years of wandering are a paradigm of life as process, a suggestion of the sacrifices demanded of anyone who hopes that his children will live securely in a promised land, an intimation of our frailty and mortality. For a Jew these events are not distant historical events or mythic symbols; they are the concepts which allow him to comprehend reality and are the building blocks of conscious thought.

Second, the editorial treatment of Moses. I have never been able to convince myself that a Biblical editor invented Moses. Had Moses been invented by the scribes of any of the successive rulers of Israel—tribal chiefs, kings, or theocrats—they would likely have taken pains to attach their leaders' lives and authority to him, the noblest figure of the people's early history. No Israelite or Judean king claimed descent from Moses. The priests claimed descent from Aaron, Moses' brother. The authenticity of such priestly claims remains a complex problem of Biblical scholarship, not to be solved here, but its relevance to the question of whether Moses existed or was invented is plain: if the priests had had the opportunity to invent Moses, they would surely have claimed direct descent from him rather than from his brother Aaron who was Moses' subordinate in rank and authority. Moses is identified as a Levite, but, according to the text, so were the notables who rebelled against God and Moses. A good Levite editor with a free hand could easily have done better by his tribe.

I know of no other ancient saga which diminishes the role of its national founder. Sagas tend to embellish, not restrict, telling us in rhapsodic detail of the courage and generalship with which a Sargon or Cyrus led their armies to unsurpassed victories. Moses never straps on a sword, rides out in a war chariot to do battle, or devises a battle plan. Most epics seat their kings on ivory thrones, dress them in purple, and crown them in gold. Moses is never described as wearing special robes or seated on a throne. Kings prove their power by dispensing summary judgments. Their palace guards swiftly dispatch any who rebel. Moses has no private bodyguard and, when challenged by Dathan and Abiram, can only ask God for help against his rivals (Num. 16:12–35). Emperors promulgate their nation's laws. Moses is a scribe who copies the laws as God dictates them to him. Great leaders build massive mausoleums to guarantee their immortality. Moses disappears into the wilderness, his burial place deliberately anonymous: "No man knows his burial place to this day" (Deut. 34:6). What marked the man, and what remains of him, is the memory of his service to God and the Instructions from God which he relayed to Israel.

Kings establish dynasties and plan carefully for the transfer of their power. Moses had no voice in the choice of his successor: "Let the Lord . . . appoint someone over the community . . . so that the Lord's community may not be like sheep that have no shepherd" (Num. 27:15–17). His sons did not share in their father's authority, and Moses apparently did not seek power for them. They were not even considered for the group of spies selected to assay the Promised Land, who would, it was clearly understood, be the future leaders of the people (Num. 13). The Torah reports only the names of Moses' sons, Gershon and Eleazar, and the fact that Moses delayed the youngest's circumcision, for reasons not given. Beyond this they are not in view, except for a single mention in an archaic fragment embedded in the Book of Judges, which seems to indicate that descendants of Gershon, "son of Moses," were officiating as minor priests at a local shrine in the territory of Dan (Judg. 18:30). None of Moses' descendants made capital of his name, and there is no indication that Moses sought to make any arrangements to benefit them. The Torah editors took every possible precaution to drive home the point that power and authority belong to God and that the community must be conscious always that Moses is simply God's agent, God is the Master.

I invite you to reread the Torah texts which deal with Moses. They are limited to the books of Exodus through Deuteronomy. (That the remaining Biblical books make only a few passing references to Moses and add no significant details to his biography is another indication of Biblical Judaism's interest in limiting Moses' role in Israel's history.) Pay particular attention to those chapters which describe Moses after he assumes his public role. Begin, say, with the third chapter of the Book of Exodus, the commissioning scene at the Burning Bush. Skip the lists of laws and instructions which follow the theophany on Sinai and read the narrative paragraphs right through to the end of the first telling of these events in the last chapters of the Book of Numbers. Then ask yourself if you can point to a text which states, or even suggests, that Moses led the Israelites from Egypt. Instead, you will find yourself remembering texts like "That very day the Lord freed the Israelites from the land of Egypt troop by troop" (Exod. 12:51). What about a statement that Moses' diplomacy was persuasive with Pharaoh? What is written is that "the Lord struck down all the first-born in the land of Egypt" (Exod. 12:29). Will you read that Moses led his people in the wilderness? Instead, you will find "The Lord went before them in a pillar of cloud by day, to guide them along the way, and in a pillar of fire by night. . . ." (Exod. 13:21). Does the Torah claim that Moses introduced Israel to the God whom they afterward worshipped? No. You will read, "The Lord called him [Moses] from the mountain saying, 'Thus shall you say to the house of Jacob . . . if you will obey Me faithfully and keep My covenant, you shall be My treasured possession among all the peoples' " (Exod. 19:3–5). Is there any report that Moses led the tribes during the forty years of the wilderness trek until they approached the borders of the land that was to be their home? You will read, instead, "And the Lord continued: 'I have come down to rescue them from the Egyptians and bring them out of the land to a good and spacious land, a land flowing with milk and honey, the home of the Canaanites. . . .' " (Exod. 3:8).

The language consistently affirms that God, not Moses, made the Exodus possible, established the terms of the covenant, and enabled the tribes to make a successful passage through the wilderness. The Torah depicts Moses not as a self-reliant leader but as a faithful courtier whose virtue consists in loyally carrying out the royal will. Moses makes no move to return to Egypt until God orders him to go. Moses does not develop a strategy for the slaves' escape. He listens to God's Instructions and follows them to the letter (Exod. 6:13). Moses' mission in Egypt is to relay God's messages to the Hebrews and to announce God's miracles to Pharaoh. He has no latitude to act on his own. It is not, after all, Moses' skill as a diplomat, his nimble or his slow tongue, but the irrefutable logic of the plagues that finally persuades Pharaoh.

I suggest that this editorial treatment of Moses was deliberate. The poets of Israel could create heroic sagas as exuberant as those of any other people, and there was an audience for rousing tales of courage and valor. The story of David is such a saga. That saga, embedded in the Deuteronomic his-

tories, contains many expressions of conventional piety—
"and David waxed greater and greater for the Lord was with
him" (2 Sam. 5:10)—but such sentiments in no way diminish the lusty feelings, daring exploits, and patriotic gore reported there. David's story is stock hagiography, the tale of a
hero who is darling youth and daring soldier, a man of overwhelming ambition and lust, a capable political organizer
and shrewd manipulator, but with it all a man of sensibility,
a larger-than-life figure whose virtues and vices are out-
sized—in short, a hero.

A brief comparison of the Moses and David episodes is
instructive. Moses is married before his public career begins
and once he accepts God's commission there are no indications that he has any further sexual interests. David's love
affairs are amply described and unceasing. God commissions
Moses directly and thereafter Moses has no private life.
Samuel anoints David in the name of God and tells him to
return to private life. Moses is depicted as unwilling or unable to act, except when God gives him specific instructions.
David rules by fiat, his every whim becomes law. When
faced with a difficult decision, Moses has no alternative but
to wait in the Tent of Meeting to receive God's Instructions. David takes advice from a variety of counselors and
makes his own decision. Moses plays no part in developing
battle plans and never enters the battlefield. David is a master strategist and trained soldier who leads his troops with
skill and courage. When Korah rebels, Moses prostrates
himself before God to ask for help and is saved only when
God orders the earth to swallow up the opposition. When
Absalom rebels against David, the king dispatches mercenaries to put down his son's uprising. Moses' sin is a purely
formal one: he fails to follow with absolute fidelity God's

Instructions for a specific ritual. When David sins, his are the sins of imagination, cruelty, lust, and power—the sins of a heroic figure.

That most Bible readers have come away from the text without a clear impression of Moses as agent rather than as principal, as ambassador rather than as leader, testifies to our habit of rationalizing saga, to the force of pious tradition, and to our familiarity with the stories of Moses' life before his commission, when the narrative allows him some measure of independence. The conviction we bring to the text that a leader is a particular kind of man—a strong, vigorous, and decisive man—influences our reading and defines what we take away from it. What is really there is a depiction of Moses as agent, as faithful ambassador, almost at times of Moses as a puppet manipulated from above.

Moses' birth story is conventional epic. Many years earlier the tribes had entered Egypt with Pharaoh's permission. A change of dynasty occurs and the new government revokes their original privileges, enslaves them, and embitters their lives with harsh labor. The new dynasty sees the large and growing Hebrew population as a potential threat, fears they might support a bid by some other alien ruler to control Egypt, and determines to break the tribes' will by forced labor and to reduce their numbers by infanticide. The decree goes out: all newborn Hebrew males will be killed. The future hero escapes the fatal decree. When the infant can no longer be hidden at home his mother and sister construct for him a watertight cradle which they place in the bullrushes at the bank of the Nile. A daughter of Pharaoh sees the cradle, discovers the child, provides a wet nurse for him, and presumably, raises him at court.

Moses' youth is passed over in silence. The story resumes

when Moses is full grown and circumstance removes him from his comfortable life. One day in the fields he sees an Egyptian taskmaster beating a Hebrew slave. The text uses active verbs to describe the incident: "When Moses had grown up, he went out to his kinsfolk and witnessed their toil. He saw an Egyptian beating a Hebrew, one of his kinsmen. He turned this way and that and, seeing no one about, he struck down the Egyptian and hid him in the sand" (Exod. 2:11–12). Moses acts on his own when he kills the overseer and again the next day when he interferes in a quarrel between two Hebrew slaves (Exod. 2:13–14). Alone he decides to flee Egypt. He acts on his own when he protects Jethro's daughters from local bullies bothering them at the village well (Exod. 2:16–21), when he marries one of Jethro's daughters, and when he agrees to work for his father-in-law (Exod. 3:1). In these domestic scenes there was no need to force theology on hagiology.

But once Moses is commissioned at the Burning Bush, once he exchanges private for public life, the text routinely and with obvious deliberation subordinates Moses' actions and authority to the expressed will of God. "Come, I will send you to Pharaoh" (Exod. 3:10); "and the Lord called Moses to the top of the mountain and Moses went up" (Exod. 19:20); "the Lord said to Moses: 'Carve two tablets of stone like the first' " (Exod. 34:1, 4). Throughout his public life Moses appears fully aware that his is an ambassador's rather than a principal's role. When he is challenged by various factions with the sin of nepotism, of favoring his brother over more senior Levites, he responds simply: "The Lord sent me to do all these things. They are not of my own devising" (Num. 16:28).

A curious aspect of the four precommissioning chapters is

the impression they give that the editor has deliberately set out to belittle the character of Moses in this period before God's commission transforms him into a man of consequence. The description of Moses' attack on the slavemaster is a case in point: "He saw an Egyptian beating a Hebrew, one of his kinsmen. He turned this way and that and, seeing no one about, he struck down the Egyptian and hid him in the sand" (Exod. 2:11–12). When he discovered the next day that the matter was known, "Moses was frightened" and he fled to Midian (Exod. 2:14–15). Heroes attack their enemies openly and defiantly proclaim their deeds. They do not strike down unsuspecting victims, surreptitiously hide all traces of their act, and flee into the night. A hero may retire for reasons of prudence, but he does not flee in panic. If he retires he plans to return to fight another day, as David did after he had fled from before Saul. Another example: Moses' long pastorale in Midian is set against the background of the Hebrews' continuing enslavement in Egypt, but the text reports no act, or even plan, by Moses to return to help them. Indeed, until God orders him to go, the thought that he had some responsibility to the slaves seems not to have crossed his mind. When God finally orders him to Egypt, Moses doesn't jump at the chance. The text depicts a man trying every way he can to get out of an unwelcome assignment: "Please, O Lord, make someone else Your agent" (Exod. 4:13).

Once he enters public life, Moses' freedom of judgment and action—and simultaneously his timorousness and self-indulgence—disappear. So consistent is the new image of Moses as a man without independent authority that we cannot assume it is accidental. It extends to costume as well as to characterization; from the time he enters public life

# The Diminished Hero

Moses keeps by him the staff which was the easily recognized symbol of his ambassadorial rank. This staff, which had begun life as an ordinary shepherd's crook, is not only an appropriate symbol of Moses' commission but is the instrument through which God's power is made known. God had empowered the staff at the Burning Bush:

Moses spoke up . . . "What if they do not believe me . . . but say: The Lord did not appear to you." The Lord said to him, "What is that in your hand?" and he replied, "A rod." He said, "Cast it on the ground." He cast it on the ground and it became a snake . . . then the Lord said to Moses, "Put out your hand and grasp it by the tail" . . . and it became a rod in his hand . . . "that they might believe that the Lord, the God of their fathers . . . did appear to you" [Exod. 4:1–5].

When God wishes to display His power He orders Moses to lift the rod and the skies darken or the Nile runs red. When, on God's command, Moses holds the rod above the rock, water gushes forth. The rod's power is not at Moses' disposal; he cannot summon it at will. Moses is not a magician but God's resident agent. His power is derivative. The man who carries the staff is *ish-elohim*, God's man, and not his own master (Deut. 31:5).

The most unlikely explanation for this editorial treatment is that the Torah somehow reflects an attempt to discredit a leader whose policies fell out of favor, as Krushchev encouraged revisionist biographies of Stalin. There is no indication of such a purpose in the text. Quite the contrary. Every line of the literature points to growing veneration for the Instructions which Moses had mediated.

The most likely explanation, in my judgment, is that the editorial determination to present Moses as an obedient servant rather than as a decisive leader reflects the Torah's overriding interest in presenting the power of the redeemer God. For centuries Jews recited litanies of the Exodus narrative at shrines on festivals and other holy occasions, always in the hope—and expectation—that rehearsing God's role in the nation's redemptive history would summon His help in the nation's immediate need and hasten the ultimate redemption, the Day of God. The consistent presentation of Moses as agent, not hero, reflects one of the significant but often-overlooked formal aspects of the Torah literature, its intended use as a recital evoking God's redemptive power.

There are good reasons to believe that the earliest portions of Exodus, Leviticus, and Numbers, and to a certain degree also Deuteronomy, are, in fact, early narrative psalms which exalt various details of the nation's early history in order to praise God for all He had done for His people. The litanies rehearse the details of the historic moments of election and covenant when the community first came under God's protection and the possibility of redemption first became real to them. The litanies were intended as more than pious commemorations; they were recitations designed to evoke God's redemptive might and His will to save His people. The use of such evocative ritual was not uncommon in the ceremonies of West Asia. Bravery in battle was evoked by the ritual of simulated bravery in a war dance, and the need for rain was ritualized by pouring libations of water on the altar. What little we know about early Israelite rites— unfortunately, most of our knowledge comes from analogizing the rites of neighboring communities to Israel—suggests that in the hope of hastening redemption, the people assigned a major role to the public recitation of psalms memorializing those acts by which God had redeemed the ancestors, bound them to Him by covenant, and brought them to a Promised Land which He had helped them to conquer. Not to put too fine a gloss on such recitals, they can be legitimately characterized as sympathetic magic.

There are a number of indications in the Bible text of the use of such recital as a means of evoking God's power. The priestly histories use the common verb for prophecy, *navah*, to describe the chanting of the Temple singers, a clear suggestion that their songs praising God's power, just like prophetic speech, were credited with the power to call forth future events. Then, too, there is the interesting succession of verb tenses in the song Moses chants once Israel is safely on the far side of the Reed Sea: "I will sing to the Lord for He *has* triumphed gloriously. . . . He *is* become my salvation. . . . In Your strength You guide [Your people] to Your holy abode. . . . You *will* bring them and plant them in Your own mountain" (Exod. 15:1–17). In another early song Deborah reviews victories the tribes had achieved through God's help and then shifts to the purpose of her song: "So may all Your enemies perish, O Lord, but may His friends be as the sun rising in might" (Judg. 5). Lest anyone doubt the efficacy of such a litany a later editor appended a postscript assuring the reader that "the land was tranquil forty years" (Judg. 5:31).

The Israelites may have come to this piety—that reciting God's past triumphs could evoke His power to save them— by unconscious mimicry of traditional West Asian court practice. Oriental courtiers knew that the powerful had to be softened by praise, and that the surest way to touch a royal heart was to remind the ruler of his past victories. Such liturgical praises seem to be religious counterparts of the fulsome praises West Asians routinely offer their sovereigns in the expectation that, having been reminded of his power and magnanimity, the king might be encouraged to display them again. Apparently the Israelites hoped, similarly, to move God to open His heart, to recognize His power, and use it in their behalf.

Such liturgies, if they mentioned Moses at all, treated him—as we have seen—as God's faithful agent, not as a major actor in the redemptive drama. The community looked forward eagerly to their deliverance, and to secure it they praised the God Who alone had it in His power to fulfill their dreams. Moses was dead. He could no longer help.

A review of the earliest liturgies reveals that Moses appears in none of them. Deuteronomy contains this early Passover formula:

When, in time to come, your son asks you, "What mean the exhortations, laws, and rules which the Lord our God has enjoined upon you?" you shall say to your son, "We were slaves to Pharaoh in Egypt and the Lord freed us from Egypt with a mighty hand. The Lord wrought before our eyes marvelous and destructive signs and portents in Egypt, against Pharaoh and all his household; and us He freed from there that He might take us and give us the land that He had promised on oath to our fathers. Then the Lord commanded for us to observe all these laws, to revere the Lord our God, for our lasting good and for our survival, as is now the case. It will be therefore to our merit before the Lord our God to observe faithfully this whole Instruction, as He has commanded us" [Deut. 6:20–25].

Moses does not appear in a formula for recitation by farmers at harvest time when they brought the first fruits of their field to a shrine:

My father was a fugitive Aramean. The Egyptians dealt harshly with us. . . . We cried to the Lord . . . and the Lord heard our plea and saw our plight. . . . The Lord freed us from Egypt by a mighty hand, by an outstretched arm and awesome power, and by signs and portends. He brought us to this place, and gave us this land. . . . Wherefore I now bring its fruits of the soil which You, O Lord, have given me [Deut. 26:5–10].

Nor is Moses mentioned in Psalm 135, a preexilic cult hymn where the relationship between the list of God's saving acts and the people's national expectations is clearly stated:

> I know that the Lord is great. . . .
> He struck down all the first-born in Egypt,
>   both man and beast.
> In Egypt he sent signs and portents
>   against Pharaoh and all his subjects.
> He struck down mighty nations
>   and slew great kings,
> Sihon king of the Amorites, Og the king of
>   Bashan, and all the princes of Canaan,
> And gave their land to Israel,
>   to Israel His people as their patrimony.
> O Lord, Thy name endures forever;
> Thy renown, O Lord, shall last for all generations.
> The Lord will give His people justice
>   and have compassion on His servants [Ps. 135:5, 8–14].

Students have recognized these sections in Scripture as paragraphs from Israel's original liturgy, but they have not recognized that the tendency of the Torah narrative to diminish Moses' role suggests that it took shape also as an evocation of God's redemptive power. As the Torah grew, a variety of materials were added to these liturgies—including lists of covenant law and various well-known chronicles of Israel's early history—and the new materials in time ex-

ceeded the old. The expanded Torah no longer read as a
straightforward evocation of God's power, but the community never completely lost sight of the Torah's original purpose. It was to be the text which they recited publicly in
order to please God and to appeal effectively to Him for the
support they needed.

No matter how much was added over time to the liturgical recitations—the creation saga, geneologies, law, psalms
of praise and prophecy, other history—the original purpose
of the Torah remained its central purpose: to state clearly
and forcefully God's power and His interest in Israel. The
recitation of history is here a praise to God, the expected
preface to a petition for His help. So, although the extended
Torah narrative, unlike the brief hymns, gives Moses a role
in the Exodus, there was no reason to embellish his role.
God needs agents on earth to carry out His work; but the
agent in place was carefully kept in his place. Given the
Torah's underlying purpose, to summon God's redemptive
powers, it is not surprising that the Moses who appears on
its pages is someone who is a diminished version of the actual historical figure.

So far, we have examined the narratives of Exodus
through Numbers. Pause a moment to turn to the Book of
Deuteronomy. Deuteronomy, of course, had its own distinct
textual history, and its narrative style suggests that it was not
as closely tied as Exodus through Numbers to the early liturgical forms. The description of Moses as "a very humble
man, more so than any other on earth" (Num. 12:3) is not
as consistently developed in this scroll. Deuteronomy claims
to record Moses' valedictory speeches which suggest, at the
very least, that he was an orator of considerable skill. Moreover, in the course of his talks, Moses asserts that he, on his

own initiative, determined the division of land among the tribes, selected appropriate cities of refuge, organized the judicial system, and nominated the spies who were sent into Canaan. The picture of a leader of stature and skill—and self-confidence—begins to emerge.

Even so, the list of Moses' accomplishments remains modest. God determines the time and line of march. God "scouts the place where you are to camp" (Deut. 1:33). "The Lord our God spoke to us in Horeb, saying: 'you have stayed long enough at this mountain. Start out and make your way to the hill country of the Amorites. . .' " (Deut. 1:6–7). Victory on the battlefield is God's achievement (Deut. 2:32). God determines which kings should be fought and which conciliated (Deut. 2:9). God, not Moses, determines that the generation who were slaves shall not enter the Promised Land because they defied His order at Kadesh Barnea to begin the conquest (Deut. 1:34). Throughout, Moses reports God's Instructions without change or addition.

In Deuteronomy, as in the other three books, it is taken for granted that God, not Moses, made the Exodus possible, offered the Covenant to Israel, and guided the tribes in the wilderness. Some of the editor's efforts to underscore the limited nature of Moses' role are still visible. One example: on the day that the tribes suffered a costly defeat at a place called Hormah, it happens that Moses had stayed in camp; lest anyone ascribe defeat to Moses' absence, the text declares that the army had been defeated because God had not gone out with the host (Deut. 1:44). Another: in summing up his career and the national experience to date, Moses himself reminds the people that their survival is not his doing, saying that God had carried the tribes "as a man car-

33

ries his son, all the way that you traveled until you came to this place" (Deut. 1:31). Moses' eulogy, which concludes Deuteronomy, might be expected to enlarge his accomplishment; instead, it emphasizes his role as God's most obedient servant, the prophet-agent

whom the Lord singled out, face to face, for the various signs and portents the Lord sent him to display in the land of Egypt, against Pharaoh and all his courtiers and his whole country, and for all the great might and awesome power that Moses displayed before all Israel [Deut. 34:10–11].

Moses makes his way through these pages as a holy man armed only with the staff which defined him as God's ambassador. He comes to the battlefield not as a strategist or general but as bearer of the symbols of God's power: "Whenever Moses held up his hand [with the rod of god in it] Israel prevailed, but whenever he let down his hand, Amalek prevailed" (Exod. 17:11). As was the familiar custom of holy men, Moses lived apart. His tent was set up ". . . at some distance from the camp . . . Whenever Moses went out to the Tent all the people would rise and stand, each at the entrance to his tent" (Exod. 33:7–8). His tent was taboo. When God visited the holy man there, the tribal leaders would prostrate themselves wherever they happened to be in the encampment (Exod. 33:10). After he had been with God, Moses veiled his face as was the custom among shamans and holy men (Exod. 34:29).

A word should be said about the courage required of holy men and prophets. Popular understanding linked, in a cause and effect relationship, the messenger with his message. When the holy man spoke an oracle, he activated the event and so was, in a sense, responsible for it. If a holy man

The Diminished Hero

prophesied defeat or national disaster, he was seen as responsible for any tragedy that might follow on his speech;
had he not spoken the disaster would not have happened.
Holy men and prophets often acted in ways contrary to the
king's or the community's perception of the national interest. One *ish-elohim* had to announce the end of Eli's
priestly dynasty (1 Sam. 2:27–36). Another denounced King
Jereboam for setting up an altar at Bethel (1 Kings 13), and
a third warned King Amaziah against a military campaign
he was contemplating (2 Chron. 25:7). It was always dangerous to cross such powerful men, yet the holy man was protected by the credulities of his society.

But as Jeremiah's fate makes clear, these protective taboos
could break down. Moses, of course, never brought words
which threatened national extinction—in fact, as we shall
see, he often interceded to protect the nation from God's
harshest judgments—but the oracles he delivered were not
always cheerfully received. After the apostasy of the Golden
Calf, Moses delivered God's death sentence against many of
the most powerful men in the camp. When the camp ve-
toed God's command to move out immediately and begin
the conquest of Canaan, Moses spoke the words which condemned the Exodus generation to die in the wilderness.

The holy man in West Asian society proved the power of
his god and the authenticity of his closeness to his god by
carrying neither weapons nor shield and living without
bodyguards—in a society where all men of consequence had
such protection. Moses, therefore, has no bodyguard.
Moses' lack of formal protection, despite his vulnerability
and repeated threats to his life, allowed the editors to display dramatically and repeatedly God's saving power.
Moses' frequent escapes from danger proved that God pro-

35

tected His servants. If Moses had hired janissaries, the implication would have been that God's power could not shield him, the very position Biblical narrative was shaped to deny. The Torah's theme is that God's power protects His ambassador-holy man in every court and situation.

Why make an issue of God's power? The Torah's purpose is messianic rather than historical. Israel's long hope depended on God's power to save. The drama of God protecting the holy man from harm, this proof of God's power, was designed to remind an Israelite audience that the nation, too, if it is a "holy community," could confidently place its trust in God. The holy man has been chosen by God for a special role and, in measure as he is faithful to God's will, God's protection is so sure that he can be indifferent to armor and enemies. Israel has been chosen for a special role. God has entered into a special covenant with Israel and when Israel fully obeys its terms, the nation, though small in comparison to other nations, can be confident of victory, security, and prosperity. A faithful Israel need fear no army or enemy.

The Torah's way of deliverance is a joyous confidence in God's beneficence coupled with a life of disciplined obedience to the Covenant, God's Will. The Torah section read in the synagogue every Yom Kippur—"I have put before you life and death, blessing and curse. Choose life, if you and your offspring would live, by loving the Lord your God, heeding His commands, and holding fast to Him" (Deut. 30:19–20)—is not, as commonly interpreted, a call to a fuller, more capacious life. It is, rather, the promise of security and of God's protection, if the nation fulfills the obligation of obedience.

Moses' trust is based on faith rather than fatalistic resignation. Moses is presented as a paragon of calm patience and steady hope; the Hebrew word for these qualities is *bittahon*. Moses is praised for his faithful obedience, his willingness to go and do, a virtue not to be confused with stoic passivity, simply letting things happen. What *bittahon* shares with stoicism is a profound sense that man cannot on his own change the human condition. But the stoic copes without any sense of hope. Moses' trust in God is an act of faith that the Exodus will take place, the Covenant will be empowered, and the Promised Land attained.

Although Moses is a model of the man who, once commissioned, faithfully obeys God's will, he is presented as a mortal, not a demigod. As a mortal he must die, but in a world which believed death was related to sin, of what sin could God's man be accused? The when and where of his disobedience is not clear. Most commentators are reduced to discovering Moses' sin in a minor and purely formal violation. The most likely episode takes place at Meribah where God had told him to hold his staff over the rock so that water would gush forth and Moses had instead struck the rock (Num. 20). What is clear is that Moses did not die of natural causes—the Torah says specifically that his strength had not abated—but as punishment because his obedience had not been total.

To understand the Torah's presentation of Moses, we must see him as a holy man, with everything that role implies. The holy man customarily acts as an intercessor or prayermaster, a role worth careful delineation, for we are no longer familiar with such men and it take a bit of imagination and some intellectual effort to perceive what is involved. It is an archaic function, and I think it fair to say that even those who participate in what are today called ministries of healing generally fail to think of Moses as one of their predecessors. But he was so known in ancient Israel.

Beyond his fundamental role as God's agent, who simply does what he is told to do in God's governing of Israel, Moses can and does petition God on behalf of individuals or the community, usually to spare them defeat or danger. The Torah editors tell the stories of Moses the intercessor with obvious awe and respect. When God bitterly and peremptorily sentences the nation to extinction after they fashion the Golden Calf, Moses steps out of his role as ever-obedient courtier and pleads: "Let not Your anger, O Lord, blaze forth against Your people." His prayer is effective: "And the Lord renounced the punishment He had planned to bring upon His people" (Exod. 32:10–14). Indeed, the text suggests that God acknowledges Moses' intercessory powers even as He mitigates His sentence: "Now, let Me be, that My anger may blaze forth against them" (Exod. 32:9). A year later, when the spies return to the Kadesh Barnea camp and frighten everyone with reports of impregnable Canaanite forts, the tribal council balks at God's specific order to begin the invasion immediately. Again, God is angry enough to pronounce the nation's doom. Again, Moses intercedes: "Let my Lord's forebearance be great . . . Pardon, I pray, the iniquity of this people according to Your great kindness, as You have forgiven this people ever since Egypt," and the Lord said: "I pardon, as you have asked" (Num. 14:19–20).

The Israelites frequently seek the benefit of Moses' proven competence in his role as holy man-intercessor:

They set out from Mount Hor by the road to the Sea of Reeds to skirt the land of Edom. But the people grew restive on the journey, and the people spoke against God and against Moses, "Why did you make us leave Egypt to die in the wilderness? There is no bread and no water, and we have come to loathe this miserable food." The Lord sent seraph serpents among the people. They bit the people and many of the Israelites died. The people come to Moses and said, "We sinned by speaking against the Lord and against you. Intercede with the Lord to take away the serpents from us!" And Moses interceded for the people [Num. 21:4–6].

As an intercessor Moses was generally, but not always, successful. When Miriam criticizes Moses' marriage to a Cushite woman, God punishes her with "snow white scales," presumably leprosy. "Moses cried out to the Lord, saying: 'O Lord, pray heal her' " (Num. 12:13), but God refuses an immediate reprieve, agreeing only to reduce her sentence to a week's discomfort and quarantine.

To the Biblical editor and the Biblical audience, Moses' actions as an intercessor offer the ultimate demonstration of his courage. While he is on God's business, Moses is protected by God's power; but on those occasions when Moses tries to change God's mind, he is without protection. The facts of court life would have been in everyone's mind. The power of an emperor protected his ambassador at a foreign court, but an ambassador or courtier who tried to change the royal mind risked the royal anger and summary punishment. Men of power do not like to be crossed: "The wrath of a king is as messengers of death" (Prov. 16:14). When Moses intercedes with God after the sin of the Golden Calf, he knows that his life is on the line: "If You will forgive their sin, well and good; but if not, erase me from the record You have written" (Exod. 32:32). Here we touch a courage which the ancients readily understood but which modern readers often fail to notice. God might grant Moses' petition or strike him dead on the spot.

In theory, the independent power of a prayermaster-intercessor is incompatible with teachings that emphasize God's control of history and God's *hesed*, His covenant loyalty. If God is just and dependable, what reason or right would anyone, even His holy man, have to ask Him to change His mind? But religions exist to help people in their need and theology must always accommodate human need. It is always in man's interest to discover ways to persuade God—or whatever power he acknowledges—to his benefit. Today, to assure ourselves a desirable future, we tinker with political structures or develop new technologies. We have powers the ancients could not even imagine, and experience has shown us that men, as well as God, can change the course of history. We assume a can-do attitude. The Biblical tradition operated with the assumption that only God can do. The Israelites looked to God as the source of all power. Biblical folk lived where their parents had lived, served at the same shrine, tilled the same fields, used the same tools. Their experience seemed to confirm the observation that God, not men, controlled history. In such a world it was critically important to know someone who had the qualifications which allowed him to plead with God. The Israelite knew that he could not in all respects live up to God's instructions; even Moses had sinned. He knew that he needed help if he hoped to satisfy God, and he sought this help in a special hero type, the holy man-intercessor, of whom Moses was the preeminent model.

In West Asia during the second millennium B.C.E., historical writing had been limited to formal materials: reports of imperial victories, lists of donations by rulers grateful for these victories, and documents which supported a shrine's claim as the home of a national god. The Deuteronomic histories, Judges through Kings, present a new kind of history which goes beyond the simple recording to facts. With the records comments are introduced to explain *why* events had worked out as they had. The "why" in every case was the will of God. When Israel lives up to the Covenant, the community deserves reward, and God sends peace and prosperity. When the nation or its kings prove themselves disobedient or indifferent, God withholds rain or victory or even independence. Where most West Asian chronicles recorded only the ruler's victories or major national accomplishments, the Deuteronomic histories cite both victory and defeat. They explain every event by what is called Covenant Theology—simply put, a kind of grading system under which a people, or an individual, is rewarded or punished according to their efforts to live up to the terms of behavior required by God and accepted by the community.

The narrative imbedded in the Five Books of Moses, particularly in Exodus, Leviticus, and Numbers, reflects the covenant themes but was shaped by a different set of concerns. These narratives centered on the promise of redemption. Their reading served a primarily evocative purpose. By rehearsing God's redemptive acts, ancient Israel summoned God to act again as a redeemer. The Torah narrative is, therefore, closer to liturgy than to chronicle, though it is presented chronologically. It sets out the framework of history rather than a record of its unfolding: creation, Israel's election, the Exodus, the Covenant, and the promise of the land provide prototypical terms which explain all that was, is, and will be.

The events of the Exodus are also rehearsed each year on the Passover, when Jews sit down to the ritual *seder* meal. The *seder* service is organized as a *haggadah*, a retelling. In song and story and by citation of various Torah texts, the ancient liberation is commemorated. God as liberator is praised. Israel's redemptive needs are suggested. According to tradition, on this night the Messiah or his forerunner, Elijah, will appear. Moses is not mentioned in any of the early versions of the *Haggadah*. Those who look on the *Haggadah* simply as a historical narrative find Moses' absence from the recitation puzzling. But to understand the *Haggadah* as a liturgy that evokes redemption, as sympathetic magic, is to understand readily why Moses is absent and God is omnipresent. Passover is an anticipation of the messianic deliverance. *Seder* night is to be the anticipated "night of watching." Moses has no role in the eschaton. God and God alone redeems.

The *Haggadah* text has been two thousand years in the making, and there is no evidence that Moses appeared as a central figure in any version. The *seder* ritual is shaped not as a history lesson or a commemoration but as a religious exercise which attempts to vivify the power that had released the slaves from Egypt in the hope that God's redemptive might would again release Israel from the trammels of political fate.

As the Torah text presents him, Moses is an exception to the rule that the legends of great men grow through the centuries. The text deliberately diminished the historical figure. In the Torah Moses is *ish-elohim*, God's man, not his own man; he is *eved adonai*, God's faithful servitor, not a powerful leader in his own right. He displays the courage of the holy man rather than the bold initiative and physical bravery of an active leader of men. His role as lawgiver and liberator, if such had ever been his role, gave way before an insistence by the Biblical editors that the text be a hymn of praise to God's saving power. God alone is liberator, lawgiver, leader. Because the Torah editors were determined that their audience should be suitably awed by God's power to save, know their faith in God's redemptive will was well founded, and participate in acts and recitations which would hasten His decision to bring to Israel the second and final redemption, the original Moses is lost to us and the Moses offered in his place is a diminished reflection of the Moses who must have been.

# CHAPTER

# II

# Moses Returns
to Egypt

THE EXODUS is usually dated around 1300 B.C.E. when such pharaohs as Tutenkhamen and Ramesses were majestic in their imperial tyranny; it was the age of Amarna. Given the troubles attending his departure, we would not expect that Moses would be eager to revisit his birthplace. But seven hundred years later he did go home again—in a sense—as Jews, then beginning to settle in Egypt, brought with them various memories and tales of God's prophet. He did not receive a hero's welcome. After all, he was the central figure in a national history which stigmatized Egypt as a land of pharaonic tyranny and arbitrary law. From the Egyptian perspective Moses was an ingrate who had repaid royal kindness by robbing Egypt of valuable possessions.

This Egypt was a lesser place, its former glories greatly dimmed. During the first millennium a slow, and what was to be an irreversible, decline set in. Late in the sixth century B.C.E. Egypt was conquered by Persia, the first in an almost unbroken line of conquerors. Greeks, Romans, Arabs, and Turks ruled Egypt for the next twenty-five hundred years.

The first Jews—they were then called Judeans—to return in any number were mercenaries hired by Persian officials to guard Egypt's southern frontier. We do not know what stories about Moses these soldiers brought with them to military colonies like Elephantine, a garrison town on an island in the Nile opposite modern Aswan, but we do know that the Exodus history figured prominently in their religious lives. Something of the domestic life of Elephantine, which was founded in the sixth century and survived to the fourth, is known through Aramaic papyrii which have survived. The texts describe a temple at which sacrifices were offered and the observance of the annual festival of the Passover, which was the community's major rite. One of the colony's proudest possessions was an edict under the seal of the Persian emperor, Darius II (423–404 B.C.E.), specifically authorizing the Passover observance. Some friction would have been inevitable between the Judeans, who were mercenaries of a foreign overlord, and the native population; and the Passover celebration probably provided a focus for Egyptian anger. Watching Judeans annually celebrate events in which Egypt was the villain could only have offended the Egyptians they were paid to protect and control. I can almost hear the natives mutter, "You wanted so much to leave. Why did you come back?"

Passover is the only festival we know to have been observed in the Temple of Elephantine. There undoubtedly were other celebrations, but Passover was clearly the most important, and so from the beginning of the Jewish return to Egypt, the Exodus story was the event associated with Jews. In the inevitable competition for place and privilege which occurs in every society, the role of Moses—by birth Hebrew, by upbringing Egyptian, by God's command leader of a slave outbreak—became a public issue. No records have survived which document the arguments made by both sides of the Egyptian-Judean controversy during the period of Persian domination in Egypt, but there is solid evidence that the Elephantine community was not made welcome. In 411 B.C.E. Egyptian priests of the god Khnub destroyed the Judean shrine at Elephantine. A fully developed Egyptian polemic attacking Moses survives from the years immediately after the Greek conquest (325 B.C.E.), so that we must assume it was not a new issue.

Following the Greek conquest the center of the Jewish diaspora in Egypt shifted north to the Mediterranean coast. Faced with the prospect of ruling a large and culturally alien population, the Ptolemies, made wary by their experience at home in Greece, where the city-states were often ruined by popular uprisings, feared that they might become virtual prisoners of the masses whom they had conquered. To reduce this danger, Ptolemy I (Soter), Alexander's general and Egypt's first Greek emperor (d. 283 B.C.E.), decided to build a new capital, Alexandria, on virgin land and to settle the place with non-Egyptians who would be economically useful and politically impotent. Alexandria was to be the capital of Egypt, but not an Egyptian city, pros Aigypton, "by" but not "in" Egypt. Ptolemy brought sizable drafts of Judean captives—one report mentions the number of one hundred thousand—to build his city. He undoubtedly saw the Jews as a hardworking, largely rural population who possessed many useful crafts and skills, who would live on in the city they had been conscripted to build, providing it with a useful and docile artisan class. Given the privilege of governing

49

themselves by their special law, Judeans could be expected to be indifferent to the competition for power within the Gymnasium and the Forum. Ptolemy may also have known something of and been comforted by the antagonism that existed between Judeans and Egyptians.

Alexandria proved an instant success. Within a generation it had become the economic capital of the Hellenistic world. The Judea they had left behind was poor, and the conscript labor force willingly settled in the new capital. Ptolemy II (Philadelphus) (283–246 B.C.E.) provided the community a charter. Soon cousins and neighbors, attracted by the sudden prosperity of their compatriots, left home and migrated to Egypt. It is estimated that by the first century C.E. one in eight who lived in Egypt was a Jew. One wonders if an observer with an eye for statistics noted that more Jews had returned to Egypt than the six hundred thousand the Torah reports had left with Moses.

To appreciate the terms of the Egyptian-Judean polemic, it is necessary to keep in mind that it was conducted within and deeply influenced by the varied and contradictory cultural assumptions which affected all who lived in the urban centers of the Hellenistic world. That world's attitudes toward heroes and hero worship were particularly significant and greatly influenced the age's understanding of Moses. Hellenistic literature is lavish in its praise of the achievements of extraordinary men. Hellenistic heroes were men of exceptional capacity, of physical courage and political acumen, more like the Bible's David than the Torah's Moses. Where the Biblical world praised God, the Greek world praised famous men. Such is the power of cultural assimilation that, in the hands of Hellenized Jewish writers, Moses comes out from under God's shadow and becomes a man of initiative and accomplishment, a hero.

This new cultural world exalted two main hero types: the indomitable warrior and the wise community leader, or *sophos*. It was widely believed that men of the latter type, by their mastery of all learning, particularly the discipline of philosophy, had come to recognize the world of appearance for what it is, a camouflage of reality. They had achieved an understanding of reality which made them incapable of error and capable of organizing their lives rationally. Conventional Hellenistic wisdom held that the formative and guiding principle in nature was reason and that consequently those who *knew* were free to *do*. The exceptional person, who coupled enlightenment with determination, could overcome the contradictions evident in most lives. Erratic and self-defeating behavior was seen as the result of ignorance and weakness, not as the inevitable mistakes of human beings.

Some philosophic schools published an authorized life of their founder, believing that his teaching would be reflected in his life and that his achievements would prove the virtue of his teaching—in short, that you could tell what was in a man's mind by the way he lived. Such a *vita* was both a lesson in morality and a presentation of a teacher's thinking since, presumably, a thoughtful reader could deduce the master's philosophy from his actions, particularly from his management of his city's affairs. Josephus' paraphrase of Deuteronomy's eulogy of Moses reflects this approach:

He departed . . . having surpassed in understanding all men that ever lived and put to noblest use the fruit of his reflections. In speech and in addresses to a crowd he found favor in every way, but chiefly through his thorough command of his passions, which was such that he seemed to have no place for them at all in his soul, and only knew their names though seeing them in others rather than in himself . . . Nor was he regretted only by those who had known him by experience, but the very readers of his laws have sadly felt his loss, deducing from these the superlative quality of his virtue [*Ant.* 4:329–31].

The Greco-Roman world paid little attention to the masses but carefully observed and recorded the characteristics and accomplishments of powerful and distinguished individuals. Those who make history are worth knowing. The original Torah story is filled with nameless walk-ons; a pharaoh, a pharaoh's daughter, a taskmaster, several sorcerers, two quarreling Hebrew slaves. Now everyone is named. The naming procedures vary, but the process of naming is itself proof that the "I" has emerged out of the clan and the crowd.

Although we cannot explain each and every name assigned to an anonymous Biblical character, it is clear from an examination of the different names that various writers, in retelling the Exodus story, gave to the Pharaoh whom Moses confronted that serious thought went into the selection. Anti-Judean writers, eager to brand Jews as an alien community, chose names which identified the Jews as relative latecomers. An Egyptian priest, Manetho (third century B.C.E.) calls him Amenophis, whom he seems to identify as a nineteenth-dynasty king (1225–1205 B.C.E.). Another Egyptian, Lysimachus (second to first century B.C.E.), an even more strident detractor of the Jews than Manetho, identifies Moses' Pharaoh with Bocchoris, a king of the twenty-fourth dynasty (718–712 B.C.E.). The Jews for their part preferred an early date. A second-century B.C.E. Jewish historian, Artapanus, names Moses' protagonist as Pharaoh Chenephres, a fifth-dynasty king (ca. twenty-eighth century B.C.E.), thus placing Jews in Egypt almost at the beginning of Egyptian civilization.

Moses becomes a visible and definable person, possessing the virtues most admired by the elites who dominated this Hellenistic world. God's most humble servant recedes into the Torah text and a vigorous prophet-philosopher-king emerges. Moses is endowed with a physical presence which would have won the applause of the spectators in one of Athens' better gymnasiums and a gravity and sober demeanor which would have earned the approval of Alexandria's most serious-minded citizens.

In his *On the Jews*, Artapanus offers the earliest known description of Moses, drawn, to be sure, not from life but from the conventions of Hellenistic portraiture. The holy man whom the Torah hides from view is here provided with the well-muscled frame of an Olympian athlete gracefully grown to maturity. Moses is big boned, of ruddy complexion, with a white beard, a full head of hair, and a commanding presence (Eusebius 9:28). Artapanus' contemporary, the playwright Ezekiel, put Moses on the stage. The actor who played him was probably tall and well formed, dressed in a tunic, or chiton, and certainly spoke his Greek lines without stammer or stutter. Several portraits of Moses occur in a series of frescoes executed in the fourth century C.E. by professional artists hired by the board of a synagogue in Dura Europus, a Roman garrison town in eastern Syria. In one scene Moses is shown as a dark-haired, dark-eyed, light-skinned baby being lifted out of a watertight cradle. In another he is a stalwart athletic young man, slightly bearded and dressed in a white linen pallium, standing barefoot beside a burning bush. His laced boots are placed neatly beside him, illustrating the Torah text: "Remove your sandals from your feet, for the place on which you stand is holy ground" (Exod. 3:5). One fresco shows Moses standing straight and tall on the far side of the Reed Sea and another has him in the same posture before a desert well from which water flows through twelve substantial hoses into the tents of the twelve tribes. In dress and look Dura's Moses is a Roman nobleman; his pallium is banded by horizontal rows of royal purple, such as a Caesar might wear.

Moses, who had spent his life with a group of wandering tribes, becomes a city man. Long removed from their nomadic origins, the Greeks associated civilization with city living. They assumed that men of courage and shrewdness could lead a confederation of tribes on a long march—such rude folk were always coming out of the steppes of Asia—but only a man of wisdom and courage, a philosopher-king, could successfully manage the more difficult task of founding a peaceful and flourishing city. Cities could not exist without law and good law established the prosperity of a city. That Greek writers did not recognize tribal custom as law and could not imagine a lawgiver who was not connected to a city accounts for their frequent and anachronistic identification of Moses as the founder-lawmaker of Jerusalem.

A travelogue-history, *Aegyptiaca*, written around the year 300 B.C.E. by Hecateus of Abdera, a Greek rhetor who had attached himself to the court of Ptolemy I, relates this account of the original Jewish community in Egypt. A serious plague ravaged the kingdom, due, many believed, to the presence of aliens on Egypt's sacred soil. The oracles are consulted and word is given that the plague would subside once the land was purified. All aliens, including some Greeks and a nameless group under the leadership of a "man called Moses," are immediately and unceremoniously bundled out of the country. This Moses is a leader "outstanding both for his wisdom and his courage" who not only leads his party ably during a long trek to a new home but enables them to establish a successful colony in a hitherto uninhabited place in the land now called Judea. Moses divides the tribes into twelve, a sacred number corresponding to the divisions of the zodiac; publishes appropriate laws for his colony, Jerusalem; builds there a temple; and organizes its cult. Believing that God was beyond representation, he orders that no idols or images be placed in the shrine. A priest class consisting of the most respected citizens is made responsible for the national rites, justice, and political administration. This Moses is a successful general who combines excellent recruitment and training practices with first-rate field tactics and a competent administrator who fairly apportions the conquered territories among his people, appropriately reserving some large grants for the priests. Moses' laws include rules designed to prevent the poor from selling their holdings, lest monopolists control the land and reduce the small farmer to serfdom. He also outlaws child exposure which, according to Hecateus, helps to account for the present large Jewish population (Stern 26–27). Hecateus' Moses is a respected figure, the founder and first citizen of a Jewish *polis,* or city-state, on the Greek model. He is pious and careful of the rites but, clearly, a citizen-priest and not a shaman, or prayer master-intercessor. It seemed self-evident to Hecateus that Moses was cut from the same cloth as the revered founders of Athens and Sparta, Solon and Lycurgus, a noble fellow, a city man, not a nomad sheik.

The Jewish community in Egypt during the Persian period had been small and scattered and Jewish-Egyptian tensions had probably been rather sporadic. With the rapid increase of Egypt's Jewish population in the early years after Alexander's conquest, intercommunal friction became a serious problem. The real issues were political and economic, but the Moses-Exodus story, the one well-known piece of Jewish history, became the vortex around which a literary polemic swirled, with Egyptians and Jews offering versions that suited their particular purposes.

Around 280 B.C.E. Manetho published a history of his nation in which, among other things, he attacks the Jews as criminal aliens and Moses as a defrocked priest of the devil god Seth. Manetho charges the Jews with atheism, miserliness, and misanthropy: the Jews refused to serve the city's gods, hence they were atheists; they claimed the Torah's rules against idolatry prohibited them from sponsoring the public rites and games which were a costly responsibility of wealthy residents, hence they were misers; and they could not or would not eat in neighbors' homes because their dietary laws imposed social distance, hence they were misanthropes. Manetho had other complaints against Jews, chiefly their deferment from duties in the home guard. The rules of Sabbath observance led Jews to request, and the Ptolemies to grant, release from service in the civil defense forces, a service that involved not only military duty but also the expensive purchase of arms and armor.

Although Manetho's original *Egyptian History* is lost, a long passage which paraphrases his version of the Exodus story survives (Stern 78–83). The reigning Pharaoh, Amenophis, suddenly decides he wants to see the gods. A courtier with a reputation as a seer reveals to him that his wish will be granted if the land is purified of all who are leprous or diseased. Amenophis promptly rounds up eighty thousand unfortunates and sends them east to work the mines and quarries of the Sinai. In time they are joined by a defrocked priest of Heliopolis, one Osarseph (the name seems to be drawn from the god Osiris who had been worshipped at Heliopolis before Manetho's priestly ancestors established there a cult of Serapis). Osarseph assumes command of this legion of the diseased and damned, equips them with arms, and adds to his force a legion of tribesmen from Jerusalem who are identified as Hyksos, those former conquerors of Egypt still hated for a rule marked by cruelty and disregard for Egyptian values or sensibilities. Once in command of this army of Hyksos and lepers, Osarseph sets out to conquer Egypt. Amenophis and his court flee to Ethiopia, carrying Egypt's sacred animals. Osarseph's army ravages Egypt for thirteen years until Amenophis, supported by his son Ramesses, mounts a successful counterattack.

Elements of the Exodus story can be recognized here. The *asafsuf*, rabble, who went out with Moses have become the "lepers and other polluted persons" whom Osarseph rallies in the stone quarries. The Biblical comment that the Israelites went out armed (Exod. 13:18) is probably the basis of the tradition that turns the Hebrew slaves into a well-equipped army. Egypt's initial defeat at the hand of Osarseph echoes the Biblical description of the debacle at the Reed Sea. Among other elements not so readily identified, one—the detail that Pharaoh took the sacred animals with him as he withdrew—probably reflects the disgust Egyptians felt at descriptions of the sacrificial cult in the Jerusalem Temple since some of the animals Jews routinely sacrificed there were of species protected in Egypt as totems of gods.

Moses is missing in this version of the Exodus story which assigns his role to Osarseph, but a postscript makes the identification. "It is said that the priest who framed their constitution and their laws was a native of Heliopolis named Osarseph after the god Osiris, worshipped at Heliopolis; but when he joined this people he changed his name and was called Moses" (Stern 83). Manetho, a professional historian despite his anti-Judean bias, first reported a version he had heard or read and then made the correction he knew to be necessary.

The Ptolemaic plan for Alexandria was as futile as it was ingenious. The city's economy grew so fast that imported labor alone could not carry out the city's work. More and more Egyptians crowded into the city, and by the end of the third century B.C.E. and for several centuries thereafter, the street mobs that Ptolemy I had feared made their presence felt. Riots generally led by priests became increasingly frequent, violent, nativist, and anti-Jewish, and the theme of the Jew as unwanted intruder became a staple in some circles. The angriest attack came from the strident pen of Lysimachus. He describes the Jews of Moses' time as a scurvied and diseased lot who took to begging and became such a great nuisance and financial burden that Pharaoh Bocchoris was advised by the oracle of Ammon to expel or drown them. The lepers are drowned. All others are "exposed in the desert to perish." Those who survived draw together and one among them, Moses, a charlatan and an imposter, becomes their leader. He leads them to Judea, conquers it, maltreats the native population, and builds there a capital. Moses promulgates for Jerusalem, his new city, laws which require its citizens to mislead all who are not of their kind and to set fire to all temples not their own. According to Lysimachus, Jerusalem was first named Hierosyla to suggest that its inhabitants had "sacrilegious propensities" and the Jews later altered the name to Hieroslyma to avoid the disgraceful implication (Stern 384–85).

In the early first century C.E., Chaeremon and Apion, the former a priest-scribe, the other a rhetor, both from Alexandria, published separate anti-Jewish versions of the Exodus story. Chaeremon's account drew on Manetho's. The goddess Isis blames Pharaoh Amenophis for allowing her temple to be destroyed during a war. A priest of the court tells the king that he can atone by purging the land of all who are polluted. Amenophis rounds up and banishes a quarter of a million aliens and diseased persons. Two priests of Egypt— Tisithen, identified as Moses, and Peteseph, identified as Joseph—become leaders of the exiles who are later joined by a legion of ex-prisoners of war. The exiles and their new allies arm themselves, return, and conquer Egypt. Amenophis flees to Ethiopia, but later his son, Ramesses, recaptures the country and chases out the intruders (Stern 419–29).

Apion, who also quoted Manetho, pictures Moses as a resident alien of Heliopolis, where he participates in the worship of the sun and builds a prayer house oriented to the east. The reigning pharaoh orders an expulsion of aliens and lepers. After a six-day journey led by Moses, the exiles arrive in Judea where Moses establishes a *polis* and organizes it around his form of worship. Because Apion had some reputation as a Homer specialist, his attack was particularly influential though it popularized such absurdities as the charge that once a year Jews seized and sacrificed a non-Jew at a ceremony where they swore eternal hatred of all non-Jews, and the calumny that a gold-plated head of an ass was kept in the Holy of Holies in the Temple of Jerusalem, which implied that Jews worshipped the Egyptian evil god Seth or Typhon-Seth, who was commonly presented wearing an ass's head (Stern 393–7).

The translation of the Torah into Greek in Alexandria in the middle of the third century B.C.E. gave Egypt's Jews an authorized text which authenticated their version of the Exodus history. Books were costly and rare, literacy was a rare accomplishment, and books and bookmen were offered profound deference. The Septuagint was not just any translation of the Torah but an inspired achievement. Egyptian Jews believed that seventy-two men had worked in separate cells and had produced identical versions. Since they were confident they could trust God's description of the Exodus as an escape of slaves from intolerable conditions, they dismissed histories which described the Exodus as an expulsion of the diseased as malicious lies. Greek-speaking Jews used their "accurate" history to refute other versions, but read into the Septuagint their world's assumptions about leadership and so paid little attention to those passages which present Moses as a somewhat reclusive holy man. They expected and created the biography of an active and successful leader.

A first-century Alexandrian audience would not have fully appreciated or approved a Moses who never went to war and who hesitated to make any decision on his own. Since Torah language is spare, with little physical description and almost no indication of motives, there were large gaps in Moses' life; Hellenized Jews filled these with episodes that, in time, gave an entirely new shape to Moses' career. For the most part Jewish historians of Hellenistic times did not invent the stories they reported. They drew on a well-known, free-floating, many-sided oral tradition which existed alongside the published Torah. It included episodes which, for whatever reason, had not been included in the written text, as well as the elaborations of generations of storytellers and imaginative interpretations by teachers and preachers. A teacher had provided details of Moses' education. A storyteller had embroidered his tale with a romantic scenario about Moses' love life as a young prince. A father, eager to teach his son virtue, had compared the responsibilities of a shepherd to the responsibilities of a good citizen. From this mass of material writers shaped an old-new Moses easily recognized yet recognizably different.

In time many of these elaborations ceased to be seen as extra material and came to be accepted as *aggadah,* part of a creditable oral tradition. Today the term *aggadah* is used to describe the nonlegal materials contained in the Talmudic literature, but originally it simply described the episodes and details which accompanied the constant retelling of Biblical history. Because the early *aggadah* did not ask for or receive formal authorization but aimed at winning the interest of an audience, it was rich, varied to the point of inconsistency, sometimes imaginative to the point of being incredible. Over the generations *aggadah* reshaped the popular understanding of the Biblical narrative by establishing through repetition various stories and elaborations as authoritative.

The process of expansion, elaboration, and explanation which created *aggadah* is almost as old as the earliest sections of the Torah text. The Torah text itself contains *aggadah.* One example: the Torah records that the ex-slaves had among them enough gold to mold a Golden Calf and sufficient gold, silver, and jewels to fashion the sacred utensils of the sanctuary. The report raises an obvious problem: how came these slaves to possess such wealth? An *aggadic* solution appears in Exodus: on the night of deliverance the Israelites borrowed gold and precious stones from the plague-weary Egyptians who were so eager to speed the Jews on their way that they let them have all the Israelites wanted (Exod. 12:35, 36). Many *aggadot*, like this one, not only solve a textual problem but seek to make a sermonic point, in this case the operation of divine retribution: the Egyptians had despoiled the Israelites who had freely come down in Joseph's day so now, measure for measure, their enslaved descendants free themselves at Egyptian expense.

When Greek-speaking Jews read about Moses, their understanding was affected by the changes of meaning and emphasis which occur in any translation. The Septuagint translators used the Greek noun *Kyrios* for YHVH, Moses' name for God. *Kyrios* suggests lordship and creative power but lacks the implication of a personal God. *Elohim* became *Theos*, pure being, a denationalized creative power. Both Greek terms emphasize God's transcendence and come out of a philosophic culture which preferred to speak of man perceiving God's will, rather than of God speaking to man. In the Torah Moses is unexpectedly summoned by God. The Hellenistic understanding of prophecy is much less accidental. The Moses who is summoned to the Burning Bush had prepared himself for his prophetic vocation. Where the Torah assumes that God put every idea into Moses' mouth, Artapanus assumes that Moses had to be a learned man before God chose him as His prophet, and he earnestly gives us details of Moses' education. A Palestinian text, *Jubilees*, explains that Moses learned elementary things from his mother and advanced Judaism from his father, Amram, with whom he remained for twenty-one years before returning to the palace. Josephus reports "that he was educated with the utmost care" (*Ant.* 2:236).

These schooling reports have another purpose. Jewish writers insist that Moses was tutored by his natural parents, which is to say that his character is the result of Hebrew, not Egyptian, learning. The point here, in these and similar tales, is the Jewish insistence that Moses' virtue was thoroughly Jewish in inspiration rather than derived from alien sources. No people wants its most famous progenitor to have been weaned on alien, in this case idolatrous, milk. Modern Jews were agitated by Sigmund Freud's Egyptianization of Moses in *Moses and Monotheism*, less on the quite defensible grounds that the psychoanalyst's venture into Biblical scholarship is unscholarly and unsubstantiated than out of a visceral feeling that Judaism's worth is brought into question by a description of its founder as one who brings foreign ideas and values.

Perceiving God in largely transcendent terms, Hellenized Jews could no longer use God as a role model. How does a man pattern himself after *Kyrios* or *Theos*—nameless, formless, creative power? Obviously, he cannot. Those who conceived of God as creative power, divine intelligence, or pure being were no longer comfortable using the list of God's attributes in Exodus 34:6–7—"The Lord! The Lord! A God compassionate and gracious. . . ."—as the basis for their ethical standards. Philosophers made the point that no one could define what compassion or mercy meant as an attribute of God. In discussing virtue, Hellenistic teachers turned more and more to the patriarchs and Moses as patterning models. Now, despite the Bible's insistence that, including Moses, "there is no man so righteous that he sins not" (1 Kings 8:46), Moses' virtues are inflated, incidents unflattering to his character are reinterpreted, and he is presented as a model of virtuous behavior.

It was an age which loved biography, but Hellenistic biography must not be confused with our own. Where current biography tends to focus on the quirks and ambivalences of its subject, Hellenistic *bios* chose as subject only the superior person and focused on his nobility, believing that virtue was more effectively taught by concrete example than by theoretical discussion. Hellenistic biographies of Moses are, in fact, long sermons on virtue.

But he, before this mob so excited and embittered against him, confident in God and in the consciousness of his own care for his countrymen, advanced into their midst and, as they clamoured upon him and still held the stones in their hands, he, with that winning presence of his and that extraordinary influence in addressing a crowd, began to pacify their wrath. He exhorted them not, with present discomforts engrossing all their thoughts, to forget the benefits of the past, nor because they suffered now to banish from their minds the favours and bounties, so great and unlooked for, which they had received from God. Rather ought they to expect relief also from their present straits to come from God's solicitude, for it was probably to test their manhood, to see what fortitude they possessed, what memory of past services, and whether their thoughts would not revert to those services because of the troubles now in their path, that He was exercising them with these trials of the moment. But now they were convicted of failure, both in endurance and in recollection of benefits received, by showing at once such contempt of God and of His purpose, in accordance with which they had left Egypt, and such demeanor towards himself, God's minister, albeit he had never proved false to them in aught that he had said or in any order that he had given them at God's command. So they should not despair even now of His providence, but should await it without anger, not deeming His succour tardy, even if it came not forthwith and before they had had some experience of discomfort, but rather believing that it was not from negligence that God thus tarried, but to rest their manhood and their delight in liberty, "that He may learn (said he) whether for once ye have the spirit to endure for its sake both deprivation of food and lack of water, or prefer slavery, like the beasts which slave for the masters who feed them lavishly in view of their services." He added that, if he feared anything, it was not so much for his own safety—for it would be no misfortune to him to be unjustly done to death—as for them, lest in flinging those stones at him they should be thought to be pronouncing sentence upon God. [*Ant.* 3:13–21].

In emphasis and definition, as the preceding passage demonstrates, the virtues and attitudes Moses displays—patience, forbearance, stoicism—match the preconceptions of upper-class Hellenistic society. Not unexpectedly, Moses is also made to fit its prejudices. Ezekiel's stage portrait of Moses includes a deliberate attempt to refute the suggestion that Moses had married a black woman. A somewhat enigmatic verse in the Book of Numbers reads: "When they were in Hazeroth, Miriam and Aaron spoke against Moses because of the Cushite woman he had married" (12:1). The Septuagint, the Greek translation of the Torah beloved by Egypt's Jew, identified Cush with Ethiopia, home of the black tribes who periodically invaded and plundered Egypt. While the idea of a black wife had not troubled Biblical Jews—Solomon is reported to have been attracted to the Queen of Sheba and *The Song of Songs* includes the verse: "I am black but comely" (1:5)—in Alexandria the upper classes held antiblack prejudices and skin color was a sufficiently sensitive issue for acculturated Jews to want to disencumber Moses of his black wife. Ezekiel manages this by having only one wife appear in his play, Zipporah, who pointedly informs her future husband that her father is king of many cities of mixed population, including some blacks. Her intention (that is, Ezekiel's) is to make it clear that she herself is not black.

The tendency to glorify great men led inevitably to what I can best label "fig leaf" descriptions of Moses. Jewish writers and storytellers covered up any aspect of his life they deemed unseemly. One of the charges raised by Manetho and his intellectual heirs was that Moses was an ingrate who had returned little but trouble to Pharaoh and his adoptive mother for the care they had lavished on him; he had not even bid them a formal farewell before he took precipitous flight. Moreover, when he returned to Egypt it was to plague the land and free its slaves without any recompense to their masters. These charges concerned writers like Artapanus who answered them in several ways: Moses had returned to Egypt more than he had received from it, for he was no other than the father of Egyptian civilization; moreover, the young Moses had served Pharaoh faithfully and would have continued to do so had not jealous courtiers intrigued against him, threatened his life, and forced him to flee.

The claim that Moses was the originator of Egyptian civilization necessarily assumes that Moses is something of a demigod and seems outlandish at first blush; but at least three Egyptian-Jewish writers of the first century B.C.E.—the historian Artapanus, an author named Eupolemus, and the playwright Ezekiel—repeat the claim. Artapanus described Moses as an engineer of note, the inventor of hydraulic lifts and war machines, the discoverer of various navigational skills, a capable administrator who had established the accepted system of weights and measures and devised the division of Egypt into administrative units called nomes, and a skilled architect-priest who knew precisely where to locate and how to build Egypt's temples. Incredibly, the founder of the Jewish religion, whose laws against idolatry were by Artapanus' time well known, is described by a committed Jew as the organizer of Egypt's idolatry. Moreover, Moses possessed knowledge of the secret meanings of the ancient hieroglyphs and of the rituals appropriate to the various gods—particularly the cat god, Bubastis; the dog god, Canubis; the ibis-headed god, Thoth; and Apis, the sacred bull—powerful esoteric knowledge which he willingly passed on to the priests of his native land. Artapanus contrasts Moses' willing and generous instruction of all who wished to learn with the well-known secretiveness of Egypt's priests (Eusebius 9:27:1–6). Only a few fragments of Eupolemus' history *On the Kings of Judah* (second century B.C.E.) have survived, but we know that in it he described Moses as the "first wise man" and made him responsible for, among other inventions, the discovery of the alphabet, that most revolutionary of all cultural tools which, according to Eupolemus, passed from the Jews to the Phoenicians and then to the Greeks (Eusebius 9:25).

The playwright Ezekiel in his Greek-style, Greek-language tragedy—titled *Esagoge,* or the *Exodus*—gives Moses a speech whose impact depends on the audience's belief that Moses was more than a mere mortal. The two hundred and sixty-nine lines of this play which survive include Moses' description to Jethro, his father-in-law, of a dream in which he finds himself on a mountain crest before a throne whose canopy touched the skies. A noble person wearing a crown and carrying a scepter in his left hand sits on the throne and bids Moses welcome, provides him with a scepter of his own, and seats him on another, lower throne. Once seated Moses looks about and sees the far reaches of the universe; below are the arch of the earth, the sweep of the firmament, and a parade of stars which bow to him as they pass. Jethro interprets the dream as a prophecy of Moses' ultimate leadership, and we note that he does not dismiss as arrogance Moses' vision of himself as a familiar and welcome member of God's court (Eusebius 9:28).

The image of Moses as a semidivine father of civilization was not only a dramatic way of refuting the charge that Moses was an ingrate but was a forceful argument for the importance and universal value of Moses' law. In the Oikoumene—the larger ecumenical world in which Hellenized Jews desired to live—the charge that the Jewish way was a parochial culture was damaging. These "histories" neatly countered such disparagement. How can Torah be parochial if it is the brainchild of the master of all knowledge and the father of all civilization? Moreover, since Moses was the father of civilization and the Torah was his rule, it followed that Jews had more to teach than to learn and therefore had no reason to subordinate their wisdom to that of any Greek or Egyptian philosophic school. Moses had brought something unique, fresh, pristine—revealed, not borrowed; universal, not parochial. Moses' specific rules reflected general truths proper for all men.

Artapanus' and Eupolemus' description of Moses as the father of civilization presented the Judean version of a common theme of the time, which tended to trace the arts of civilization back to a single inspired thinker, usually a demigod, who had taught mankind the practical skills by which it had prospered. Moses played this role among Egypt's Hellenized Jews, Orpheus among Egypt's Orientalized Greeks, Hermes-Thoth among the more Hellenized Egyptians. Other Egyptians ascribed the role to an early Pharaoh, Sesostiris, who was described as the father of Egyptian learning, organizer of the rites, and source of all useful knowledge, or to Imhotep, builder of the first pyramid and counselor of Pharaoh Zoser.

As the first wise man and as one who had lived long before the Golden Age of Greek thought, Moses could be seen, if one was so inclined, as the father of that ultimate discipline, Greek philosophy, and the Torah could be seen as the original statement of truth and the source from which all philosophers derived their knowledge. A second-century B.C.E. Jewish philosopher and exegete, Aristobulos of Paneas, said bluntly, "Plato followed our laws" (Eusebius 13:12). He argued that, since truth must be one, the familiar Greek philosophic categories and the Torah laws were simply different ways of expressing the same single truth, and he set out to demonstrate this claim in a voluminous commentary on the Torah of which, unfortunately, only a few fragments survive. The commandments were what they seemed, specific rules, and, at the same time, specific examples of the general principles of philosophy. The Sabbath, he asserted, was a specific day of rest; a sign of a sacred number important to the rites; a statement of the existence of the seven heavenly spheres which circumscribe and animate the earth; and a description of the seven potentialities or senses which constitute the mind. The Ten Commandments were commandments and the sum of the original numbers $1 + 2 + 3 + 4$ and, thus, a quintessence of all truth. The Torah, properly understood, presents not only the ideal constitution of a *polis* but a blueprint of the cosmos, the rules of natural law. To Aristobulos and his readers Moses is not simply the prophet who brought God's Instructions or even the wisest of all lawgivers but the master of those who know.

Erudition and superstition coexisted comfortably in this Greco-Roman world, often in the same person's mind. The educated recognized that some of the gods were ancient kings who had been deifed by pious legend, yet they continued to participate in the deification of kings and philosophers. Remarkably advanced theories about the origin of myths were often held by the same people who consulted magic books and took part in the mysteries of Serapis or Thoth-Hermes.

Egyptian magic and esoteric wisdom were acknowledged throughout the Mediterranean world as unmatched, and Moses was widely acknowledged by Jews and non-Jews as a master thaumaturge. In early Egyptian painting and sculpture, male gods were routinely depicted holding a staff, an iconographic sign of their civil and/or divine authority. During the Middle Kingdom the rod ceased to be a god-identifying symbol and became the sign of the wizard. In Hellenistic times Moses is rarely described without his rod, and all the attributes of the wizard are attached to him. By keeping the wonderful rod front and center, Ezekiel indulges in quite effective show business to reinforce the image of Moses as a wizard. Ezekiel's Moses can make the rod do anything he wants, and his powers are plainly superior to those of Egypt's famous wizards. Ezekiel knew his audience—like them, he paid little attention to the Torah's insistence that the rod's powers could be released only by God.

Artapanus' Moses may have been the father of civilization, but he was not above a bit of magic. Artapanus reports that at one point during the lengthy negotiations which preceded the Exodus, Pharaoh has Moses thrown into a dungeon. Moses' incarceration doesn't last the night. Using his knowledge of the powers associated with God's Name, Moses commands the gates to open and open they do, commands the guards to sleep at their posts and sleep they do. Once free, Moses does not flee into the night but goes directly to the palace. He enters unchallenged, casts a spell over the palace guards, and makes his way to Pharaoh's bedroom. The sleeping monarch awakens to find Moses at his side. Recognizing that Moses' presence is no ordinary event, for only a mighty god could have enabled Moses to escape from jail and enter the palace, the king does not shout for help but, instead, asks Moses to reveal the name of his god (Eusebius 9:27).

Pompeius Trogus (first century B.C.E.), a rather naive Roman historian, misrepresents Moses as Joseph's son and establishes him as "heir of his father's knowledge," which he describes as consisting largely of mastery of the art of magic, the gift of second sight, and an infallible ability to interpret dreams (Stern 336–38). Pliny the Elder (first century C.E.) in his *Natural History* refers to Moses only once and then in connection with magic: he speaks of a branch of magic "derived from Moses, Jannes, Lotapes [Balaam's two sons] and the Jews" (Stern 498). A number of Egyptian books on magic exist, dealing with such subjects as the proper writing of charms and amulets; they bear titles like *The Eighth Book of Moses, The Key of Moses,* and *The Secret Book of Moses.* Several alchemical texts of the time also bear Moses' name: *The Chemistry of Moses, The Maza of Moses, The Diptosis of Moses.* Amulets found in both

Jewish and non-Jewish graves in Egypt dating from the Greco-Roman period bear Moses' name and feature a rod-like symbol; clearly Moses ranked high on any list of well-known Merlins familiar to the credulous of the age—which means to almost everyone.

How had Moses acquired the secret and esoteric knowledge which enabled him to be a wizard? He had asked for it and at the Burning Bush God had provided it. Moses says: "When they ask me, 'What is His name,' what shall I say to them?" God answers: *Ehyeh Asher Ehyeh* (Exod. 3:13–14). The passage was read as the gift to Moses of God's Name and of the knowledge necessary to use its power. Nearly everyone in that time and place took for granted that the use of a power-laden Name could heal the sick, bring the rain, or strike one dead if used in a curse. Readers of the time would not have thought it curious that Artapanus identifies the weapon Moses had used in the murder of the Egyptian taskmaster as the utterance of God's Name. One who knew The Name had no need of a knife.

The Hellenistic world reshaped the image of classic Greece's civic hero, the politically active sage whose learning informs and shapes his character and consequently his service as lawgiver and magistrate, into another hero-type, the politically active seer whose learning is not just a personal attainment but also a gift of the gods. The leader's wisdom now includes matters esoteric and magical as well as scientific and philosophic and Moses is made to fit easily into the new heroic mold.

As wizard, prophet, and founder of a nation, Moses must have been accepted by many besides Jews as one of the demigods who were widely venerated throughout the Hellenistic world. Hercules, Orpheus, Zoroaster, Imhotep—and even Alexander—were widely accepted as both human and more than human. Had they not revealed what otherwise would not have been known and accomplished what no mortal could accomplish? Their lives evidenced no contradictions, presumedly because they governed themselves by the light of reason. As perfect men they were fit objects not only of veneration but of adoration.

Greco-Roman biography was the near cousin of apotheosis. Perhaps it is not so suprising, therefore, that one finding of my study of Moses' place in Hellenistic culture is the suggestion dug out of its literary remains that there was an early Judean shrine in Egypt where Jews worshipped Moses as a divine being. The literary materials we must examine developed as part of the Jewish response to the attacks by Manetho and his heirs. Although the detractors could invent their canards out of whole cloth, the Jewish advocates could not; Hellenistic Jews felt free to go beyond Torah but not to contradict it. They reshaped the Moses episodes by wrapping Moses in *aggadah*. Where the detractors picture Moses as an upstart who became leader of a band of ne'er-do-wells and lepers, Jewish apologetes pictured him as a loyal prince who served his adopted father faithfully until envious courtiers and fanatic priests maliciously conspired against him. To those Egyptians who argued that Moses had fled out of fear that his murder of the taskmaster would become known, Jews responded that Moses had left because powerful and jealous courtiers, envious of his closeness to Pharaoh, had intrigued against him, leaving him no other intelligent course. And, as we have seen, several argued that Moses was, far from being a defrocked priest or a recent immigrant, the founder-benefactor of Egypt's world-renowned civilization. Their general theme was the nobility of

Moses and the tales that they told reveal a good bit about Jewish life and concerns, including the probable existence some time in the past of a Moses cult.

I believe that at one time, probably during the Persian occupation, a formal cult of Moses flourished at a shrine where Moses was the object of Jewish devotion, probably at Leontopolis near modern Memphis. I am convinced that even after the shrine was abandoned many Egyptian Jews continued to think of Moses as a divine being. I do not mean that they acknowledged Moses as the son of God, but that they knew him as a man whose nature was free of the flaws and passions which lesser mortals cannot escape and whose accomplishments were so extraordinary as to seem supernatural. Let me develop that tale.

No specific reference to a Moses shrine is to be found in the surviving literature. We would not expect to find one. Greeks would not have recognized the uniqueness of such a place, Egyptians would not have wanted to publicize the fact that such a shrine had ever been built on their sacred soil, and—most important—later rabbinic Jews would have expunged all reference to such a shrine as a religious scandal.

I believe the shadow of the shrine can be found in two *aggadot* current during this period, one published by Josephus, the other by Artapanus. The versions published by these two historians are composite reports of long-circulating stories presented as history but given without indication of source or date. We must proceed by inference and analogy from hidden clues buried in them. Unravelling *aggadah* requires the skills of Sherlock Holmes. Our investigation will proceed through three stages: a critical review of the two relevant "histories," both of which use the ibis bird as a central figure; an investigation of the possible polemical purposes of these histories; and an analysis of the elements in them that suggest a Moses cult.

Josephus' version opens when young Prince Moses is still a favored member of Pharaoh's court. Marauding Nubian troops have penetrated into Egypt where they meet such light resistance that their leaders decide to press on and loot the entire country. The reigning Pharaoh consults an oracle and is told to replace his defeated generals with Prince Moses; he consults with Thermuthis, his daughter and Moses' adoptive mother, and acts on the oracle's advice. Moses accepts the commission. His decision pleases both Egyptian and Hebrew leaders but for different reasons. The Hebrews look to Moses' rise to power to increase their chance of release from slavery; the Egyptians expect Moses to defeat the army and then fall prey to court intrigue. Moses musters his troops and leads them into Nubia. He does not proceed south along the Nile, the usual invasion route into the Sudan, but follows a circuitous overland route which veered east into the dry and forbidding interior. His route was considered impassable because it was infested with poisonous vermin and snakes "which the region produces in abundant varieties, remarkable for their power, their malignity, and their strange aspect; and among them are some which are actually winged so that they can attack one from their hiding places in the ground or inflict unforeseen injury by rising into the air." Moses is prepared. On his orders the troops carry with them baskets of papyrus bark, each containing an ibis, a tame bird but the snake's deadliest enemy. On reaching the danger zone Moses orders the birds released, and they go to work with good appetite. As things turn out, the Nubian capital falls without a costly frontal attack—in part because the city's princess, Tharbis, notices the handsome prince as she watches the battle from her city walls and decides to become his bride. The marriage is celebrated and Moses presumably enjoys both victory and the fruits of victory (*Ant.* 2:242–76).

Artapanus' fragment presents Pharaoh's daughter, here called Meroe, as wife of Chenephres, who rules in the delta lands. Because she is sterile she adopts a young Hebrew whom she calls Moses. He is widely loved for his many benevolences—Artapanus interpolates here the description of Moses as the father of civilization, which we have already examined—and honored by the priests with attributes normally ascribed to the gods. Artapanus informs us that the priests called Moses *hermes*, interpreter, possibly because of his ability to interpret the esoteric meaning of sacred texts.

Chenephres becomes jealous of Moses and seeks a chance to undo him. The opportunity presents itself when Chenephres must order a punitive raid against Nubia; he commissions Moses as general of Egypt's forces but tries to insure his defeat by providing him with a conscript army of unskilled farm boys. Moses accepts the commission and foils Chenephres. The war lasts ten years, during which Moses builds a sizable camp-city near the enemy capital. He names the camp-city Hermopolis after Hermes and consecrates it to the ibis, "because this bird slays the creatures that injure man." The siege is a long one and during its course the Nubians come to appreciate Moses' character, courage, and chivalry. They conclude an honorable treaty with General Moses which includes an unusual act of respect: "they learned from him to circumcise their sons."

When Moses returns to the Egyptian capital, Chenephres and the priests feign pleasure at his success but continue to plot against him. His army is demobilized. Some soldiers are sent to garrisons on the Sudanese frontier, others are ordered to demolish an old brick Temple at Diospolis and to build there another of stone, quarried and cut by hand from the nearby hills. Then Chenephres sets in motion a murder plot against Moses. He hires Chanethothes, apparently a Hebrew, to do the killing. When Meroe dies, Chenephres believes that her funeral procession will provide the assassin a good chance at Moses. The plot misfires because Aaron hears of it and informs his brother; Moses awaits the would-be assassin's attack, kills him, and withdraws to Arabia (Eusebius 9:27).

These "histories" conform to a popular Hellenistic literary device, *aretas legein*, the recital of the virtues of a founder-hero. But these histories are Jewish histories, hence they are also *aggadah*, concerned with putting a good face on the Torah narrative.

Since the Torah narrative is silent on all details of Moses' life until the events which precipitate his flight to Midian, a tale of Moses as a field commander of Egyptian forces in no way contradicts God's word. The treacherous Hebrew who accepts the murder contract might easily be identified with one of the quarreling Hebrews who had challenged Moses on the day after he killed the Egyptian taskmaster. The discovery of this identification is indeed worthy of Holmes. One of the Hebrews accused Moses of the taskmaster's murder (Exod. 2:14); yet, on the day of the murder, Moses had made certain there were no witnesses to the deed. The murder could have been known only to Egyptian officials who would have received a missing persons report, and only from them could the accusing Hebrew have learned of it, which suggests that he was a paid informer, precisely the kind of man to whom the court would have given the assassination contract. Moses' attention to his adopted mother's funeral arrangements would win him praise in both Egyptian and Jewish circles and can be connected to a virtue the Torah specifically ascribes to Moses: at the time of the Exodus, he carries the bones of Joseph out of Egypt as the patriarch had requested on his death bed so they could be reburied in the family's cave near Hebron (Exod. 13:19).

The final element of the story—that pertaining to circumcision—is an *aggadic* detail which helps smooth over a problem in the Torah narrative. An eliptical passage in Exodus (4:24–26) can be interpreted to suggest that Moses had been lax in this all-important duty, having either overlooked or delayed the circumcision rite, at least for his second son. The "fact" that the Nubians used Moses as a model—men fought naked in the Sudan's broiling heat—and "learned from him to circumcise their sons" is a neat and dramatic way to eliminate the unacceptable possibility that Moses was indifferent to Judaism's rite of initiation. This *aggadah* may have served an additional purpose. During Hellenistic times monotheism became an increasingly attractive alternative to idolatry among the urban upper classes who felt that they had outgrown belief in the ancient myths. Non-Jewish men who found the Jewish way attractive would have found the initiation requiring circumcision less so; for an adult it was painful and possibly dangerous surgery. From within and without the Jewish community there must have been pressures to set aside a physical requirement that stood as an obstacle to conversion. If so, this *aggadah* was part of the loyalist response: No.

The basic intent of these histories is to counter charges made against Moses by anti-Judean polemicists. Manetho had said that Moses and his people served the devil, acted barbarically toward their neighbors, were untrustworthy and physically offensive. These histories "prove" that Moses and the Jews were loyal, circumspect, virtuous, and of acceptable appearance. Moses' body is healthy and well formed, countering Manetho's description of Moses as a scabrous alien who, with other lepers, had been driven out of Egypt.

Four elements in these histories do not immediately suggest familiar Biblical themes: Moses' brevet as a general; the cabal against Moses by Egyptian courtiers; the ibis; and the Nubian woman. It is these elements which principally interest us. The unexpected image of Moses as victorious general allows him to exhibit the physical courage and strategic brilliance that Hellenistic convention required of its heroes. These writers could not display Moses' martial virtues by citing any of the battles described in the Torah because, as we have seen, the Torah indicates at every turn that Moses neither set battle strategy nor fought in the lines. Each of Israel's victories was God's doing. To prove his military craft and martial valor, therefore, Moses had to mastermind and command a battle fought before he was commissioned as God's agent. The blank period in Moses' life, his years in Egypt, provided plenty of room to invent battle and battlefield.

For the battlefield to be in Nubia was logical enough. Sudanese and Ethiopian tribes periodically plundered Egypt, and Egypt's soldiers routinely retaliated. Their campaigns, if successful, brought rich booty into Egypt, primarily amber, slaves, hardwood, and ivory. There was also a textual reason to place Moses' campaign in Nubia. The Book of Numbers includes the report that Miriam and Aaron "spoke against Moses because of the Cushite woman he had married. . . ."

(12:1). Who was this woman? The Bible makes no other reference to her and some medieval commentators try to identify her, without much success, with Zipporah. The problem is that the Torah plainly identifies Zipporah as a Midianite. The Bible suggests two identifications for Cush: one Cossaea, the country of the Kassites in Mesopotamia (Gen. 2:13, 10:8); the other Nubia, another name for the Sudan (Gen. 10:6). The Sudanese identification, the more common one, was made official in the Septuagint. Since Moses' life is fully accounted for after he flees Egypt, he must have visited Nubia earlier, as a youth. No Egyptian prince—and Moses' life in Egypt, we are always reminded, was the life of a prince—would have gone to that barbaric land unless he had been ordered by Pharaoh to head a punitive expedition; and had he married there his wife would have been none except a princess.

The fact that the ibis served Moses in his campaign was proof of his loyalty. The Roman zoologist, Aelian (ca. 170–220 C.E.) reports an Egyptian tradition which described the ibis as a consummately patriotic bird. "Of its own free will the ibis would never quit Egypt and should some men lay their hands upon it and forcibly export it, it will defend itself against its assailant and bring all his labor to nothing. For it will starve itself to death and render its captors' exertions vain" (Aelian 2:38). Ornithologists report that most species of the ibis do migrate, but no matter, this legend of the patriotic bird who would not leave the motherland was widely credited.

The ibis is firmly identified as a predator. Five centuries earlier Herodotus had reported that a particular species of black ibis with legs like a crane and a strongly hooked beak protected Egypt from the hordes of winged serpents which migrate from Arabia each spring and that the ibis was revered by Egyptians for this service. Aelian adds the report that another species of ibis encounters the serpents which come down the Nile in flood time and destroys them, thus saving many Egyptian lives. Plainly, Moses' use of the ibis as mine sweeper through vermin-infested lands was a dramatic way of proving his loyalty.

The ibis was useful on another count. Here was proof that Moses was sensitive to Egyptian religious feelings. Had he not dedicated his military camp to Egypt's sacred bird? Had he been a disloyal ingrate or a rogue priest, the ibis would not have served him. Rather, Egypt's priests were deceitful men, disloyal to the crown when they conspired against Moses, one of the king's most loyal and obedient subjects, he who had organized Egypt's sacred rites, aided its priests to locate their shrines properly, and revealed to them secret lore.

The next step in the argument—that these two histories, with their references to Moses' military, magical, and religious use of the ibis, refract memories of a syncretistic cult which had worshipped Moses as healer and intercessor—depends in part on recognizing the importance of the ibis in two of the most popular Hellenistic-Egyptian healing cults, those of Thoth-Hermes and Imhotep-Asklepios, and on noticing the numerous similarities between these two cults and elements in the two Moses stories. The gap between conjecture and conclusion cannot be closed, but the weight of the evidence is impressive.

Given Judaism's traditional stand against idolatry, the existence of a Moses shrine violates our assumptions about Jewish monotheism, but we must guard against assuming that ordinary Jews were immune to the syncretistic pressures of Egypt. The Elephantine papyrii indicate that at least two goddesses were worshipped along with the Judean God at that island shrine. Some Jews would not have found the idea of a Moses shrine sinful so long as God also would be worshipped there. The existence of such a shrine must be seriously considered for it alone allows us to explain two otherwise inexplicable facts: the existence of the histories linking Moses with the magical-religious use of the ibis, and Moses' appearance in Ptolemaic magic and alchemy.

Thoth-Hermes and Imhotep-Asklepios were cults of healing and immortality. The shrines of these two cults at Sakkara and Tuna El Gebel, respectively, were places of initiation and healing, where worshippers were not only treated and cured but reborn. The ibis was intimately associated with both cults. During the second millennium Thoth had been known as patron of wisdom and healing and was often pictured as a seated god with an ibis head. In Hellenistic times the ancient Egyptian cult of Thoth was merged with a Greek mystery associated with Hermes, and Thoth-Hermes became the central figure in the age's most popular syncretistic cult.

Sometime during the sixth century B.C.E. the worship of Imhotep, designer of Egypt's first stepped pyramid and chancellor of Pharaoh Zoser of the Old Kingdom, as a god of wisdom and healing became popular. During Ptolemaic times the deified Imhotep was identified with the healer god Asklepios, and his shrine at Heliopolis became the Lourdes of its day. In the late 1950s and early 1960s Walter B. Emergy excavated the Imhotep shrine complex at Sakkara North, the necropolis of Memphis, and discovered several tunnels packed floor to ceiling with earthenware pots, each containing a wrapped and mummified ibis. Research determined that most of the bird offerings had been left there in

Greco-Roman times. The mummification of the ibis bird was based on the belief that something of the god was incarnate in every living member of the sacred species. It was therefore deemed a pious act to bring a dead bird to the shrine, where its share of the god's presence could be reunited with its heavenly source and where the pious pilgrim could expect to be rewarded with a cure, a heartfelt desire granted, or even life eternal. In a niche in an underground mummy chamber, Emery discovered a demotic ostracon on which, under a picture of an ibis and a hawk, someone had written a plea for protection in the next life. A Ptolemaic tomb painting shows an ibis-headed god holding the staff of life and emblem of years, speaking words of promise, "I bring to you millions of years, life, well-being and the attainment of eternity."

Artapanus specifically identifies Moses with such a cult figure. He does so on the basis of a crude etymology which identifies Moses with Musaeus, whom he describes as the teacher of Orpheus, the poet-musician who became the focus of one of the age's best-known mysteries. That his Jewish readers would accept the implied relationship despite its polytheistic implications suggests that they were not unaccustomed to thinking of Moses in these terms. Artapanus' and Eupolemus' references to Moses as patron of Egyptian culture, inventor of the alphabet, organizer of Egypt's cult, and source of the theory and practice of medicine, also ascribe to Moses precisely the gifts and skills which Egyptians and Greeks specifically associated with gods like Thoth-Hermes and Imhotep-Asklepios.

There are numerous thematic links between Thoth-Hermes and Moses. Thoth was known as a moon god, regulator of the calendar, and heavenly scribe, all attributes that could easily be associated with the founder of a Jewish cult which organized its calendar on the basis of visual observation of the new moon and centered its practice on a scroll containing God's Instructions written out by the founder. Thoth-Hermes was viewed as the source of both sacred and general law and, by inference, as the organizer of the social order. The parallel to Moses' career as legislative prophet is obvious.

Thoth-Hermes was the protector of the goddess Ma'at who personified cosmic and earthly order. Several bronze and wooden sculptures survive which present Thoth as a sacred ibis, towering protectively over Ma'at, suggesting that the ibis symbol may have been associated with Thoth-Hermes' function as protector of justice. Moses not only mediated the law and organized the legal system but also sat in judgment. In Greco-Roman times Thoth-Hermes took on many of the attributes of Asklepios-Imhotep, and their shared totem, the ibis bird, came to be associated with the art of healing. Moses' powers as a faith healer were related to his role as intercessor; he had interceded with God to withdraw Miriam's leprosy. As inventor of writing, Thoth-Hermes knew the sacred and secret meaning of the hieroglyphs and his shrine contained a library of sacred books said to contain the secrets of the universe. Moses' Torah was believed to contain depths of meaning recognizable only to those to whom he had provided the interpretive key. In Roman times Thoth-Hermes became Hermes-Trismegistus, the thrice-blessed dispenser of esoteric wisdom, acclaimed by various gnostic and other writers as the source of their revelation, as the revealer of texts full of divine secrets—in much the same way as Hellenized Jews knew Moses.

Despite these associations between Moses, the ibis bird,

and the syncretistic cults, I would be reluctant to suggest that a shrine dedicated to Moses as healer and psychopomp, where the ritual involved the mummification of sacred animals, may have operated at some early stage of the Egyptian diaspora were it not for another set of associations which specifically places mummified ibis birds within a Judean Temple. After putting down the Jewish Rebellion (66–70 C.E.), Rome took severe measures to eliminate potential centers of revanchist activity. As part of this program of suppression the Roman Emperor Vespasian signed an order in 73 C.E. requiring the Jews of Egypt to dismantle a temple and altar at Leontopolis in the nome of Heliopolis. Leontopolis had been founded as a military camp by Onias IV, a Judean nobleman who commanded a legion of Jewish mercenaries in the service of Ptolemy VI (Philometer) (181–145 B.C.E.). Onias had built in his garrison city a temple "to the Most High God in the likeness of that of Jerusalem and with the same dimensions" (*Ant.* 13:3).

Onias' temple featured an altar and a sacrificial ritual similar to that practiced in Jerusalem. Its priests claimed this privilege on the basis of one of Isaiah's prophecies: "In that day there shall be an altar to the Lord inside the land of Egypt . . . and [it] shall serve as a symbol and a reminder . . ." (Isa. 19:19–21). Vespasian apparently ordered its destruction to prevent the place, founded on a messianic prophecy, from becoming a rallying spot for zealot diehards.

Josephus provides unusually extensive detail about this temple's history, including correspondence about its founding. This correspondence, which we now know to be forged but which Josephus accepted as authentic, was ostensibly found in the temple archives and includes the letters presumedly exchanged between Onias and the reigning Pharaoh which led up to Onias' acquiring the site. Onias' initial request reads in part, "I have found a most suitable place in the fortress called after Bubastis of the Fields which abound in various kinds of trees and is full of sacred animals. . . ." Ptolemy expresses surprise at the choice of a site "so wild and so full of sacred animals." He is willing to grant title but wonders if Onias really wants a ruined temple full of animal mummies which must not be moved or violated. Onias answers that he does.

It is most unlikely that Onias or the forgers, probably temple priests, would have been so insistent that their temple be located at this particular place if the site had not been previously associated with Jewish worship. Jews shared a common belief of the times that once a place was consecrated to a particular faith it remained so for all time. The report of mummified animals at this temple site leads us to ponder again the significance of the Egyptian *aggadah* which speaks of Moses dedicating a town to the sacred ibis. The suspicion is strong that the mummies of Leontopolis were ibises and that sometime before Onias built his temple there a group of Jews, perhaps another paramilitary colony during the Persian period or a draft of Judean workers early in Ptolemaic times, dedicated a healing shrine to Moses and worshipped there, using the rituals customary at such a shrine. If this be so, it was later abandoned for reasons which can no longer be recovered, and Onias, hearing that this place had been consecrated by his countrymen, established there a more orthodox center of Jewish worship. The existence of the forgeries might also reflect the desire of the Judean priests who served at Onias' temple to counter charges that they had at one time engaged in the Moses cult. The letters say, in effect, it happened but long before we came here. All these documents somehow relate: Artapanus' report of the military camp General Moses built and dedicated to the sacred ibis during his Nubian operation; the report that Moses' demobilized army demolished an old brick temple and built another of cut stone quarried by hand from the hills nearby; Onias' request of Pharaoh "to permit me to cleanse this Temple which is in ruins, and to build a Temple . . ." (*Ant.* 13:3).

Rabbinic Judaism had little use for the literature of the Alexandrian diaspora and, for the most part, set it aside. Artapanus, Ezekiel, even Josephus, are never quoted by name in rabbinic texts. In traditional Jewish circles the usual explanation is that these omissions were the natural result of the fact that these men had not written in Hebrew and so, over time, as vernaculars changed, lost their readers. It is equally likely that their works were deliberately put aside by the rabbis who gained control of the structures of Jewish life after the destruction of the Jerusalem Temple and who were determined to weed out all vestiges of idolatry.

The significance of these facts, if facts they be, is not that a group of Judeans in a foreign land at an early period in the faith's development violated the Torah's rules against idolatry, but that given a cultural environment which encouraged the glorification and adoration of noble heroes—witness emperor worship, witness Christianity—the Jewish tradition pulled back from Moses worship despite the popularity of hero worship all around them. Burdened or blessed, depending on your point of view, by the Second Commandment, Judaism disentangled itself from cultural pressures which encouraged hero worship and apotheosis, in the process not only exalting God but reaffirming Biblical Judaism's candid and realistic assessment of man.

CHAPTER

# III

# Of Biography
and Biographer

I WAS SEATED in the standardized discomfort of a commuter flight, working my way through Sholem Asch's romantic and self-indulgent novel, *Moses*, when a young teacher from our local yeshivah who had been assigned the next seat turned and peered intently at my book. "What are you reading?" I told him. He frowned. I thought I knew why. During the 1930s Asch had published novels about Jesus, Paul, and Mary, an ill-timed ecumenical undertaking which had earned for him the deepest suspicions of many in the beleaguered Jewish community. I found I had jumped to a wrong conclusion; my neighbor knew nothing of Asch. He was exercised by the very idea of a novel about Moses. "Who needs a book about Moses? The Torah tells it all." For him a novel about Moses bordered on the blasphemous. Novels were trivial, and a novel about Moses would diminish the greatest man who ever lived.

Asch's work is more a historical reconstruction than a

novel, I explained, and other writers—Louis Untermeyer and Howard Fast came to mind—had tried their hand at biographies of Moses with no great success. Moses is a difficult and intimidating subject, and the Torah provides few insights into his personality. A writer needs the genius of a Thomas Mann to write about people who talk familiarly with God, and so far no one of that caliber has attempted a life of Moses. My neighbor had completely lost interest. He had time and thought only for Torah.

The conversation pointed up a cultural divide which today often separates Jew from Jew and also suggests a difference of attitude and approach which over the centuries has distinguished classic Christianity from rabbinic Judaism. The rabbinic tradition is singularly devoid of biography. The pages of the Talmud and the *Midrashim* are sprinkled with anecdotes about the patriarchs and various sages, but not even Abraham or Akiba ever became the subject of a "life." On the other hand, the Christian tradition is rich with the lives of saints and deems it an act of devotion to re-tell the life of Christ. Christianity saw the lives of the saints as eloquent testimonies to the transforming power of faith and the rewards of faith. It looked on biography as a tool of evangelism. Christianity emphasized the moment of illumination as the moment when a person was "born again"; there was no need for the saint's life to have been a consistent model of virtue, for all that was necessary was that the life had been transformed by the acceptance of Jesus as Lord. Though it acknowledges the transforming power of a mystical experience, the rabbinic tradition does not focus as sharply on it, denying that a person's life can be neatly divided into before illumination and after. The rabbis taught that believers and nonbelievers alike are inextricably caught up in the contradictions of human nature. Within us are two drives or life forces: one assertive, competitive, self-concerned; the other cooperative, loving, and empathic. Both have their use and place and neither is ever completely displaced. The rabbinic view of human development emphasizes habit, discipline, and community rather than the transforming spiritual experience. For Jews biography could do little to provide confirming evidence of the incessant moral struggle in which all are forever engaged. The rabbis had no reason to encourage testimonies by those who felt themselves saved since Judaism, as they understood it, rejected the Christian gospel that a person is saved through faith.

Rabbinic literature is often subtle, generally informed, sometimes brilliant, but rarely personal. There are no intimate memoirs. There is no rabbinic parallel to Augustine's *Confessions.* Anyone who teaches post-Biblical Jewish literature to undergraduates sympathizes, as I do, with the students' initial disappointment in the rabbinic classics. The rabbis preferred the theoretical to the personal; their writing lacks the tug of immediacy and reveals little of the inner life and spiritual struggles of a believing Jew. To make matters worse, most of this literature is graceless and shapeless; notes, mountains of notes, rather than a crafted work.

It was a matter of perspective. Rabbinic literature was created by a community which felt itself under divine sentence. The Temple was destroyed. The nation was in exile. Conventional rabbinic wisdom blamed the worldly ways of the Hellenized generations for having earned for the whole community God's severe judgment. The nation had sinned when it had taken up worldly ways, with disastrous results, a message the holiday of Chanukkah annually reinforced. Sermons routinely urged the faithful to reject the world of appearances, the world of passion and indulgence, including the world of art, theater, and literature, in favor of God's world, the world of Torah. Poetry, theater, music, and the arts had no place in the rabbinic curriculum. For the rabbis the goal was not the development of each person's individual and varied talents but *teshuvah,* a return to the old ways through obedience to God's unchanging Instructions. The community's goal was to realign Israel with God and so end the exile. The individual's goal was to survive life's tests by steadfastly following the commandments and so merit life in the World to Come.

In this burdened world there was only one legitimate subject for thought and study: Torah. Any theme or text which did not flow directly from this source was suspect. Literature, however imaginative, was not Torah, neither were the philosophic texts of the Greek schools. Rabbinic Judaism did not encourage any and all learning, but only *Talmud Torah,* Torah learning. Study was encouraged only within the perimeter of a special and specific curriculum. *Talmud Torah* sanctified Torah learning and discouraged wide, indiscriminate, or secular reading. Neither personal narratives nor political chronicles were Torah. The rabbis were interested in God's thoughts, not those of human authors.

Some traditional Jews may object to my description of rabbinic Judaism as self-confident of its truth and self-enclosed. They will point out, and correctly, that every generation had sages who were abreast of the state of learning in their day. Some were expert mathematicians and astronomers. Many were physicians. Fathers encouraged their sons to master the practical subjects. Of course, ideas of all kinds floated in the air of the great urban centers, but during the

Talmudic period, that is, approximately from the fall of Jerusalem in 70 C.E. to the rise of Islam in the seventh century, there is no evidence that any sage trained himself systematically in philosophy, rhetoric, or literature. The great rabbinic academies of the period did not possess general libraries. The rabbinic curriculum consisted of Torah and Talmud and not the trivium or quadrivium.

Since the synagogue never developed a Holy Office or an Index of Prohibited Books, many are under the impression that the virtue of *Talmud Torah* describes love of all learning. It does not. Rabbinic Judaism treated study as a discipline of piety, but it did so at the same time that it was effectively burying the whole literary output of the Hellenistic diaspora and limiting the curriculum of Jewish education to Torah-related subjects. This special focus was to determine the content of the rabbinic curriculum over the centuries.

I once wrote a book about a controversy which broke out in thirteenth-century Southern France over the orthodoxy of Maimonides' master work, *The Guide of the Perplexed.* Some Jews were so troubled by Maimonides' philosophic approach to Judaism that they denounced *The Guide* to the Inquisition whose Dominican organizers were only too glad to add this Jewish volume to their bonfire of forbidden books. Many sixteenth- and seventeenth-century printed Hebrew books, particularly if their provenance is Italian, are spotted with inked-out passages and conclude with a censor's signature. Because the censors were Christians, often converted Jews, these episodes have been explained away as the result of external pressures on the Jewish community. But it was not long before rabbinic councils in Italy and Poland began to anticipate censorship and to threaten Jewish printers with various penalties if they published works without an authorization of reliability issued by responsible Jewish authorities (*Haskamah*). The list of writings which were, at one time or another, excluded)by rabbinic fiat is long: all Karaite works, various books of philosophy, Shabbatean pamphlets, Hasidic work, Kabbalistic works, Frankist texts, Zionist pamphlets, Haskalah writings, materials by religious liberals and reformers.

Censorship is a harsh term to those of us who have been trained in a society which accepts the free exchange of ideas as a necessary and inalienable right. The rabbis were not so certain that there were benefits in the dissemination of folly or error. They lived in a world which believed in ultimate truths and in a pre-Freudian culture which believed that actions conform to knowledge and, consequently, that the control of error, the elimination of *sefarim hitzonim* (outside books, non-Torah), was a necessary step in insuring the moral growth of the individual and the moral welfare of the community.

The rabbis were not interested in books as shaped literary products. Their books are, in fact, *yalkutim*, mixed grab bags of comments, commentaries, and class notes which, for all their insight, are often graceless in style and formless in structure. The Talmud and the *Midrashim* are for the most part little more than compilations of academic notes made by many hands, none of them editorial, until at some point a decision was made to publish the existing deposit. A librarian of the Talmudic period could not have shelved *the* Talmud or *the Midrash*. The two Talmuds are accumulations of legal materials. The various *Midrashim* are anthologies of discrete commentaries on Biblical texts. None of these anthologies of the Torah tradition had originally been planned as a book.

## Of Biography and Biographer

Torah describes a single continuum, not a library of discrete texts. Books have a beginning and an end. Torah is eternal and endless. Books are self-contained. Torah is an ongoing process. Books present an author's ideas; Torah is concerned only with God's ideas. Biography reflects an individual's philosophy; Torah reflects God's will. During the Talmudic period most sages ceased referring to Moses as *Safrah Rabbah b'Yisroel*, Israel's premier scribe, though it was a fundamental doctrine of their faith that he had written down the entire Five Books of Moses, and adopted for him a title which suggested his role as a Torah teacher, *Moshe Rabbenu*.

Mohammed was the first to call Jews the people of the book. But the rabbis were not bookish men; they were schoolmen, classroom teachers. Rabbinic Judaism put aside serious consideration of all books save Torah. The philosopher-liturgist, Gaon Saadiah b. Joseph (882–942 C.E.), was perhaps the first rabbi-author who set out to write a book whose purpose and scope were announced in the preface, the whole designed as a self-sufficient unit. The cosmopolitan Islamic milieu of the tenth and eleventh centuries encouraged writers to break with these rabbinic restraints, and Jews began again, as they had in the Hellenistic diaspora, to publish their own works. The trickle was soon an avalanche of collections of poetry full of adroitly used Biblical phrases, philosophies which carefully developed the relationship between reason and revelation, grammars which set out the structure of the Hebrew language, manuals of medicine, and long essays on particular subjects in Jewish law. Even when books became common, the distinction between Torah and non-Torah was clear. Students were regularly warned to avoid love poetry and tales of questionable moral effect.

97

Surviving shelf lists reveal that Jews who owned sizable library collections distinguished Torah from other books and felt no obligation to treat with other than formal care books which were not clearly Torah. The tenth and eleventh centuries were a book-filled era, but there were no biographies or autobiographies among them. There was still no religious need for personal testimonies.

I no longer find it surprising, as I once did, that it was a Christian publishing house, that of Daniel Bomberg in Venice, which first edited the vastness of the Babylonian Talmud and provided it with citations, standard pagination, and editorial precision (1520–23). By research standards the Bomberg text was a distinct improvement and was accepted, but it also marked the creation of separations, of beginnings and ends, which eventually transformed an unbroken creative activity called Torah into various discrete works which could be studied separately rather than treated as part of an on-going, unified tradition. When I handle in the same day a printed Masoretic text of the Torah and a Torah scroll, I sense the emotional consequences of dealing with a published work rather than with a manuscript. A Torah scroll belongs in the ark. It suggests holiness and draws my life into its teaching. To handle or read the Torah scroll is a religious experience. A printed Bible is a book. I read it critically as I might another classic text. I even make notes in the margin.

My seatmate had been conditioned by a rabbinic culture which values only Torah. From his perspective a novel about Moses is not Torah and, therefore, suspect. When nearly two millennia ago—just before the rabbinic tradition emerged as the dominant force in Jewish life—a Greek-speaking, thoroughly Hellenized Jew of Alexandria, Philo

Judaeus (20 B.C.E.–50 C.E.), wrote a biography of Moses, the only such work until this century, the sages managed to set it aside for all the reasons we have been discussing, probably without reading it.

An intellectual ascetic of a mystical bent, Philo knew his Plato and he knew his Torah. Indeed, he is the only Hellenistic Jew we know who mastered both the Torah curriculum of his day and the curriculum of the Greek schools. In his writings, most of which are Biblical commentaries, Philo set himself the task of showing the correspondence between these two distinct ways of approaching the basic ethical and metaphysical questions. I find it comfortable to think of Philo as a Jewish rhetor who developed with considerable skill an allegorical interpretation of Torah which "proved" that God's word was both the useful constitution of the Jewish community and a universal prescription for virtuous living and philosophic enlightenment. Philo accepted the Torah law as law and its history as history. He was a pious and observant Jew for whom the Torah was a many-splendored source of wisdom and truth. To discover this truth Philo approached the Torah text allegorically and through a sophisticated and imaginative analysis uncovered meaning beneath the obvious meaning of the text. Working with a text he believed to be inspired, this well-educated commentator turned the Torah into a guide to intellectual and spiritual enlightenment.

As a Biblical exegete rather than a systematic philosopher, Philo ties his ideas to separate texts rather than present them in separate essays. His outlook must be drawn together from his discrete comments. This commentator's approach, which has challenged generations of interpreters, interests us primarily because Philo did not put aside his exegetical interests even when his purpose was to present a *vita* of Moses. His *Life of Moses* is both a panegyric to the prophet and, at the same time, a defense of the Mosaic law. Plutarch would have been interested only in the man and would have written a very different biography. Philo is interested in the man and the law and digresses at length, particularly in the second volume, on such topics as the details of the construction of the Tabernacle, the shape of its vessels and the weave and color of the priest's vestments (*DVM* 2:71–158), and the rules which govern the observance of Passover, laws of inheritance, and violations of the Sabbath (*DVM* 2:192–245).

Philo wrote to praise Moses and to prove to his neighbors, the elite of Alexandria, as well as to the more Hellenized Jews of his city who instinctively thought in Greek categories and felt comfortable with Greek ways, that the Torah, the acknowledged constitution of the Jewish community, was not a parochial document but a constitution without equal and a consummate expression of truth. He did so in part by explaining the underlying purpose of specific laws, but his major tactic was to glorify the prophet-legislator who had brought the Torah. This approach reflects Stoicism, the Greco-Roman intellectual tradition Philo prized. The Stoics assumed that a man's achievements reflect his character and found the man in his achievements. They argued that a sensitive observer of the Parthenon could deduce not only the technical skill of the architect but his knowledge of the laws of nature, the harmony of his soul, and the soundness of his character. Only a superior person like Solon could have promulgated the much-respected Constitution of Athens. Plato had argued that the perfection of the lawgiver validates the wisdom of his constitution. Philo had read Plato and agreed. To praise Moses was to praise his Torah. To ascribe perfection to Moses, as Philo does, was to ascribe perfection to the Torah.

Modern editions of the *Life of Moses* are printed in two volumes, though Philo may have originally divided the essay into three parts. Philo portrays a Moses who excels in each of the four conventional categories which, according to the Stoic fellowships, establish the merit of a superior person. According to the Stoics, a great man proved himself by competently discharging the responsibilities of government; by wisely organizing the laws of his community; by carefully managing his city's rites; and by bearing himself with dignity and honor in his daily life. Philo related these four categories to the four offices Moses had occupied during his lifetime—political leader, lawgiver, priest, and prophet—and defended the proposition that Moses had not only excelled in all, but had no peer. In his view Moses deserves the title of "the most perfect of men" (*DVM* 1:1). He marshals the evidence for his claim in successive sections which discuss Moses' unrivaled capacity as a ruler, his unique abilities as a lawgiver, his unequaled record as priest, and his singular role as prophet.

The *Life of Moses* is more panegyric than biography, and more aretology than either. *Arete* denotes prowess or excellence, hence *aretology*, praise of a hero's virtues and excellence. A "life" of this type was essentially an illustration of nobility and a manual for moral development. Modern biography explores the tangle of relationships and contradictions in which the subject, like every human being, is caught and examines everyone close to its subject. Philo's spotlight is on one person. Only Moses is mentioned by name. Everyone else is a shadow: it is "sister," not Miriam; it is "the father of the girls," not Jethro. Only Moses is in the foreground. Panegyric's aim is to praise rather than provide a critical assessment of a person's character and in the process glosses over flaws and errors. Philo honestly believed Moses had been ever and in all ways virtuous. The encomia that Philo lavishes on Moses suggest a perfection that both our Freudian age and the Bible would, out of hand, declare impossible of human attainment. His parents were the best of their contemporaries (*DVM* 1:7). The Egyptian princess adopted him because she "approved of his beauty and fine condition" (*DVM* 1:15). Even as a child he was never childish, diligently applying himself with a modest and serious mien to learn what was sure to profit his soul. As a youth he was serious, never frivolous. He was taught by tutors, each a master of a specific branch of knowledge. Egyptian masters taught him arithmetic, geometry, poetry, music, astrology, and the sacred meaning of the hieroglyphs. Greek masters taught him grammar, rhetoric, and logic and instructed him in the various alphabets and astronomy. But Moses swiftly outstripped his teachers: "His seemed to be a case of recollection rather than of learning" (*DVM* 1:21). As a youth he was not enticed by wild adventure or attracted by palace courtesans. There were no romantic escapades. He was clean in body and in soul, "purifying himself from all the calls of mortal nature, food and drink, and intercourse with women" (*DVM* 1:25). He was moderate in diet and severe in habit. His was a life of denial verging on the ascetic. Every act was carefully and wisely conceived and executed.

Physically, Moses was without blemish. When he was carried about on a litter people from all walks of life stopped to look, transfixed by his beauty. He was "noble and goodly to look upon ... advanced beyond his age" (*DVM*

# Of Biography and Biographer

1:18–19). Moses' speech was fluent. Moses' need for Aaron
as a spokesman is interpreted as a matter of court etiquette:
it was not fitting for Moses to shout so Aaron stood beside
him on great public occasions and bellowed out the words
that Moses spoke quietly to him (*DVM* 1:84). Philo's
Moses is stoic, disciplined, self-controlled, master of every
appetite and passion, learned in that wisdom which distinguishes truth from appearance, virtue from the semblance of
virtue (*DVM* 1:24). Though adopted by Pharaoh's only
daughter and seemingly destined to become the next Pharaoh, Moses put aside the allure of pleasure and the advan-
tages of position to recover for himself the high discipline
and philosophic culture of his ancestors (*DVM* 1:32–33).
His mind was incapable of accepting any falsehood; he
adopted no idea or concept without the closest examination.
Though a prophet, Moses was not an Amos, a rude dresser
of sycamore trees suddenly seized by the word of God, but a
well-dressed and carefully manicured gentleman whose
mind was accustomed to dwell on high thoughts and spiritual subjects.

Philo's Moses is incapable of sin or even of acting on impulse. He never spoke angrily or out of turn. Philo's version
of the murder of the Egyptian taskmaster turns the killing
into a bit of deliberate surgery done to protect and benefit
all mankind rather than an impulsive act by one who surprised even himself and did not stay to face the consequences. While the young prince was out charioting, he observed the working conditions in Goshen and was angered
by the oppression of his birth people; but wise beyond his
years, he knew that a single individual, even a prince, was
powerless against pharaonic absolutism. He could do little
more than offer an occasional encouraging word to the

slaves and deliver an occasional warning to the taskmasters
about their excessive use of force. Some of the overseers
were "wild beasts in human shape," sadists, and it was one
of these Moses killed. He was not guilty of murder for murder involves the taking of a human life; Moses had killed a
wild animal, not a human being. "Righteous it was that one
who lived only to destroy men should be destroyed" (*DVM*
1:44). Philo's re-creation of this story omits the subsequent
scene where Moses steps between two quarreling Jews, and
there is not even a whisper about his precipitous flight.
Rather, Moses calmly and publicly defends his actions before Pharaoh. Only later does he retire to Midian when he
discovers that jealous courtiers have maliciously lied about
him to Pharaoh, who has been taken in and has authorized
an attack on his life (*DVM* 1:47). Men such as Moses do
not flee. He retired gracefully, all the while praying to God
to relieve the oppressed and punish the oppressors (*DVM*
1:47). As we have noted, the Biblical account leaves open
the possibility that Moses dallied in Midian with his new
wife for a considerable period, despite the slaves' continuing
pain. Philo's Moses, immediately on arriving in Midian, intercedes with God to protect the helpless and to destroy the
tyrant (*DVM* 1:47). It is God Who requires Moses to delay
his return so he can be properly trained for his task. When,
finally, the order comes, "Go, return," Moses responds with
dispatch and leaves immediately for Egypt (*DVM* 1:74 ff).

Philo tirelessly underscores Moses' virtue. He is free of
ambition. Proof: he did not attempt to establish a dynasty
by designating his sons as his heirs. He was free of greed.
Proof: unlike most tyrants, Moses did not levy tolls. There
was no greed or avarice or vanity in his nature. Proof: the

Bible is silent about Moses' dress or the management of his household.

Philo emphasizes in Moses' life those acts which illustrate the four cardinal virtues of the superior man: prudence, justice, temperance, and bravery, as these were described by the Stoic tradition. A modern reader finds himself contemplating the disciplined sobriety of a substantial citizen of a Hellenistic city-state, whose virtues seem just a bit out of focus when applied to the Moses we know from the Torah. At one point Philo lists four qualities which are especially important to the legislative condition of mind and which Moses uniquely exhibited: "Love of humanity, of justice, of goodness and hatred of evil." One could interpret these qualities in Biblical terms, but note Philo's Hellenistic specification: "By love of humanity he is bidden to produce for public use his thoughts for the common weal; by justice to honor equality and to render to every man his due; by love of goodness to approve of things naturally excellent, and to supply them without reserve to all who are worthy of them for their unstinted use; by hatred of evil to spurn the dishonourers of virtue, and frown upon them as the common enemies of the human race" (DVM 2:9–10). Only a Greek could find these virtues in the Biblical account of Moses or, at least, so express what he found there. Philo's Moses exhibits wisdom, endurance, sufficient political sagacity to be a good citizen, self-restraint, continence, temperance, realism, good sense, knowledge, endurance of toil and hardships, contempt of the pleasures, justice, advocacy of excellence, censure and appropriate correction of wrongdoers, praise and appropriate honor to the just . . . (DVM 1:154). This Moses is a gentleman of consequence, of many parts and calm demeanor. He is the only man ever to capture all the laurels in the game of life which Philo describes as the only worthwhile game.

Let us examine this approach more systematically, beginning with Philo's interest in promoting respect for the Torah as the ultimate source of truth and enlightenment. The Stoics believed that a city's well-being depends on the virtue of its king. If the king is unenlightened, his laws cannot be consonant with the basic realities of the universe and therefore cannot create or support a properly ordered or stable community. Equally, the laws of a philosopher-king whose mind comprehends the nature of the intelligible world will reflect the ultimate harmonies and be able to support and sustain a stable and just society. Philo used the term democracy to describe the harmony which the philosopher-king develops in his mind and spirit as reflected in the society he organizes, since his city-state inevitably reflects in its operation his mind's clarity and balance.

A number of superior men have established the basic law of their communities, but time has shown that each of these constitutions was flawed. The founding laws of Athens and Sparta have had to be revised from time to time. Every *polis* has amended its laws. Only Torah law remains immutable. No situation has arisen which required these Instructions to be enlarged or changed from the day the Torah was promulgated at Sinai. "His [Moses'] laws are most excellent and truly come from God since they omit nothing that is needful" (*DVM* 2:12).

What accounts for the Torah's superiority? The Torah's unique virtue is partly grounded in Moses' exceptional mental and spiritual endowment and partly in the fact that after Moses had disciplined his senses and passions and fully developed his mind, God gave him the added blessing of prophecy. Other lawgivers had fully activated their minds. Only Moses had received from God that wisdom which no man, however brilliant, can attain through his own efforts. "Moses necessarily obtained prophecy also, in order that through the providence of God he might discover what by reasoning he could not grasp, for prophecy finds its way to what the mind fails to reach" (DVM 2:6). Various schoolmasters had taught Moses much and he had taught himself much; but when he ascended Sinai there were still gaps in his knowledge. Philo accepts the basic Hellenistic intellectualist premises, except one: he denies that reason unaided could discover and establish the full truth. There were limits to what could be known by experience or logical demonstration. On Sinai's top Moses entered into contemplation and "through inspiration sent from Heaven above, he grew in grace, first of mind, then of body also through the soul, and in both so advanced in strength and well-being that those who saw him afterwards could not believe their eyes" (DVM 2:69). The last is, of course, a reference to the Biblical description of Moses at his descent, his face alight with the divine light (Exod. 34:30). Until Sinai Moses had been like the explorer who enters the darkness and searches everywhere to find God. Moses did not find God. In the end God came to him. Here Philo reveals his Jewishness. The Moses who ascended Sinai's height was an educated man. The Moses who descended was fully enlightened. The communion at Sinai was the climax of Moses' life. His advantage over all other philosopher-kings lay in God's having made known to him the perfect law, the Torah. Only Moses among history's lawgivers had been granted the added understanding which can come only from God; therefore, only his law is not subject to the inherent limitation of human reason. Prophecy is the gift which keeps a lawgiver's pen from faltering.

His understanding of prophetic enlightenment led Philo to omit the story of Moses' second ascent of Mount Sinai. On his first ascent Moses hears a murmuring in the camp below, and though he is loath to break off communion with God, he knows he must. After first interceding with God for Israel, he descends to the drunken mob busy at the rites associated with the golden image—here identified with the Egyptian bull god Apis—and commands the punishment of the idolators. Philo does not indicate that Moses carried down with him the stone tablets. For Philo the tablets were only an external sign of the law. Since Moses had achieved full knowledge of God's Instructions during his stay on the mountain, he did not need a text to remind him of God's Instructions, and had no reason to spend another forty days with God; there was no need for a second ascent, and none is described.

Philo's purpose is to exalt the Torah's value. The Torah is not a special set of laws for one of the world's many nations but laws appropriate to all men and any society. Moses was lawgiver to all. God's laws are too good to be limited to any one city, "too good and Godlike to be confined within any earthly walls." They are laws suitable for all people, a faithful image of the proper constitution for the whole world (DVM 2:51). Since the Torah presents a rule in full conformity with the laws of nature it is an ideal constitution and will one day be understood and adopted by all. Philo puts it this way: when the veil is lifted from the eyes of the nations, "I believe that each nation would abandon its peculiar customs and turn to honouring our laws" (DVM 2:44).

Philo insisted men need look no farther for the perfect law. Moses was the perfect philosopher-king; consequently, only Torah law is without error and will never need to be amended.

Given his apologetic interests, it is not surprising that Philo treats Moses as the model philosopher-king; but it is somewhat surprising that he should describe Moses as a model priest (*DVM* 2:66 ff). Although the Torah reports several occasions when Moses offered sacrifices, the rabbinic tradition rarely mentions Moses' activity as a priest; it was Aaron who was the High Priest and his descendants in Philo's day still controlled The Temple and the altar.

Philo does not have in mind a professional priest. In Alexandria, Philo's home, as in every other Hellenistic *polis*, a man was chosen from the most distinguished and respected citizens to hold the office of priest for a specified period during which he was expected to pay for various rites and preside at the attendant sacrifices. To be chosen was a mark of distinction, as well as evidence of one's wealth; and to carry off the role successfully was important for the well-being of the entire community. Patterns were important to the Greco-Roman world and, therefore, to Hellenized Jews. Strict custom governed the relationship of officials to citizens, of citizens to their families, of neighbors to each other, and of the city to its gods. Everyday life was full of confusion, governed by opinion rather than truth. Civic ritual, properly conducted, signaled the order which lies at the center of things and the desire of a city to be in order. Proper ritual was the religious equivalent of court etiquette, and its proper execution showed the community's concern that it please its heavenly protector. If those who acted on behalf of the city were men of proven quality who did their part properly, then the city could rest secure in its relationship to its god. It could face the future with confidence. Jews adopted this pattern, admitting only the "best and worthiest" to serve the King of Kings. Moses was the ideal choice to be such a priest, the representative of his people before its God, because he had the requisite qualities of character and knew exactly how to discharge his duties appropriately. Note the succession of ideas in Philo's discussion of Moses the High Priest: "Great natural gifts . . . improved by philosophy . . . fruits of virtue brought to perfection. . . . He came to love God and be loved by Him . . . inspired by a heaven-sent rapture. . . . An honor well becoming the wise is to serve the Being Who truly is, and the service of God is ever the blessing of the priesthood. . . . This privilege was given to him as his due" (*DVM* 2:66–67).

We have come a long way from the Torah's description of Moses as holy man who lives apart from the camp and from Ezekiel's Moses as Merlin. Philo's Moses is a man of substance, quality, dignified piety, and consummate wisdom. There is also a defensive note in his description. Remember how Manetho had charged the Jews with miserliness? By having taken the leading role in such civic duties, Moses showed that Jews did not shirk those duties, however costly, when they could serve the true God.

Philo's work suggests some striking distinctions between Biblical and Hellenistic thought. The Biblical ethic was horizontal. Man is born. He walks life's way wrestling with duty as best he can. He wins many battles with himself and loses some. He is at times virtuous and at times a sinner, his fate tied inextricably to that of other men. It is Philo's interest in presenting Moses as a model of virtue which sets his *Life of Moses* outside the Torah continuum. The Torah's position is that man is an inconstant being; that virtue develops from habit, and that where the commandments do not provide clear guidance, God's attributes suggest the moral way: Leviticus' "You shall be holy, for I, the Lord your God, am Holy" (19:2). If you must have a pattern, imitate God, not another fallible mortal. Philo thought vertically. The world and the worldly must be transcended. It is in separating himself from the common herd that man is saved. Philo valued the life of contemplation even more than the life of the active citizen. Contemplation is necessary to enlightenment. The Midian years are not simply an interlude as shepherd of Jethro's flock but a long period of withdrawal and seclusion, which Philo insists is necessary after one is educated to allow the mind to transcend schooling and gain clarity and certainty. It was in Midian that Moses digested philosophic doctrines and mastered the distinction between truth and semblance. When Moses had achieved this capacity, the knowledge of God poured into him in a blessed stream. But once one has gained enlightenment, he must put quiet behind him. Moses left Midian to do God's bidding, and after Sinai he remained with his people though his tent was set apart and he retired there often to be with God.

Biblical thought assumes that human nature is contradictory and never wholly transcends its conflicts; that though the commandments had been given and a way charted, man cannot fully free himself of the inherent contradictions of his nature. He could never become anything but man. Biblical man never loses his libido, is always capable of sin, and so always is in need of the gift of God's grace. In the Hellenistic world, at least in the elite intellectual circles Philo frequented, the emphasis was more on man's attainments than on God's grace.

# IMAGES of MOSES

The Greeks adored the hero crowned victor in the games and the heroic leader. They wrote about divine poets, divine athletes, and holy philosophers and held such men up as fit models. Ethics was for them a political, hence conditional, science, concerned with the formation of character traits rather than with the delineation of absolute ethical standards. They believed that an enlightened man could live a wholly virtuous life and so they confidently provided—in the *bios* of superior men—praiseworthy role models.

As was noted in chapter II, in this Greek-speaking world the Septuagint, the Hellenistic translation reflected a cultural tendency to retire God to an existence of transcendent perfection. God lost His easy familiarity with man, His ability to walk in the cool of the garden, and His ability to act as a model for human behavior. Philo again and again uses the term, *To On*, Existence, for God. His is an intellectual world in which God is variously conceived as pure being, an unmoved mover, thought thinking itself, pure existence, transcendent; a world which has lost the ability to communicate simple, commonsense moral ideas by reciting God's attributes: merciful, gracious, long suffering. No one was any longer certain what these attributes meant when they were posited of God. A God Who is pure existence cannot be a model for the human being. Philo does say "a man should imitate God as much as may be" (*Vir.* 168), but the context makes it clear he means no more than that man should obey Torah law and follow the spiritual course which it maps out. So Moses and, to a somewhat lesser degree, the other patriarchs necessarily took God's place as exemplars of appropriate and virtuous behavior.

A Moses or a Solon could be conceived as a paragon, a man who had achieved such clarity of mind that his actions faithfully conformed to an absolute standard of virtue. If human is defined as conflicted and divine as controlled and of single purpose, such a man had, in effect, become divine.

Behind these assertions lay certain psychological assumptions. In his undeveloped state the human being is a complex creature of body and soul who is inconstant in his actions because his passions are undisciplined and his mind is full of doubts and uncertainties. Most minds remain shadowed by confusion and therefore hesitate between the demands of truth and those of passion and appetite; and when the moment of decision arrives the appetites generally win out against an uncertain will. Character depends on will, and wisdom frees the will. Right and effective living requires that a person put behind him what is only beguiling, misleading, seductive, all that belongs to the world of appearances, and develop the habits of mental and physical discipline. He can do so in measure as he comprehends the world as it really is. When he truly knows what is right, he can do the right. A man can marshal the full force of his will only when philosophy has clarified what he must do. There is for Philo no such person as a saintly innocent. Moses was the magnificent leader he was because he was a man of character and wisdom. The Moses who met God at the Burning Bush is not a half-educated, and probably spoiled, Egyptian princeling or a simple shepherd, but a mature individual and an accomplished student who has done the Hellenistic equivalent of postdoctoral work in philosophy. Moses has outgrown the temptation to sin because he understands clearly what needs to be done and, in that sense, has become divine. He is singular, *the* appropriate model, because his mind is singularly clear, fully and truly aware, and his spirit is singularly controlled and balanced.

# IMAGES *of* MOSES

Philo had many labels for Moses: the chief prophet, teacher of divine lore, lawgiver of the Jews. But the most important thing he could say about Moses was that he was "the greatest and most perfect of men" (*DVM* 1:1), a man who not only had reported God's law faithfully but had always lived by its explicit rules and in accordance with its implicit values. Ordinary men obey the Torah as best they can. Moses had brought the Torah into his soul and since God's law is perfect so was Moses' soul and his every act. Moses was without fault, "the fruits of virtue showed in word and deed here brought to perfection" (*DVM* 2:66). It could be said of him that he had become a living Torah, a model of God's way (*DVM* 1:162).

How close does Philo come to the transformation of Moses into a God-man? In one essay Philo interprets *ish-elohim* by saying, "The man who is wholly possessed of the love of God ... is no longer a man, but actually God" (*Prob.* 43). His Moses clearly does not share the familiar human frailties; but "God" as applied to Moses must be taken figuratively. To paraphrase Philo, The wise man is said to be a god to the foolish man, but in truth he is not god ... for when he is compared to God he will be found to be a man of God, but when compared with a fool, he will seem a god in appearance and opinion (*Som.* 2:234). God is a metaphoric label which suggests Moses' accomplishment and perfection but not actual divinity. Philo's Moses is mortal; he dies, though his death, like his life, is extraordinary. He is summoned to immortality by God Who resolves his twofold nature of soul and body into a single unity, transforming his whole being into mind, pure as sunlight.

If you had asked Philo whether Moses was a divine being

he would have answered unequivocally no. He did not worship Moses. His Moses was not a son of God. Moses' life and death had not changed the fundamental nature of existence. No one is saved through Moses. But Moses has become something more than a human being. The contradictions inherent in human personality have disappeared. His nature is such that foolishness could no longer be spoken, ignorance is no longer possible, and sin is entirely out of the question. In that sense Moses is "a divine man."

When we look beyond the distinct list of virtues with which Philo and the rabbis separately endow Moses and search out the structure of ideas implicit in both, an unexpected similarity emerges. Both assume the transforming virtue of study. The rabbis often taught that through study man learns to do the right and that when study has become a familiar discipline the right becomes second nature. *Torah Orah*, Torah study, enlightens the mind, sets one on the path of discipline, and leads to the development of a righteous man who merits blessing in this world and in the World to Come. The rabbis generally did not go as far as Philo and the Greeks in assuming that man can, through study and discipline, overcome the contradictions of his nature, but their conviction that Torah gives life in this world and in the World to Come strongly suggests that through the discipline of Torah study a person's character is significantly transformed. A late Talmudic source quotes a long paragraph ascribed to R. Meir (second century C.E.) which details how this transformation occurs:

He who occupies himself in the study of Torah for its own sake merits many things and, still more, he is deserving of the whole world . . . [The study of Torah] clothes him with humility and reverence and prepares him to become righteous, saintly, upright and faithful. It keeps him far from sin and brings him near to virtue. From him men enjoy counsel, sound knowledge, understanding and might. . . . It gives him kingship and dominion and discernment in judgment; to him are revealed the secrets of the Torah and he becomes like a never-failing spring and like a river that flows on with unceasing force. He becomes modest, long-suffering and forgiving of insult. It magnifies him above all things [M. Avot 6:1].

Philo could not have described the transforming capacity of disciplined study any better. Through study man learns to control his passions, to understand the idea of justice so as to be able to administer a community and give sound decisions, and not only merit authority but manage office without being corrupted by it. Learning is for the rabbis, as for Philo, the pearl beyond price. "Lessen your occupation with business and busy yourself with Torah" (M. Avot 4:10) and again, as in Philo, ultimately learning is not for its own sake. The sage owes the duty of leadership to his community.

As biographer Philo has created Moses as the ultimate philosopher-king—*nomos empsychos kai logicos*, a law incarnate and made vocal. As an allegorist and teacher of a way of religious enlightenment, Philo transforms the events of Moses' life into guideposts for those who seek the goal of enlightenment. Philo has set aside the Biblical approach to the Torah as a liturgical document whose recitation would encourage God to hasten the second redemption and replaced it by a sustained allegorical commentary which treats all the events of Moses' life as signs pointing the way to the illumination of the individual mind and the consequent deliverance of the individual soul from the web of passion, ambition, and appetite. Philo assumes that the community will be saved through the governance of an enlightened leader, as Moses had saved Israel. Philo believes in the Great Man who will make things right. The Torah affirms the great God Who redeems.

The rabbis paid as little attention to Philo's *Life of Moses* as my seatmate did to Asch's. Philo's *Moses* is never mentioned in rabbinic literature. It was not Torah, for all the reasons which have been cited. But Philo's *Moses* has been read in recent years by another generation of Jews who are conditioned to see Moses in heroic terms rather than as the mythic figure of the Torah narrative. Philo's Moses has no libido, but he is a person and, therefore, easier to grasp than the shadowy Biblical figure.

The natural child of Philo's *Moses* is Gregory of Nyssa's (fourth century C.E.) similarly titled *Life of Moses* which presents the details of Moses' life and then a point-by-point meditation, *theoria,* on its spiritual meaning. His interest is not in the Torah law—Gregory was a Cappadocian monk, theologian, and mystic—but in the mystical process by which Moses ascends to God. Like Philo he emphasizes Midian as a place of silence and meditation where Moses gains the special insights which come only from communion with God. Sinai is significant not simply as the place where the Torah is given but as the moment when Moses completes his ascent along the mystic way. Bishop as well as ascetic mystic, Gregory delights to detail how, once enlightened, Moses returns to the community to lead his people according to his new understanding of God's nature and will, to witness before them to the marvels he has seen. It is a beautiful book and, despite the writer's antinomian principles, it suggests what the Talmudic sages might have written if they had not been so zealous for the law. I prize the Torah but I miss the books that might have been.

# CHAPTER
# IV

# Another Moses

WHEN an anti-Semitic cartoonist in the USSR draws a Jew, he gives him a long nose and the name Moses. A tired stereotype, but apparently there is a receptive audience. Even non-Jews recognize that Moses has been a favorite name among Jewish families. We Jews have a saying meant to praise our premier scholar-philosopher by comparing him to our only legislative prophet: from (the original) Moses to Moses (Maimonides) there was none like Moses (Maimonides). The name Moses seems elementally Jewish but after the original Moses nearly seventeen hundred years passed before another Jew bore the name.

I have searched the lists of Biblical and post-Biblical personages, scanned the names of Judean mercenaries and merchants who appear in the Hasmonean chronicles, conned the Aramaic and Greek papyrii written by the early diaspora communities, and investigated the lists of the Tannaim and Amoraim who taught in the Talmudic academies. Not one includes the name Moses. The Babylonian Talmud mentions a certain fourth-century C.E. merchant, Mesah b. Arzi, a miserly man who owes his place in the literature to his unwillingness to give his son-in-law, Huna, a brilliant but impoverished scholar, the cash dowry stipulated in his daughter's wedding contract, preferring to promise payment in case of future need (b. B.B. 174b). Since the Talmud is the work of scholars like Huna and represents their interests, Mesah is soundly abused. But he has the distinction of being the only Moses, beside the original, we know of during the first two thousand years of Jewish history, and he lived at least seventeen hundred years after the man whose name he seemingly carried.

The eighth century C.E. marks the end of the Moses hiatus. Jewish boys bearing the lawgiver's name are suddenly everywhere. This change coincides with the swift and dramatic conquest by the armies of Islam of most of the world in which Jews lived and is, in fact, a consequence of the Arab victories. The Quran refers often to Musa (Moses), who is listed along with Adam, Abraham, and Jesus, among others, as one of God's chosen messengers, a link in the line of caliph-apostles of whom Mohammed claims to be the last and culminating figure. There were many young Musas in the Muslim world and, as has been the case throughout history, the minority adopted the naming patterns of the dominant culture. An old taboo had worn thin and, seeing Muslims at ease with the name, Jews broke with centuries of inhibition and reclaimed the name for their own.

How had a taboo against naming a son after the most famous Jew of all originated? It must be remembered that in most societies the process of naming a child was considered a terribly serious business. Priests and sages, and probably astrologers, were consulted. Folk wisdom insisted that "the name of a person determines his destiny" (b. Ber. 7b), and there is no indication the sages disagreed. The sages interpreted the maxim "a good name is rather to be chosen than great riches" (Prov. 22:1) literally, as well as figuratively, and advised parents that "none should name their children after the wicked" (b. Yoma 38b), citing the text: "the memory of the righteous shall be for a blessing, but the name of the wicked shall rot" (Prov. 10:7). A quick look at the names which appear in rabbinic sources indicates that, in fact, the names of those whom the Bible labeled wicked (Jereboam, Korah, Ahab . . .) were avoided.

Names were seen as part of a person's persona and believed to play a major role in determining a person's fate. The story of David, Abigail, and her short-sighted and parsimonious husband Nabal (literally, churl) turns on the proverb, "As his name, so he is" (1 Sam. 25:25). It was commonly believed that a person acquired the characteristics and the destiny of the person whose name he bore, that the namesake inherited his *mazzal*, his sign. Thus the tradition developed of naming a child after a rich or long-lived progenitor. A more sophisticated version of the idea considered that a name was a form in an Aristotelian sense, a reality, independent of any particular person, whose essence affected all who bore the name. It was not uncommon for a man or woman to take or be given a new name as a symbol of some change in their situation or in the hope of changing that situation. When a slave earned his freedom he took a free man's name as a sign he had broken with his past. A king took a throne name upon his ascension for the same reason. According to the Torah God Himself had renamed Avram (Abraham), Sarai (Sarah), and Jacob (Israel) in order to describe a new relationship to Him or a major change in their lives.

Moses is one of the few major figures whom the Torah calls by only one name. The Talmud is less reticent in this regard, referring to Moses by any number of names: Jered, Gedor, Heber, Socho, Jekuthiel, Sanoah. . . . The multiplication of names was seen as a way of honoring Moses. In the Byzantine and Sasanid empires where the Jews now lived, a ruler was invested with a seemingly endless list of names and titles, and a slave was lucky to have a name at all. Why these particular names for Moses? The rabbis found them in Scripture. Among the interpretive principles which they accepted was one which held that everything in Scripture was related to everything else: "All Your Words are One." A daughter of Pharaoh who appears in one of the long, confusing, and deadly dull genealogies which begin the Book of Chronicles, is imaginatively connected to Moses. The relevant passage reads: "His Judean wife bore Jered the father of Gedor, Heber the father of Socho and Jekuthiel the father of Sanoah. These are the sons of Bithiah, the daughter of Pharaoh" (1 Chron. 4:18–19). Any daughter of Pharaoh with Judean family connections had to be Moses' foster mother, and once that identification was made, imaginative etymology connected each name in her family tree with Moses: Jered because in his day manna came down (*yarad*) for Israel; Gedor because he fenced in (*gadar*) the breaches of Israel. The modern critical spirit cries out, "But the princess was not Moses' natural mother." The rabbis had a ready and lovely answer. "This teaches us that anyone who brings up an orphan boy or girl in his house, the Scripture accounts it as if he had begotten him" (b. Meg. 13a).

The cultures of West Asia were steeped in the belief that

the past could not be escaped. Christianity taught that human beings had inherited the sin of Adam. Rabbinic Judaism taught that the Jewish people were supported by the merit of Abraham, Isaac, and Jacob. The concept of the transmigration of souls was widely credited. Everyone's experience validated the concept of reward and punishment expressed in the Second Commandment: "... Visiting the guilt of the fathers upon the children, upon the third and upon the fourth generations . . . but showing kindness to the thousandth generation . . ." (Exod. 20:5). We may protest the whole idea of inherited punishment and find this calculus of rewards and punishments unjustly balanced, but an Israelite would have accepted it as an accurate assessment of life. If a father sold himself into slavery, the son became a slave and the grandson after him. A leper's child was born in a leper colony, that is, into ostracism. A king's child was a prince. Assumptions about the continuing influence of the past should have made Moses' name a favorite. Moses had lived a full life, to one hundred and twenty years, and when he died he was as vigorous and physically sound as he had ever been. He had been honored by God with the most important mission ever entrusted to a mortal. Yet, for almost two thousand years none were named after him. Why not?

Because Moses had died but was not dead. According to the *aggadah*, after his death Moses was translated into Heaven where he was warmly welcomed, clothed with light, and made a member of God's court (ARN 157). There were even some who said that Moses had been an immortal, who entered Heaven without passing through the gates of death. The Talmud, the authorized work of sages and rabbis, was not ready to sanction this idea, but neither was it willing to discredit it. "There are those who maintain that Moses did not die but continues to administer above" (b. Sotah 13b). However Moses got to Heaven, his presence there was universally accepted and there was general agreement on his heavenly tasks: when he is not studying Torah with God, he is busy in God's court defending Israel's interests. It was universally believed that he who had defended Israel when alive continued to intercede for Israel in his afterlife.

If there had been only the Torah's Moses to consider, there probably would have been a flock of namesakes in every generation, but an immortal Moses who worked in God's ministry of justice might not take kindly to those who bore his name. The rabbinic culture, like most cultures of the time, considered it prudent to keep at a safe distance from heavenly beings. An angel might take it amiss if an ordinary mortal bore his name or brought his name into disrepute, and no one knew what damage an indignant angel might cause. To people convinced that the human voice carried to Heaven, it seemed only logical that celestial personages would not appreciate being disturbed every time a namesake was addressed. Experience with the unpredictable power of the local sheik made it quite clear that it was best not to call attention to yourself except when the matter was urgent. Being prudent folk, parents in Biblical and rabbinic times did not name their sons after the ministering angels; such names as Gabriel, Raphael, and Michael do not appear in the lists, and when Abraham and Moses joined the ministering angels their names were inevitably included in this taboo. To speak Moses' name casually, say, when calling a son to dinner or, worse, when chiding him, was to disturb unnecessarily an important heavenly personage and to run the risk that he would not respond when you really needed a friend at court.

Many are surprised to hear that the rabbis tended to look on Moses, Abraham, and a number of others in much the same way Buddhists think of their Bodhisattvas, as superior men who had attained Heaven, where they enjoyed the peace that passes understanding and busied themselves as earthly courtiers do, recommending the petitions of favored commoners to the king's attention. This surprise, testimony to the loss of the rich and colorful world of legend and lore which once enveloped Jewish life, indicates how different today's mindset is from that of the rabbinic world. Despite the insistence of various Jewish apologists, it simply is not true that archangels belonged solely to the Zoroastrian tradition and that Judaism's virtue lay in a stubborn adherence to a pristine monotheism, violated only by the ignorant and the credulous.

Heavenly beings were acknowledged by all the cultures of West Asia out of which the Israelite religion evolved. The ark in the Holy of Holies of the Jerusalem Temple was supported by cherubim and seraphim. God was defined as singular and omnipotent, yet He was never alone in Heaven. The Bible frequently speaks of the messengers of God, and the noun it uses, *malach*, also signifies an angel. Theoretically, the angels were only go-betweens, but the *aggadah* often blurs the angels' dependence on God and suggests their autonomy—Satan is the best-known example—probably because many Jews had trouble ascribing to God's will and wisdom all the confusing things that happened to them. A popular *aggadah* recounts that various angels opposed Moses when he entered Heaven to receive the Torah, despite God's announced decision to make the Torah known through him (b. Shab. 88b). Jews found it only natural that God's court should be as busy and crowded a place as their ruler's, and as full of scheming courtiers. Since God's power, unlike an earthly king's, could never be successfully challenged, angelic treason would ultimately fail, but in the meantime a willful angel could create a good bit of havoc on earth. When someone would congratulate himself on a piece of good work, another was sure to say, "Don't open your mouth and give Satan a reason to do mischief."

The Talmud frequently reports on the *famalia shel ma'alah*, the celestial family, which it describes as a large community of angels, archangels, and a few patriarchal figures who had been translated after a life of loyal service to God. As in any family, there were quarrels, and at least one sage was sufficiently worried that angelic strife might have dire consequences for mankind that he closed his devotions with this prayer, "May it be Your will, O Lord, our God, to keep peace among the members of the heavenly family and among the members of the earthly family" (b. Ber. 17a).

A society invests considerable emotional energy in its taboos. They are rarely quixotic and generally represent a protective reaction to a perceived threat to the group's survival or interests. The taboo against using Moses' name began as an attempt to reduce the danger of angering a supernatural power and was reinforced by fear a new Moses might grow up and, because he bore the name—and therefore the destiny—of the original, become a prophet whose words could bring the authority of the Torah into question.

No thesis is more frequently reaffirmed in Biblical and rabbinic literature than the immutability of the revealed Torah. The law was "throughout their generations, for a perpetual covenant" (Exod. 31:16). The sages taught that the Torah had been created before the first day of creation, had been presented to Moses in its entirety and had been transmitted over the generations by an unbroken chain of competent leaders and teachers. God's Instructions, as they had been communicated through Moses, were immutable, not subject to revision or amendment: "You shall not add nor subtract from it" (Deut. 13:1). The *Yigdal,* one of the most beloved medieval hymns (fourteenth century) put it this way, "This law God will not alter nor change for any other, through time's utmost range." During a state of emergency a prophet or group of sages might temporarily suspend a rule, but no permanent changes were permitted (M. Ber. 9:5).

Judaism, like all living things, necessarily adapted itself to new situations, yet Jews did not recognize that fundamental changes had taken or were taking place, that the Torah was continuously being reshaped by commentary on it. Since the sages attached their ideas to the fixed Torah text and drew their authority from it, the art of commentary camouflaged the extent of their changes. The sages acknowledged that Moses might not be familiar with some of their formulations and practices, but they insisted their commentaries did no more than explore the deeper reaches of Torah and express what God had placed there and always intended for them to discover and obey.

We face here one of the great cultural divides which separates the modern person from his ancestors. We pride ourselves on being adaptable. For us change equals improvement, suggests miracle drugs and computer banks, progress. Though in our soberer moments we recognize that change can be disruptive both to the social order and to an individual's emotional equilibrium, we accept the risk because mobility, research, and invention have enhanced the possibilities of our lives. We prize creativity. The rabbinic world prized constancy. In their experience change meant no more than the exchange of the poverty and the narrowness of the village for the poverty and alienation of the city, of one avaricious and unpredictable overlord for another, changes without clear benefit. Life was brief, bruising, full of anxiety, and people desperately needed the support of the familiar. Neither Biblical man nor the Jews of rabbinic times shared our predilection for change. Jeremiah spoke for many generations of teachers when he advised: "Stand at the crossroads and ask after the ancient ways, where the good way lies. Take it and you shall find rest for your soul" (6:16). Wise men taught that the world would remain pretty much as they found it, "that which has been is that which shall be" (Eccles. 1:6), until End Time when God would ring down the curtain on this world and bring a new world into being.

A major part of the Torah's appeal and authority derived from the universal conviction among Jews that it contained God's Instructions, that these would always and in all situations be valid, and that the Torah's wisdom was elemental and incontrovertible. In the midst of life's confusions it was good to know that one stood on the solid ground of Torah. Proof of this confidence was that no human council would ever need to amend or void the Torah. But what if God spoke again and ordered changes?

The major danger of such an upheaval came from those who claimed to mediate God's will, the prophets. Like their contemporaries among other West Asian nations, Biblical men believed in prophetic revelation, stood in awe of prophets, and often consulted them. The Bible reports a number of roving seers and professional court prophets. Since no one knew what The Voice might say, the Torah tried to set up safeguards against any unwanted oracle by suggesting a standard which would enable the nation to distinguish the "true" from the "false" prophet (Deut. 18:15 ff), and by giving the community authority to put to death any prophet who "makes you stray from the path the Lord your God commanded you to follow" (Deut. 13:6). The suggested test is verifiability: "If the prophet speaks in the name of the Lord and the oracle does not come true, that oracle was not spoken by the Lord, the prophet has uttered it presumptuously" (Deut. 18:22).

Scripture includes the description of prophetic acts and the text of speeches by the so-called literary prophets (Isaiah, Jeremiah, Ezekiel) in which they spotlight the sins of the nation and present their understanding of the Covenant. Judaism would have been less, much less, without the prophets. But Israel always had an anxious relationship with them. Prophecy cannot be precensored. There is always the possibility that a prophet might bring new Instructions from God. The idea of an open line to God raised the possibility that Sinai had not been as complete and final a revelation as claimed. One senses a definite sigh of relief among the religious establishment when, after the Babylonian exile, these messengers of God are moved off center stage and the gates of prophecy are declared closed.

Judaism could not deny the not uncommon sense of being inspired or the reality of mystical experience. But it could and did create an ethos which conditioned the prophetically inclined and the mystic not to expect that their contact with God would be as intimate as Moses'. Only Moses had spoken to God face to face. The other prophets had seen God in a vision or heard God within the context of a dream. Israel was taught that to see God face to face was to speak with Him on constitutional matters—and that only Moses achieved this distinction. Among the many prophets in Israelite times, some must have been legislative prophets, for scholarship has made it clear that the Torah is a composite work, that God's Instructions, the *torot*, originally came from a variety of sources. But all records of such legislative oracles were kept out of Scripture, and there is every reason to believe that the omissions were deliberate. As Scripture describes Israel's experiences with its prophets, Moses brought God's Instructions. Amos, Jeremiah, and all the others spoke oracles of reproof, condemnation, or promise, but did not bring new commandments.

Postexilic Judaism distanced itself from the prophet and elevated the sage into the place of religious authority. The prophet might be anyone. There is no way to predict who will have a vision and/or hear a voice. The sage is trained in, and has been shaped by, the tradition. It could safely be assumed that he would be concerned with the integrity of the tradition. A sage who heard a heavenly voice knew that he heard a *bat kol*, the daughter of a voice, a heavenly sound at several removes from God. A famous *aggadah* told of a jury of sages disputing the acceptability of an oven. The majority ruled one way. A single scholar voted otherwise. He stood his ground and called the Heavens to approve his stand. A *bat kol* was heard seconding the minority view. A new vote was taken and the dissenter was still a minority of one. A sage might put existing ideas together in a novel way, but he could never pronounce new law. He had no authority to do so.

Prophecy had been effectively staunched in the Jewish community by the fourth century B.C.E. and that should have been the end of the problem. That it was not was due almost entirely to a Torah text which seemed to promise that some day another Moses would appear in Israel. The section on prophets in Deuteronomy—the last portion of chapter 18—opens with a promise. Moses says: "The Lord your God will raise up for you a prophet from among your own people, *like myself;* him you shall heed" (Deut. 18:15). The promise is repeated three sentences later in a form altered to present God as speaking to Moses: "I will raise up a prophet from among them, from among their own people, *like yourself.* I will put My words in his mouth" (Deut. 18:18). The language is specific. God will at some point in the future send to Israel another prophet of stature comparable to Moses. Now Moses was not just another prophet. His eulogy declares him to have been incomparable in two ways: his contact with God was more intimate than that experienced by any other prophet—"Never again . . . whom the Lord singled out face to face"—and his ministry offered a unique public display of miracles which had brought about the nation's deliverance—"For all the great might and awesome power that Moses displayed before all Israel to Pharaoh and to all his land" (Deut. 34:12). Though it is never spelled out in so many words, there was a third way in which Moses' prophetic activity was unique. Other prophets warned of the severe consequences of national disobedience, held out the promise of the End of Days, or brought God's advice on how the nation should act in a particular situation. Moses alone brought Torah, God's Instructions. Thus, the promise that some day a prophet like Moses would appear raised the unacceptable possibility that his message would abrogate or amend the Torah.

The early sages drew as little attention to the text as possible; the promise of a prophet "like myself" is never cited in the Babylonian Talmud. Though a danger, the promise was still God's promise and could not be ignored. When forced to deal with it, the rabbis tried to neutralize the text by bracketing that promise with another text, the opening line of Moses' eulogy: "Never again did there arise in Israel a prophet like Moses" (Deut. 34:10). Since God's words cannot contradict themselves, the rabbis taught that this pairing makes it clear that the purpose of Deuteronomy 18 was simply to promise Israel that God would send other prophets, a promise which God had amply fulfilled.

Deuteronomy 18 was generally read as a fulfilled pledge. Most commentators, therefore, explained "like myself" as a general pledge that God would send to Israel a succession of prophets, as, in fact, God had done. Since the commentators lived long after the gates of prophecy had been sealed shut, the only open issue for them was to define the precise way in which those prophets had been *like* Moses. Some treated the phrase "like myself" as an elaboration of the preceding phrase "from among your own people," and argued that the quality all the prophets had shared was that all were Jews (Rashi to Deut. 18:15). Nahmanides translated the phrase "from among your own people" to read "from the midst of you" and drew the conclusion that the common factor was that all the prophets had preached in the land of Israel (Nah. to Deut. 18:15). This interpretation was a bit awkward since Moses never entered the Promised Land, but it testifies to the special sense of the holiness which Jews have always attached to the land. Another medieval exegete related the comparison to the fact that the prophets God would send Israel would be like Moses, "true" prophets, not diviners or soothsayers (Ibn Ezra to Deut. 18:15).

Unfortunately for the rabbis' peace of mind, the question of the proper interpretation of the promise "like myself" did not remain a purely academic exercise. In their missions to Jews some elements in Christianity advanced the claim that Jesus was the promised second Moses. Deuteronomy 18 was held up as a powerful credential by Christian preachers who claimed that Jesus' mission had been predicted in the Torah they chose to call the Old Testament. It not only "proved" Jesus out of the Torah itself but "authorized" Jesus to promulgate new Instructions. By citing Deuteronomy 18, they attached to Jesus the veneration in which Moses was held by many whom the new faith wanted to attract.

Christians could and did build a pretty convincing case that the rabbinic interpretations of Deuteronomy 18:15 ran counter to the text's explicit meaning. The text speaks of a prophet, not of prophets. Which prophet did God have in mind? None of the prophets whose activities are reported had been like Moses in the three ways which marked him as unique. None had known God face to face. None had been an agent of the nation's redemption. None had received or wielded legislative authority. A close look at the context in which the promise appears suggests that the pledge specifically alludes to a new legislator-prophet. A passage between the two versions of the pledge—"like myself" ... "like yourself"— seems to explain why God was offering it: "This is just what you [Israel] asked of the Lord your God at Horeb, on the day of the Assembly, saying, 'Let me not hear the voice of the Lord my God any longer or see this wondrous fire any more lest I die.' Whereupon the Lord said to me, 'They have done well in speaking thus'" (Deut. 18:16–17). The reference is to the first day of revelation when God spoke aloud the Ten Commandments and the people had been so frightened of the voice and of the fire that surrounded the mountain that they cried out: "If we hear the voice . . . any longer we shall die. . . . You [Moses] go close and hear all that the Lord our God says and you tell us everything . . . and we will willingly do it.' The Lord heard their pleas . . . 'They did speak well. . . . Go say to them, return to your tents, but you remain here with Me and I will give you the whole Instruction—the laws and the rules . . .' " (Deut. 5:22–28).

The Ebionites, an early sect made up almost entirely of Palestinian Jews, disciples of James, Jesus' brother—their early bishops were all of Jesus' family—followed Torah law and, at least during the first generation, regularly made pilgrimages to the Jerusalem Temple, practiced circumcision, observed the dietary rules and the Sabbath, and accepted Jesus as the Second Moses. According to their understanding, the revelations Jesus had brought dealt with messianic rather than legislative matters. The Ebionite founders were Jesus' contemporaries and immediate family and presumably knew his thinking, which suggests that Jesus probably had just such an image of himself as the Second Moses, the prophet-agent of the second redemption.

Moses is mentioned over eighty times in the New Testament, more than any other figure of the Hebrew Scriptures. The early church knew Moses as prophet, exemplar of faith, and suffering apostle of God; the first two roles were familiar, the last a particular Christian emphasis. Some Christian editors followed the Hellenistic-Jewish pattern and treated Moses as a moral paragon, removing from his portrait all suspicion of moral weakness or physical incapacity. Moses had acted deliberately and responsibly when he attacked the taskmaster: "By faith when he grew up [Moses] refused to be called the son of Pharaoh's daughter, preferring to suffer hardship with the people of God than enjoy the transient pleasures of sin" (Heb. 11:24). Moses had behaved courageously when he fled: "He left Egypt not because he feared the king's anger; for he was resolute, as one who saw the invisible God" (11:27). There was no question of any speech defect; he "is mighty in words and deed" (Acts 7:32).

The editor of the Gospel according to Matthew does not actually quote the "like myself" text, but throughout his narrative he selects traditions, or creates them, which show that Jesus' life had followed the pattern set by Moses. This is the gospel in which the apocryphal story of the slaughter of the innocents appears, a fiction whose only purpose is to analogize Jesus' life to Moses'. As the life of the infant Moses had been endangered by Pharaoh's command that all Hebrew male newborns be killed, so the baby Jesus had been endangered by Herod when the tyrant ordered the death of all Jewish boys in and around Bethlehem. Matthew reports that Jesus had been hidden and taken by his parents to Egypt where, like Moses, he had spent much of his youth. This too, is clearly apocryphal, but it allows Christians, like the editor of this scroll, to claim that Jesus, too, had come out of Egypt. When Matthew reports that God permitted Joseph to take Jesus back to Judea, he uses the same explanation—all who had plotted on his life are dead—that God gave Moses for the timing of his commission to return to Egypt (Exod. 4:19). The Sermon on the Mount is a sermon on a mount so that Jesus may be seen in the same situation as Moses on Sinai. His speech concluded, Jesus performs ten miracles which clearly are intended to parallel the ten plagues—miracles—that Moses performed in Egypt. Matthew declares that Jesus, as a Second Moses, surpasses the first. Why else should God send another? Moses was the prophet of the first redemption. Jesus is the prophet of the second redemption. Moses was the first among Old Testament prophets; but he was less than the Christ. Moses had brought his people from bondage. Jesus delivered all nations from the bonds of sin. Moses had brought a law of love to his people. Jesus brought a covenant of love to all nations. Moses was *eved adonai,* God's faithful servant; Jesus was God's faithful son.

The connection between Jesus and the promise of a prophet "like myself" is explicitly made in the Book of Acts, specifically in the speech of a certain Stephen before the Court of High Priests (Acts 7). Stephen is described as a member of a small group of Jews, not unlike those who belong to the Jews for Jesus cult. They followed most of the rules of Jewish practice but accepted Jesus as the Second Moses, God's agent in the work of the final redemption to whom He gave the authority to legislate on issues of faith and practice. The editor describes a scene which, purportedly, had taken place at Jerusalem, perhaps a decade after Jesus's death. Stephen had made a rather strident public witness to his faith in the Synagogue of Freedmen and, subsequently, had been accused of blasphemy before the Council and the High Priests of the Temple. Witnesses charged him with having declared "that Jesus of Nazareth will destroy this place and alter the customs handed down to us from Moses" (7:6). Stephen's defense is a long accusatory speech in which he gives his version of Jewish history and perfidy. He begins by summarizing the Biblical account of the lives of the patriarchs and the early life of Moses, closely paralleling the Biblical account except that he insists Moses' education had been Egyptian rather than Jewish (7:22). Moses was a fine-looking child, adopted by Pharaoh's daughter who brought him up in the palace as her own son; he "was trained in all the wisdom of the Egyptians, a powerful speaker, and a man of action;" at forty he looked into the conditions of his fellow countrymen, saw them ill-treated, avenged one of them, and had no recourse but to flee. Moses spent forty years in Midian before he was commissioned at the Burning Bush to liberate his people. Once Moses is commissioned, Stephen's account becomes a bitter anti-Jewish polemic. Stephen heaps praise on Moses and scorn on the Jews: Moses brought the tribes to Sinai where he received God's Instructions, worked miracles for forty years in the desert, persevered against all odds; but the Israelites never accepted his leadership and were never grateful. Moses is depicted as a suffering leader who must struggle every day with what Stephen clearly considers the congenital contumacy of the Jewish people: "He thought they would understand that God was offering them deliverance through him, but they did not understand" (7:25). "Our forefathers would not accept his leadership. They thrust him aside . . ." which leads to the peroration, "How stubborn you are, heathen still at heart and deaf to truth! You always fight against the Holy Spirit. Like fathers, like sons. Was there ever a prophet whom your fathers did not persecute? . . ." (7:51). Stephen counts among Moses' virtues that he relayed God's promise of a messiah. In this connection Stephen quotes Deuteronomy 18:15, naming Jesus as the Second Moses; but he twists the promise a bit to drive home his bitter attack on the Jewish people: "God will raise up a prophet for you from among yourselves as He raised me"

(7:37). The wording "as He raised me" in Stephen's context—a list of instances during which the tribes abused Moses—can only mean that Moses foresaw that Jesus would also experience the ingratitude of the Jews.

Moses fared well in early Church exegesis. The Church identified him with Jesus, the Second Moses, and believed Moses' words had promised Jesus' mission. The author of the Gospel of John writes: "Do not think that I shall accuse you to the Father; it is Moses who accuses you, on whom you set your hope. If you believed Moses you would believe me for he wrote of me" (5:45–46). Matthew's vision of the Transfiguration takes the theme one step farther. It takes place on a mountain (obviously Sinai) in the presence of Moses and Elijah, the other prophet who saw God on Sinai. The men stand there silently, obviously in the role of the two witnesses required by Jewish law to attest to the accuracy of what is seen and heard: God Himself saying: "This is My beloved son, listen to Him" (Matt. 17:6). In effect, Matthew pictures Moses passing on his mantle of prophetic authority to Jesus.

A rather impressive marble copy of Michelangelo's Moses sits in a corridor just outside my office. Whenever I analyze my emotional response to the piece, as distinguished from any aesthetic reaction, I recognize that I am slightly amused, certainly not seriously disturbed, by the horns, the result of Jerome's limited Hebrew vocabulary and the acceptance of his Vulgate translation by the Roman Church, or by Moses' athlete's frame, as if he had come fresh from the Pan-Hellenic games; but I am disturbed by the blank face of the twin stone tablets which Moses holds under his arm. Michelangelo, understandably, carved a Christian Moses; he gave us Moses as one of God's noblemen, not the prophet who had brought God's unchangeable law. One of the reasons Christian interpretations tend to emphasize Moses' fineness of spirit and character *before* the revelation of the law is to suggest that the Torah laws are largely irrelevant to the moral life. The Torah can then be pictured as a set of parochial, largely cultic and civil, rules. Moses' nobility became, paradoxically, an argument against the validity of Torah.

Early Christian writers laud Moses' virtue and capacity as a leader not only because his qualities merited acclaim but because his character, steadfastness, and patience had met the same disloyalty and ingratitude from the Jewish nations as had Jesus' witness and ministry. Here was proof of Israel's congenital stiff-neckedness. Where rabbinic commentary understood that Israel's murmurings against Moses proved the obvious—that leadership is a cruel task—Christian polemic tended to interpret Moses' heartaches in racial terms. Jews were congenitally intractable. The Church was loath to say that Moses willingly endured abuse in order to bring redemption into the world—the role of the suffering servant was reserved to Jesus—so Moses' sufferings proved only that Jews were spiritually blind and morally corrupt. Most early Christian writers explain Moses' virtue by pointing to his Egyptian rather than Jewish upbringing. Chrysostom, particularly among the Church Fathers, went on at length about Moses' palace life to emphasize that Moses was conditioned by generous royal values rather than by the narrow and legalist attitudes of a benighted Israel, that his spirit had not been twisted by the pernicious conditioning of the Hebrew way of life. Some commentators took this racism one step further and claimed that Moses was not a Jew, for no Jew could have achieved what he achieved. There were exceptions; Ephraem Syrus (fourth century) repeated an *aggadah* which described Moses' Hebrew education under his parents' tutelage (Com. to Exod. 30:4). But most churchmen preferred to elaborate on Stephen's assertion: "He was well versed in the wisdom of the Egyptians" (Acts 7:22), and so separate Moses from Judaism.

Incidentally, it is this ancient polemic that an elderly Sigmund Freud picked up in his hapless detour into Biblical history, *Moses and Monotheism* (1939). Freud's argument that Moses was an Egyptian who instructed the Israelites in a version of Egyptian monotheism and was killed for his pains by an ungrateful people is little more than the old Christian canard refurbished with a few tentative modern "facts." As mentioned, this work, published at the height of Hitler's decade of power, got a predictable reception among Jews.

If the "a prophet like myself" text was taken as a welcome confirmation by those early followers of Jesus who believed in Jesus as the prophet-herald of redemption, it presented problems to Paul and those Christians whose faith was centered in the Son of God, the Christ, rather than in the actual person of Jesus. Paul does not quote Deuteronomy 18 or explore the Jesus-Moses parallels. In his eyes the Christ was not "like myself" but incomparable, a position which became the official doctrine of the Church. The popular medieval religious play, *Le Mystere D'Adam* (twelfth century) makes the point forcefully and dramatically. In the concluding scene a succession of Old Testament prophets appear to repeat prophecies they had brought about the Christ. Moses speaks the "like myself" prophecy, using Stephen's translation, and then adds, "That which I speak, through God I saw;/ From our own brethren, from our law/God shall raise up a man who'll be/Prophet and sum of prophecy. / Heaven's secrets all shall he receive;/Him, *more than me*, shall ye believe" (*Adam* 186). Luther, with characteristic bluntness, expressed the same thought. "This is the chief passage in Deuteronomy and a clearly expressed prophecy of Christ as the new teacher. . . . Moses' purpose is to show that in the future there will be another priesthood, another kingdom, another worship of God, and another word by which all of Moses will be set aside." He handles the troubling comparison "like yourself," which might suggest an earthly prophet rather than a son of God, with equal dispatch. "He is not speaking here of similarity between Moses and that Prophet in regard to personal worth, but of similarity in authority and office. . . . Unless this Prophet was greater than Moses, Moses would not yield obedience and authority to him" (Lec. on Deut. 18:15).

Paul avoided the image of Jesus as the Second Moses because it raised the whole question of law. Moses had been a legislative prophet. Paul declared that the law was a burden and a blindness, an invitation to sin. "The Law he [Moses] engraved in letters upon stone is a dispensation of death" (2 Cor. 3:7). Moses, he believed, had brought a law that shackles and must be discarded. Paul argued that Moses had heard the law from angels, not directly from God; that the law consequently was a contingent rather than an immutable set of rules adequate for its time but inadequate for an age to which Christ had brought deliverance. Some among Paul's disciples declared that the law of Moses was in fact the law *of* Moses, representing Moses' thinking and not God's words (Mark 10:1–12). Torah law had had temporary value as a system of restraints for a world sunk in Adam's sin, but for those who affirmed the new dispensation and who had transcended Original Sin through Christ's atoning death, the law was no longer needed. Paul had little use for any law. He believed in the transforming power of faith. His interest was in the Christ, the Savior who had died to atone for Adam's sin, faith in whose spirit brought spiritual transformation and redemption. He was not interested in Jesus as a legislative prophet.

To drive home his rejection of the Second Moses analogy, Paul rewrote the Torah's description of Moses' transfiguration after his experience on Sinai. According to the Hebrew text, after Moses had been with God his face was alight and he put a veil over his face to protect others from the dazzling nimbus that played around his head. Paul insists that Moses had put on the veil to hide the fact that this light had begun to fade, a sign that the revelation he had received was only a temporary measure which would, in short order, give way to the greater glory, "the dispensation of the Spirit" (2 Cor. 3:7–11). Sinai has "faded away to make way for the radiance that will not fade." Paul also interpreted the veil as a suggestion of the blindfold that remains over Israel's eyes, blinding them to the Christ. "To this day, whenever the Law of Moses is read, a veil lies over the minds of the hearers; but when a man turns to the Lord the veil is removed" (2 Cor. 3:15). Medieval iconography picked up this highly visual theme. I remember particularly a stained glass window in the Cathedral of St. Denis in which Jesus is portrayed lifting Moses' veil, figuratively giving him sight. It also played a role in medieval Vatican ritual. When a new Pope was crowned he processed through Rome as its temporal, as well as religious, lord and received the homage of all citizens. During these ceremonies Rome's Jews were required to be present and offer to the Pope a Torah scroll which he received and returned with this formula, "May Almighty God remove the veil from your heads."

The synagogue responded to these Christian charges in various ways. A number of *aggadot* describe in detail Moses' Hebrew education: he had been taught to read by his mother, given more advanced training by his father, and only when he was twelve—or twenty, some said—did he return to the palace. The nimbus of light which radiated from Moses' head when he came down from Sinai was specifically related to the revelation of the Torah. According to one *aggadah*, when Moses finished inscribing the text on its parchment scroll, he wiped his pen on his hair, leaving there traces of the heavenly ink which gave off a glowing radiance which everyone could see (Ginsberg 6, n. 309).

Where Christian polemic used the Hebrew tribes as prototypes of all Jews, prefiguring the blindness of every generation of Jews to the true faith, the synagogue emphasized the psychological brutalization which the slaves had endured in Egypt. The rabbis gave the generation that came out of Egypt with Moses a special name, *dor ha-midbar*, the generation of the wilderness. They had been a difficult lot, but Israel was not congenitally depraved. Oppression had corrupted the Exodus generation, but their children were fit to enter the Promised Land. In a simply analogy the rabbis compared Israel to a prince who went to live in the open country, working in the fields and hunting in the forest until he was encrusted with sweat and deeply tanned; but as soon as he returned to the palace, scrubbed down and put on fresh linen, he again took on the look of nobility (Cant. R. 1:6). The rabbis noted that the Torah does not mention any communication by God to Moses' during the thirty-eight years after the *dor ha-midbar* was declared unfit to enter the

Promised Land. They explained God's silence by saying that
He had no reason to speak to Moses as leader of a generation condemned to die in the wilderness (Ginsberg 6:98, n.
550), that God had spoken to Moses only for the sake of Israel and that all God had done had been for Israel, not for
Moses. They added that the shepherd is nothing without his
flock. Despite their shortcomings, the Jews of the wilderness
generation had had their share of redeeming virtues, most
notably generosity. They had willingly given their jewelry
for the Golden Calf and later what precious items remained
to them as precious metal from which to mold utensils for
the Tabernacle. A third-century sage was awed by such indiscriminate generosity. "One cannot understand the nature
of this people; when appealed to for the Calf they gave; when
appealed to for the Tabernacle they gave" (j. Ber. 1:6).

To counter the Christian claim that the Torah was not
God's final word, a claim that attacked the authenticity of
the Jewish tradition, the rabbis not only cited *aggadic* incidents which enhanced the Torah's majesty, but preached
countless sermons on the Torah's authenticity and reinforced the people's veneration of the Torah by adding to the
liturgy innumerable formulae of praise of the Torah. A medieval commentator used a text taken from one of Moses'
valedictory speeches to make the point that all God's Instructions had been revealed at Sinai. Moses' peroration
reads: "Surely this Instruction which I enjoin upon you this
day is not too baffling for you, nor is it beyond reach. It is
not in the heavens that you should say who among us can go
to the heavens and get it for us and impart it to us, that we
may observe it" (Deut. 30:11–12). The comment reads:
"You must not say that another Moses will arise and bring
us another Torah from Heaven. I, therefore, tell you, 'It is

not in the Heaven, that is to say, no part of it has remained in Heaven" (Deut. R. 8:6).

Their liturgical efforts were probably most effective. Liturgy is the catechism of ordinary people. What was in the service became the familiar phrases by which the people defined their faith, particularly in the long centuries before books were printed, when the service was necessarily known by heart.

One example can stand for many. By the end of the first century the practice of weekly Torah reading in the synagogue had become established. To precede and follow the reading, blessings were devised which affirm that the Torah is the word of God, that the Torah contains *the* truth, that the gift of the Torah marked Israel's election, and that obedience to the Torah is the way to merit God's reward: "Praised be You, O Lord our King of the Universe, Who has chosen us from all peoples and has given us Your Torah. Praised be You, O Lord our God, Who has Given us the Torah of truth and has planted in our midst eternal life. Praised be You, O Lord, Giver of the Torah." When the Torah was returned to the ark after it had been read, a declaration was recited, composed of various lines from Deuteronomy, Proverbs, and Isaiah which affirm the Torah's life-sustaining power.

This is the Torah which Moses set before the children of Israel, according to the commandment of the Lord by the hand of Moses. She is a tree of life to those who lay hold of her. Happy is everyone who holds her fast. Her ways are ways of pleasantness and all her paths are peace. Length of days are in her right hand. In her left hand are riches and honor. The Lord was pleased for His righteousness' sake to make the teaching great and glorious.

The rabbis also enlarged Moses' achievement. Moses, too, had been a savior. A Talmudic sage, Simlai, relates the text: "He was numbered among the transgressors and bore the sin of many" (Isaiah 53:12), to Moses' prayer: "If You will forgive their sins, well and good; but if not, erase me. . . ." (Exod. 32:32), and explicitly suggests that Moses accepted death in the wilderness, though it need not have been his fate, because he hoped that his death would atone for the many sins of those whom he had led and, inferentially, of the generations yet to come (b. Sotah 14b). Another *aggadah* reported that Moses had captured and held prisoner the Angel of Death until Moses had recited the prayer which assures Israel ultimate victory over the Dark Spirit, thus insuring to mankind the possibility of life in the World to Come (PM 125 ff). Like the Christ, Moses had brought to mankind the gift of immortality, salvation.

Early Christians looked on the Hebrew Bible as a closed book. Its prophecies had been fulfilled in Jesus. Jesus was the prophet "like myself" and much more. Another Palestinian group, the Samaritans, believed that the "like myself" prophecy had not yet been fulfilled; indeed, they still eagerly await its fulfillment. Samaritan theologians frequently refer to Deuteronomy's "like myself" pledge, find the messiah predicted there, and identify their prophet-lawgiver-messiah as Moses himself sent back to complete the work of redemption he had begun so long ago.

The Samaritans derive their name from the noun, *shomerim*, the observers, or the keepers of the truth. The truth is the Five Books of Moses. They admit into the canon no other scriptural books but these five. Their Torah and the Torah of the synagogue are almost but not completely identical. Among other changes, their version includes a rule which specifies Mount Gerizim, near Samaria, as God's chosen sanctuary in the Promised Land. The Samaritans believe that the Jerusalem Temple should never have been built, that evil and self-serving priests had built and administered it and had committed the ultimate blasphemy of tampering with God's Word and amending the original text in order to authorize their shrine.

Because they settled near Samaria, it was first assumed that they were descendants of Israelites who had lived near their country's capital, Samaria, when the Assyrians destroyed the city in 721 B.C.E. but had not been significant enough to be included among the captives who had been marched off into exile and a future as the lost ten tribes. Present scholarship tends to date the Samaritan separation from the main body of Judeans to the postexilic period and to relate the schism to the many bitter arguments which raged in Maccabean times around the authority of the Jerusalem priesthood (second century B.C.E.). Today the Samaritan community numbers less than a thousand; they still guard a venerable Torah scroll, written in an archaic Hebrew alphabet, not the square script of the rabbinic scribes. They claim this so-called Abisha scroll was inscribed during the early years of the Israelite settlement in Canaan, thus antedating by nearly a thousand years any extant Torah manuscript. In their eyes it is the only authentic record of the original revelation.

Since the Samaritans have no Bible save the Torah, they interpret the line in Moses' eulogy, "Never again would there arise in Israel a prophet like Moses whom the Lord singled out face to face" (Deut. 32:10), as the statement that Moses was the only true prophet. The likes of Hosea, Joel, and Amos are dismissed as visionaries and sorcerers.

Elijah, they claim, was not transferred to Heaven by a whirl-wind but rather died unceremoniously, clumsily falling into the Jordan River and drowning. Belief in Moses as the sole prophet of God seems to have been part of the Samaritan tradition from the very beginning. They venerate Moses in their writings and prayers with language which exceeds even the rabbis' most lavish encomia. The oldest extant writings by a Samaritan theologian are those of a fourth-century C.E. poet-exegete, Markah, who published a six-part compendium of ethics and theology which centers on the role and authenticity of Moses: (1) his life and teachings from the Burning Bush to the crossing of the Reed Sea; (2) a commentary on Exodus 15, the crossing of the Reed Sea; (3) a commentary on the blessings and curses of Deuteronomy 37; (4) details of the commissioning of Joshua; (5) a commentary on Moses' psalm known as Deuteronomy 32; and (6) a description of Moses' death by the hand of God. Markah's Moses is a paragon. "The radiance of his consecrated spirit will never be matched by another mortal and remains with him even in the tomb" (5:3). When Moses ascends Sinai he parts the veil which separates this world from God's realm, the Heavens, and ascends into God's court where he receives not only the law but the fullness of knowledge. On the day of his death Moses learns what will happen on Judgment Day. When his mission is fulfilled he parts the veil which separates earth from Heaven and ascends into the realm of the angels. Moses ascends. He does not die. In life Moses gained levels of existence and perfection not attained by any other mortal, and he lives on with God.

I could match most of these Samaritan claims in rabbinic sources. The phrase, *ish-elohim*, which Jews translate "man of God," can be read, if taken literally, "man-God," which emboldened some to describe Moses as half man and half celestial being (Deut. R. 11:4). Another *Midrash* claims that when God placed all the objects of creation on one side of a scale and Moses on another, Moses outweighed all of them (PM 72–72). The Samaritan tradition went that one step further. Markah states bluntly, "He who believes in Moses believes in his Lord" (4:17). Moses is not God, nor is he the son of God; but he is of God, he is "the father of wonders, the storehouse of miracles" (6:9). Belief in this semi-divine Moses is a Samaritan article of faith. "Give ear, O Heavens, let me speak, let the earth hear the words I utter" (Deut. 32:1) suggested to Samaritan commentators that Moses could command the forces of nature. In terms borrowed from the light mysticism of popular gnostic theologies, Moses is pictured not only as the prophet-messenger of God's word but as a son of God's house, "the light of two worlds," "the living listen to him, the dead fear him, heaven and earth do not disobey his words" (Markah 6:9). Moses is the master of knowledge, the word that was, is, and will ever be. Samaritan prayer appeals directly to Moses. As far as we know, Samaritans never made an idol or icon of Moses. They, too, were bound by the Second Commandment. But he was enshrined in their prayers and a focus of veneration. "Let us follow after the great prophet Moses who leads us well, for our Lord sent him to us. Where is there a prophet like Moses, who was a good father to all Israel, bringing them up and caring for them, atoning for them . . . and who gave life through his prayer" (4:7).

At first the Samaritans seem to have expected that a prophet like Moses would be the herald-prophet, the Elijah of the Messianic Era. There are reports of a group who rallied around a certian Dositheus, a miracle-working faith healer (first-second century C.E.) who, according to Origen, called himself "the prophet" like "myself" (*Contra Celsum* 1:57), and who, on that basis, seems to have claimed God's authority to alter the law. The equally mysterious Samaritan mystagogue, Simon Magus, may have made similar claims. By the Middle Ages the main Samaritan tradition, perhaps to protect itself from the likes of Dositheus and Simon Magus, had changed its messianic vision from the anticipation of a prophet "like myself" to the expectations that Moses himself would return as the messiah. Having no other prophet to work into its imagery, Samaritan messianism ultimately shaped itself around the idea of Moses returning to earth as the prophet of the final redemption. The Samaritans call their messiah *Taheb* (literally, one who restores), generally identify him as Moses returned, and describe him as a supernatural redeemer who will bring security to the Samaritan nation, universal acceptance for its ideas, and blessing to mankind before the final Day of Judgment. It is tempting to call the medieval Samaritan tradition Mosaism since Moses is their ideal religious personality, the model for human behavior, source of God's Instructions, agent of His miracles, the central figure in their drama of redemption and the object of constant veneration. Certainly, the Samaritan tradition went further in this direction than Judaism was ever tempted to go.

One of the unexpected facets of Moses' afterlives is that rabbinic Judaism assigned him a minor role at best, and often no role at all, in the messianic drama. Messianic speculation is a huge and sometimes inchoate field—there are few limits to the human imagination—whose literature includes a few references to Moses, generally as a supporting actor in the messianic drama. Observing that the commandments were written on two tablets, one tradition suggests that in the time to come God will bring Moses and Elijah and the two will perform messianic tasks together (Deut. R. 10:1). In another *aggadah* Moses' role is as leader of the resurrected generation of ex-slaves, the *dor hamidbar*, all of whom had died during the long march, but now are finally allowed to enter the Promised Land (Exod. R. 2:4). But when all these references are brought together they make a quite meager list (Ginsberg 6:167, n. 966). Moses' messianic role is surprisingly modest.

The relegation of Moses to a role subordinate to Elijah's is surprising. The first Exodus was rehearsed every Passover as the promise and the prototype of the second. Some rabbis said that the second redemption would be like the first and that "the last redeemer would be like the first" (Num. R. 11:2). What would be more natural than to affirm Moses' messianic return? But Moses never came into his own as an eschatological prophet. Moses is not given the lead role; Elijah is.

The identification of Elijah with the messianic drama developed quite early. The scroll of Malachi, an early postexilic text, concludes with a severe judgment against the Jerusalem community, its sting somewhat mitigated by a concluding promise that God will send Elijah "before the coming of the great and terrible Day of the Lord" and Elijah will "turn the hearts of the fathers to the children and the hearts of the children to the fathers" (3:23). The oracle was widely known. Several centuries later a second-century B.C.E. teacher of Jerusalem's well-born sons, Ben Sirah, repeated Malachi on this point, "It is written that you are to come at the appointed time with warnings, to allay the divine wrath before its final fury, to reconcile father and son and to restore the tribes of Jacob" (Eccles. 48:10). It is my belief that the major role Elijah plays in rabbinic messianism reflects a desire to distinguish the Jewish vision from the Christian and the Samaritan visions and a deliberate effort to suggest that the promise of Deuteronomy 18 had been fulfilled.

The Elijah narrative in Samuel through Kings includes a remarkable number of parallels between Elijah's career and Moses', almost sufficient to suggest that the editor had set out to type Elijah in Moses' pattern, much as the editor of Matthew chose material which typed Jesus in Moses' pattern. Elijah is the only other prophet besides Moses to whom God invariably spoke directly and never in a vision. Like Moses, Elijah is the agent through whom God provides food and drink to those in need. Moses had been forty days on the mountain, Elijah remains forty days in the wilderness. Both Moses and Elijah formally empower their successors. Elijah's death, like Moses', is not described as a normal burial but a walking away from the camp and, in Elijah's case, a translation into Heaven. Whether or not the Elijah narratives were shaped by those who believed that he was the prophet "like myself," these similarities and the Malachi prophecy were too tempting for the rabbis to ignore. They told innumerable stories about Elijah's messianic role and frequently embellished the Moses-Elijah comparison. One sage reports that God revealed Himself to Elijah on Mount Sinai in the same cleft of the rock where He had appeared to Moses (b. Meg. 19b).

The rabbis substituted a well-known prophet for Moses so they could say that Deuteronomy 18 has been fulfilled. Why was Elijah the prophet they selected? Because he was mentioned in a specific oracle. From the rabbi's point of view, Elijah was a propitious choice. If Moses were to return, he might bring new Instructions. Elijah had not been a legislative prophet, and there was no reason to believe that in the Messianic Age he would become one. Even so, the rabbis made certain that Elijah was never pictured as the bearer of new Instructions. They taught that Elijah was a disciple of Moses, a disciple who lacked the full authority of his teacher (b. Sotah 13a). Elijah had heard "the voice of Great Stillness" (1 Kings 19:12) and not the commanding voice which had made known the Torah to Moses. Among the tasks assigned Elijah in the Messianic Era was that of resolving some minor points of law. It would be his task to make known a few rules which had been part of the original Torah but which had been forgotten. By specifying Elijah's *halachic* role as one in which he would not break new ground, the rabbis precluded his having any other (b. Ber. 35a). Another Talmudic passage reports that Elijah was smitten by "sixty flaming lashes" when on one occasion he exceeded his authority and revealed a secret prayer formula (b. B.M. 85b). The rabbis hoped Elijah had learned his lesson.

For all their veneration of Moses, the rabbis didn't want a Second Moses.

# CHAPTER

# V

# On the
# Mountain Top

**A**S I TOOK my seat in the tourist bus from Beer-sheba to Saint Catherine's Monastery, an active Greek Orthodox house perched on a rocky slope near the southern wilderness of the Sinai Peninsula, a guide began to prattle about its history. "Saint Catherine's was established here in the sixth century because the peak was known as Jebel Musa, the mountain of Moses, Mount Sinai. The monks claim that their building is on the actual site of the Burning Bush." He laughed knowingly at the idea that anyone knew where that particular bush had grown, but if he had doubts that Jebel Musa was Mount Sinai he kept them to himself. The identification of this particular two-thousand-foot peak as the mountain of Moses is probably based on little more than the vision of a desert monk who had settled himself near the spot and had a revelation that this was the famous Mount Sinai where Moses had spoken with God. Others heard of his vision, and soon the height came to be named

Jebel Musa. Centuries later an established order of monks learned of the tradition, found the place attractive and water available, and built here their fortress monastery, confident that they would be close to God at a place where God had so significantly revealed Himself. It helped that they were supported by a sizable grant from a Byzantine emperor eager to gain salvation and to have friendly eyes and ears in the sparsely inhabited region between his southern border and Arabia.

No one knows the actual location of the mountain of Moses. There are many similar heights in the sierra that runs north to south almost the whole length of the western edge of the Sinai Peninsula. Many who now conjecture that Jebel Musa lies too far south to be the peak the Torah describes base their theories on a text in which God gives Moses directions for his journey beyond the Reed Sea: "Turn back and encamp between Pi-hahiroth, between Migdol and the sea, before Baal-Zephon" (Exod. 14:1). After Israel's 1967 military occupation of the Sinai, archeologists located a Phoenician shrine dedicated to Baal Zephon on a spit of land which runs for some miles just off the Mediterranean coast enclosing a large dry-pan lagoon, known since antiquity as Lake Bardawil. If this shrine is the Baal Zephon mentioned in Exodus and if these directions indicate the road the slaves took, the Israelites followed a route which led them far to the north of Jebel Musa.

The entire mountain scene may, in fact, be legendary. The appearance of the High God to the sheik on a mountain top, generally in a setting heavy with thunder and lightning, was a conventional idiom in West Asian myth, where men regularly met their gods on the heights. Although piety loves the dramatic and most artists have imagined Mount

Sinai as an imposing peak, many of the rabbis would not have been disappointed to discover that few peaks in the Sinai rise above two thousand feet. Among the *aggadot* which warn against making overmuch of the revelation's stage setting, one reports that when God decided the time of revelation had arrived, several mountains, all much loftier than Sinai, vied for the honor of being the place of revelation, and that He chose Sinai because it was the lowest and least noticeable (Ginsberg 6:31, n. 183). The point, of course, is that God's Words do not need scenic embellishment.

At no time in Jewish history did Mount Sinai become a place of pilgrimage. Neither the Bible nor rabbinic writings mention organized pilgrimages to the site of the revelation. The only other person to visit Sinai, according to Scripture, was the prophet Elijah (1 Kings 19), and there is reason to doubt that Elijah actually came to this place. I have already suggested that the highly legendary account of his life which has been inserted into the Deuteronomic history seems to be the work of an editor or editors who shaped his biography on the pattern of Moses'. Christian, not Jewish, piety "discovered" the place alleged to be Mount Sinai.

Why did Jews not make Sinai into a place of pilgrimage? There was no Torah prohibition of such rituals; indeed, Torah law required that three times a year the male members of the community appear at God's shrines. *Hag*, the Biblical name for a festival, has also the meaning of pilgrimage. The answer may be that there was no reliable tradition about the physical place of the revelation. Though Scripture generally locates the revelation on Mount Sinai, in seventeen places it calls the mount Horeb and in a number of others calls the hill simply "the mountain of God." The rabbis assumed that the three names were different labels for the same place and devised sermonic explanations for the various names: "the mountain of God" because it was here that God had revealed Himself; Sinai because here *sinah*, hatred toward idolatry, became a national requirement; and Horeb because the Torah is a sword, *herev*, which defends Israel against her enemies. It is probable that several traditions circulated about the location of the high place where Moses had been with God or that no one actually knew the location. In retrospect, we can see it was best that way; reality rarely lives up to imagination, and God's Instructions might have seemed less impressive had later generations found Sinai to be an unimposing site.

The absence of a ritual of pilgrimage to the sacred mountain is consistent with the Torah's focus on the Great God Who, rather than the Great Man who. The Israelites were not to retrace their prophet's spiritual pilgrimage, but to present themselves to the Lord, "in the place which He will choose" (Deut. 16:6, 15, 16). Pilgrimages were made to God's shrines—Shiloh, Bethel, Jerusalem—not to the place of Moses' illumination or to his grave. In the first chapter we analyzed the editing of the Moses stories to enhance God's role and diminish Moses'. This theological approach remains in evidence through most of the Biblical period. None of the canonical books outside the Torah offer fresh details of Moses' life. Beyond a few mentions of Moses in geneological lists (1 Chron. 23:14–15, 26:24) and two references to Moses as builder of the desert tabernacle (1 Chron. 21:29, 2 Chron. 1:3), postexilic writings refer to Moses only to identify him with the law that he had mediated (Mal. 3:22). Given the importance of this tradition in Biblical thought, we would expect it to be continued by subsequent generations, but Hellenistic and rabbinic Jews broke away from it. Ben Sirah's review of Jewish history, written in the second century B.C.E., is little more than a list of notables with a few lines about their several accomplishments, which begins with this most un-Torahic of thoughts: "Let us sing the praises of famous men" (Eccles. 44:1), and proceeds to sing the familiar praises of David and unexpected praises of Moses. Post-Biblical Judaism developed a "mystique of the righteous," which saw the future of the nation and, indeed, of the world, as somehow dependent on the presence of men and women of exceptional quality. In Biblical times idolatry was still a clear and present danger. Apparently, in post-Biblical times the religious authorities believed that the doctrine of the absolute unity and power of God was so firmly established that they could safely accommodate the people's natural desire to cherish heroes.

Given the centrality of the Sinai event in Jewish history and thought, it is somewhat surprising to discover that the Torah is as vague on the details of the event as on its location. A brief resume of chapter 19 in Exodus which purports to describe the initial stages of the Sinai drama will make the point. Three months after crossing the Reed Sea, the tribes arrive at Mount Sinai. Moses ascends. God offers a covenant. Moses reports the offer to the elders. The people answer as one, "All that God has spoken we will do." Moses reports their answer to God. God promises to come in a thick cloud. For an undisclosed reason Moses again reports to God what has transpired. God imposes a two-day regimen of purification, declares the mountain out of bounds, and promises to come down in the sight of all of the people on the third day. The community is told that when they hear a long blast of the shofar they can approach and ascend. Moses goes down and reports. On the third day, amid nature's portents, Moses leads the people to the foot of the mountain. Moses speaks, but there is no indication what he says. God descends to the top of the mountain and Moses goes up. God orders Moses to descend to warn the people not to break the taboo limits. Moses tells God the people will not approach for they fear to breach the limits He has ordered set. God again orders Moses down with instructions to return with Aaron and to warn the priests not to break the taboo limits. Moses descends and speaks. Again, there is no indication what he says. The very next line introduces the Ten Commandments: "God spoke all those words saying: 'I am the Lord your God'" (Exod. 20:1). God appears to speak the Ten Instructions when nobody is on the mountain.

To whom does God speak? Deuteronomy reports that Moses was alone on the mountain when the Ten Commandments were spoken (Deut. 5:5). Exodus 32:17–18 seems to place Joshua on the mountain during the entire forty-day period (no length of time is mentioned in Exodus 19), apparently at a spot between Moses and the camp, since it is Joshua who brings Moses news of the Golden Calf. It does not say how Joshua brought the news to Moses. Did he shout? Did he climb to the summit to report the news directly? Was he with Moses when God was there? The medieval commentators were reduced to saying, "I do not know in what capacity Joshua was serving here" (Rashi to Exod. 24:13). Exodus 24:9 places Moses, Aaron, two of Aaron's sons, Nadav and Abihu, and seventy elders on the mountain and not only on the mountain but on the mountain top: "[They] ascended; and they saw the God of Israel: under His feet there was the likeness of a pavement of sapphire, like the very sky for purity" (Exod. 24:9-10). Clearly, at least one tradition which found its way into the Torah text knew Sinai as something other than a private dialogue between God and Moses.

There is similar confusion about Moses' activity while he was on the mountain. One narrative has him bring up tablets of stone so that God can inscribe the Instructions (Exod. 34:1-4). Another has him come up empty handed and receive on the mountain top tablets of stone which God had already prepared (Exod. 24:12). Another version omits all paraphernalia and has Moses simply report to the people the Instructions he has heard from God (Deut. 5:5).

All these contradictions of logic and confusions of chronology are evidence of the point I have been making. It cannot be said often enough. The Torah gives no indication that its editors had set out to present a history book. The Torah grew out of Israel's liturgy and Israel's law. The Sinai narratives were designed to convey the sense of awe and miracle which revelation kindles.

The term, *Mattan Torah*, the gift of the Torah, was assigned by the rabbis to the Sinai event. The mountain was not important, the message was. A miracle had taken place. Israel and the world now possessed what had heretofore been unavailable: redemptive Instructions. After Sinai Israel could say, "God has told us what is good and what He requires of us." If we understand religion as a cluster of ideas, institutions, myths, rites, and disciplines by which a group makes sense out of the confusions of daily experience, validates moral standards, defines the purpose of life, and affirms the possibility of redemption, then we must say that ever since Sinai Jews have assumed that at Sinai Judaism emerged as a complete religion. The rabbis like to imagine that Abraham knew what being Jewish required, but the Torah does not make that claim. What it does claim is that at Sinai Israel bound itself to a covenant whose terms are represented by the Torah. There Jewish life, for the first time, acquired its mature shape.

However they describe the Sinai event, the various Torah narratives take pains to underscore the reliability of the text of revelation. In one version God Himself engraves the rule on stone. In another God guides Moses' hand as he writes the Instructions. Moses repeatedly tells the people that he has reported the revelation to them exactly as God had commanded him. The Torah is careful to describe Moses when he talks with God as awake, in control of himself, his senses, and his thoughts. Although prophecy could involve ecstatic seizure or mantic activity, Moses never babbles or falls into a trance. His role on Sinai is that of a prophet who talks quietly, soberly, and responsibly with God. The only noticeable change in Moses' person is that his face became radiant after he had been with God.

Since religion constructs transcending concepts, those eternal truths all people need, over the contradictions of our experience, Jewish liturgy and *aggadah* understandably emphasize in every possible way the reliability of the Sinai scene. Sinai was not a private illumination in which God spoke only to Moses but one which "all the people witnessed" (Exod. 20:15). A true copy of the Torah in Moses' own script was put in the Ark where all could readily consult its text (Deut. 31:26). Conservative scribal traditions reinforced this sense of immutability by insisting that the Torah be copied with a scrupulous fidelity which extended to the placement of columns of text on the parchment sheets, the number of lines in each column, and the special treatment of certain passages, and it is so copied still today. Few members of nonorthodox synagogues accept the Torah as literally the word of God; yet, their liturgy still focuses on the Torah as symbol of certainty. After the Torah is read worshippers recite some verses from the Psalms: "The law of the Lord is perfect, restoring the soul. . . . The ordinances of this Lord are true, they are righteous altogether" (19:8–10).

The Torah's presentation of Sinai confronts us with many mysteries, but the most important mystery of all surrounds the most important question: what did God say or dictate to Moses during his two forty-day sojourns on the mountain? Some chapters indicate that only the Ten Instructions were spoken on the mountain, although editors have inserted a number of other Instructions in the Exodus text between the accounts of Moses' first and second ascents. Deuteronomy enlarges Moses' Sinai experience. It describes the Ten Commandments as "those words—those and no more [which God spoke]—to your whole congregation on the mountain" (Deut. 5:19), after which God instructs Moses to have the people return to their tents, "but you remain here with Me, and I will give you the whole Instruction" (Deut. 5:28). Deuteronomy later indicates that Moses wrote a book of Instructions (31:24), but neither here nor elsewhere does the Torah specify that Moses taught or wrote down any of the narrative portions which are now included in the written text. Yet, that is the understanding of the traditional synagogue. When the Torah scroll is lifted up before them, the congregation repeats a text: *"This* is the Teaching that Moses set before the Israelites" (Deut. 4:44), which in its original context referred only to a list of commandments but in its liturgical use clearly embraces the entire Five Books of Moses.

One of the hallmarks of the Jewish tradition is a determination to concentrate all revelation in the Sinai experience, despite any number of texts in the Torah itself which suggest that *torot*, revealed Instructions, were received at other times and places. To put it another way, Judaism has been shaped and controlled by the myth of a one-time, for-all-time, all-encompassing revelation.

The urge to unify, to bind into a single event, all that was held constitutional and sacred, represents the most distinguishing feature of the Jewish theological tradition. The need to incorporate into the Sinai revelation all that the community over generations came to accept as Torah was so strong that it ran roughshod over many contrary "facts." The passion was proof, if proof be needed, of the compelling power of the revelation myth. Centuries after the pious myth had become firm doctrine, an *aggadist* finally found a vivid visual image to express it: the tablets on which God's Instructions had been inscribed were of sapphire crystal like God's Throne, translucent and transparent, inscribed on all sides not only with the Ten Instructions but with all the rules of the Torah and the whole Torah.

A century of critical research on the composition of the Torah enables us to describe the process of folding all that was considered Torah into the Sinai experience. In preexilic times lists of divine Instructions, stories of the nation's beginning, creation myths, and liturgical formulae circulated independently, most often orally. Over the centuries some of these elements were attached to each other. Storytellers added saga to saga. Priests added lists of *torot* to lists of *torot*. At various times the confederation of tribes seems to have celebrated covenant renewal ceremonies during which the record of God's redemptive acts, which was in effect a review of the people's early history, were read out as a confirmation of God's authority, together with those Instructions which constituted the Covenant's terms. From time to time these narratives and lists of Instructions were set down in writing. In 621 B.C.E. a scroll of law, generally believed to contain major legal elements of Deuteronomy, was found by workmen refurbishing the Jerusalem Temple. Since no one could remember its origin, it probably had been hidden there at a much earlier time. The editorial process probably received its major impetus during the Babylonian Exile as religious leaders worked desperately to preserve the national traditions. An exiled community deprived of its Temple and cult had only its scrolls of narrative and Instructions as reminders of God's care and records of its practice. The ritual of public reading may have begun at this time. In the middle of the fifth century B.C.E. a representative of that exile community, Ezra, brought from Babylon to Jerusalem a Torah scroll which he established as authoritative by reading from it in the town square and winning the community's oath of acclamation. By the fourth century B.C.E. the present Torah text was in existence and accepted as authoritative.

The idea that the whole text of the Torah scroll had been revealed to Moses on Sinai was fully accepted by the fourth century B.C.E. and remains a doctrine of orthodox Judaism. An occasional paragraph in the rabbinic literature suggests that the brief description of Moses' death in Deuteronomy 34 may have been appropriated from Joshua's scroll (b. B.B. 14b) but this suggestion was a decidedly minority opinion. Once the thesis of unitary revelation is accepted there is no logical reason why an omniscient God could not have described to Moses the manner of his own death, including the fact that the tribes would mourn him for thirty days in the plains of Moab. A second century C.E. sage, Simeon, made the point poetically, "Let us say up to this point [Deut. 34:15] God dictated and Moses wrote it down, and that from this point on God dictated and Moses wrote it down with tears in his eyes" (b. B.B. 15a).

The interest of the Torah's editors did not extend to the removal of inconsistencies of detail. Seams between the various versions still show, and those willing to suspend belief in the myth of a single revelation can readily see where they were stitched together. But that is a modern perspective. In Biblical times this composite work became one Torah, and the one Torah became the constitution of the Jewish nation. The long unifying process, like so much else in the evolution of Biblical thought, is evidence of a cultural tendency to draw together originally diverse materials. In the beginning there were many shrines: Bethel, Gilgal, Schechem. Then there was one, Jerusalem. In the early years of Jewish self-rule authority rested with tribal councils and a series of temporary war chiefs with limited authority, and then there was a king with a centralized bureaucracy. In the beginning God was above all other gods. Then there was the uncompromising monotheism of Deutero-Isaiah, "To whom, then, can you liken Me?" (Isa. 40:25).

In the Torah and in the speeches of the preexilic prophets, God's Instructions are usually labeled simply *torot*, Instructions, or *Torat Adonai*, the Instruction of God (for example, Exod. 13:9; Josh. 24:26; Isa. 1:10, 5:24), terms which do not associate revelation with one prophet, one time, or one place. The postexilic material unabashedly makes the claim of singularity; the Torah given "through the hand of Moses" (2 Chron. 33:8, 34:14); "the Torah of God which was given through the agency of Moses" (Neh. 10:30); the Torah of Moses (Ezra 3:2; Dan. 9:13); the book of Moses (Ezra 6:18; Neh. 13:1; 2 Chron. 35:12); the book of the Torah of Moses (Neh. 8:1); the commandments of Moses (2 Chron. 8:13); the Torah in the book of Moses (2 Chron. 25:4).

Some explain the emergence of the label, *Torat Moshe,* the Torah of Moses, which identifies all revelation with Sinai and Moses as the result of cultural assimilation. In both the Persian and Hellenistic cultures in which the Jews found themselves, communities customarily named their law code after the founding king or the lawgiver; thus, the laws of Cyrus, or the laws of Solon. Others relate the substitution of the specific term, *Torat Moshe,* for the general term, *Torat Adonai,* to the increasing force of the taboo against the use of God's Name. In preexilic times the Tetragrammaton, YHVH, seems to have been part of the common speech, but during the Exile people began to use substitute names and later the use of YHVH was so effectively banned that ultimately only a small group of senior priests knew how the Name had been pronounced. I tend to feel that the use of the label *Torat Moshe* was encouraged by the rabbis to drive home the theme of the one, the only, and all-embracing revelation. *Torat Moshe* made it clear that there was and would be only one Torah.

Israelites of the Conquest period knew that Moses had heard Ten Instructions when he was with God. By the time of King David their descendants knew that Moses had heard a great number of Instructions. A half millennium later Judeans of the postexilic communities accepted the idea that Moses had received the whole Torah. By the second century B.C.E. many Judeans knew that Moses had heard not only the Torah text but all the details of the future history of the world.

Apocalypse is a literary genre which claims to reveal the future, generally knowledge given to a mortal who has been allowed to enter Heaven. Biblical prophecy had assumed that God based His decisions about the future on the nation's conduct: if the nation be willing and obedient, all will be well; if not, punishment is inevitable. Apocalypse, the stepchild of classic prophecy, removed Israel's virtue or lack of it as a determining factor in history. The script has been written, God acts "for the sake of His great Name," a nation or a person can do little but prepare spiritually for Judgment Day. Apocalypse speaks to the emotionally and politically beleaguered, and in the Greco-Roman world it spoke particularly to those groups of religious loyalists who felt that the certainties by which they lived were being swept away by the turmoil of ideas and values in the teeming and troubled urban centers of their world.

Sometime in the first century C.E. a Palestinian Jew wrote out a purportedly exact copy of Moses' valedictory speeches. This *Testament of Moses* presents itself as an elaboration of various prophecies quoted in the Torah, particularly those contained in the final chapters of Deuteronomy which include the only predictive oracles attributed to Moses (Deut. 33). The scene is Moses' investiture of his chosen successor, Joshua. The *aggadah* often describes Moses' last day on earth, and the idea that on that day he revealed to Joshua certain secrets about the future was by the first century something of a commonplace. One *aggadah* describes Moses' gift to Joshua of a book of secrets which set out the history of the people Israel from their entry into the Promised Land to the promised messianic kingdom (Ginsberg 3,

n. 401). Chapter 33 of Deuteronomy bears this superscription: "The blessing with which Moses blessed Israel before he died" (33:1). The chapter is divided into short, poetic prophecies about the future of the various Israelite tribes. These prophecies were highly valued because God Himself called them "a blessing." The *Testament of Moses* enlarges on these prophecies and sets out Jewish and world history until the final redemption. Where had Moses learned these secrets of the future? Obviously on Sinai.

Perhaps two centuries earlier than the *Testament,* during the difficult days before the Maccabean rebellion, a scroll called *Jubilees* was acclaimed as Torah by a circle of pietists, many of whose ideas closely resemble the teachings of the monastics of Qumran. These sectarians avoided social contact with non-Jews and were particularly incensed by the sins of the Jerusalem religious establishment, the priesthood, which they felt had been contaminated by alien cultural norms, worldliness, and moral laxity. They were particularly exercised that the Passover, as celebrated in the Jerusalem Temple, was not properly observed. According to their calculations the paschal sacrifice was being offered on the wrong day and, therefore, the nation's major redemptive rite was not effective. This was a matter of immense consequence to the faithful for if the Passover, "the time of our deliverance," was observed on the wrong day its force was lost and so was any chance of redemption. The proper date and ritual had been set out by God Himself, and the pietists had the word of Moses to prove that their calendar was the proper one.

*Jubilees* presents itself as Torah. An editorial superscription declares the text to be a faithful report of what Moses heard on Sinai. "This is the history of the division of the

days of the law and of the testimony . . . as the Lord spoke
to Moses on Mount Sinai when he went up to receive the
tablets of the law and of the commandment" (1:1). The text
begins with an exhortation to faithfulness much in the manner of Deuteronomy and proceeds to rehearse the events
covered in Genesis and the first twelve chapters of Exodus.
The legal sections of Exodus through Deuteronomy are not
duplicated, but various *torot* are scattered through the narrative text, not always identical in statement, though generally in import, to the authorized version. Nothing is said
about Moses after Sinai. There is no interest in the wilderness leader, the holy man who puts down rebellion. *Jubilees*
pictures Moses as a scribe. He is told to sit, listen, to "write
in a book in order that their generations may see . . ." (1:5)
and "to write for yourself all these words which I declare
. . ." (1:7). *Jubilees* claims to be that book. Its text declares
that Moses had been informed not only about the familiar
subjects of Torah but about the future.

Both the *Testament* and *Jubilees* enlarge the content of
the Sinai revelation to include certain knowledge about the
world's future. They also mark an important change in the
locale of God's meeting with Moses. In these apocalyptic
works, Moses ascends the mountain and then leaves the
mountain top for the Heavens. Despite the Torah's explicit
statement, "Moses remained on the mountain forty days
and forty nights" (Exod. 24:18), the image of Moses' ascension from Sinai into the Heavens was to become conventional in Talmudic times. The rabbinic scenario generally
pictures Moses on the mountain for a week of spiritual preparation. Then God sends down a cloud, Moses enters it and
is brought to God's Palace where he spends the forty days
learning Torah from God (Ginsberg 6:46, n. 247). In an-

other presentation of the same idea the mountain itself rises heavenward, the skies open up, and Sinai with Moses astride it, like Jack on his beanstalk, enters Heaven (PRE 41:1).

This restaging of the Sinai event corresponds to new cultural assumptions about revelation. The Biblical image had Moses ascending, God descending, and the two meeting at the summit. A simple story, but it presented problems in a world under the impress of the pure monotheism of Deutero-Isaiah—"To whom will you liken Me"—and of those elements of Hellenistic thought which emphasized God's transcendence and perfection. Everywhere challenges were being raised to the literal meaning of the old myths. At the same time, other elements of the Hellenistic ethos were insisting on distinctions between man's soul and his physical nature and suggesting the possibility of the soul disengaging itself from the worldly and the physical and rising to rejoin the Divine Soul. Moses' ascent into the Heavens was a personification of a new understanding of the mechanics of revelation. God didn't come down. The soul went up.

*Jubilees* preserves God's otherness even in Heaven. Once Moses is safely in the Palace, God orders a ministering angel, the Angel of the Presence, a personification of God's Immanence, to write out world history from creation "to the day when My sanctuary shall be built among them for all eternity" (1:27). The Angel goes to the heavenly library, takes out the "tablets of the divisions of the years" and reads from them to Moses, ordering him to make a true copy of the Angel's dictation (2:1).

Giving angels a role in the Sinai revelation is somewhat unusual. Though most Jews of Greco-Roman times believed in angels, often personified God's Immanence (*Kavod, She-*

*kinah*), and tended to picture God as communicating with man through such agents, the sages and the rabbis generally preferred to separate Sinai from all other occasions of God-man contact and to insist that at Sinai Moses' contact with God had been direct rather than through an agent. The Sinai revelation was too critical to be entrusted to intermediaries. God alone had spoken these Words, the truth, the sum of all wisdom. Moses alone, the perfect messenger, had received them.

The new image of Sinai introduces for the first time the idea of privileged communication. The Torah assumes that Moses reports all that God tells him. The *Testament*, however, describes a private briefing for Joshua's ears only. *Jubilees* publishes only part of what Moses is told. Judaism ceases to be the world's only totally open faith, without secrets, and develops its own esoteric and restricted gnosis, ideas reserved for those who have been vetted and given the appropriate security clearances. Moses is no longer confined to the mountain top, he hears more than he had heard before, and he no longer reports publicly all that he has heard. As a consequence, divisions develop within Israel between those who know all, the initiates, and the rest of the community.

The Moses who enters Heaven is in danger. Rabbinic writings clearly indicate that Heaven is not a place for mortals, even for Moses. Heaven is a place of secrets and mysterious powers surrounded by innumerable gates, each guarded by angelic watchmen. Various *Midrashim* compiled in Geonic and later times pull together the Talmudic *aggadot* which describe the dangers Moses faced. Stepping out of a cloud, Moses finds himself face to face with a certain Kenuel, captain of the guard, "What business have you here, mortal?" Fortunately, Moses is armed with knowledge of the secret Names of God and utters the appropriate incantation; the gatekeeper flees. Moses passes on to another gate and another gatekeeper, Hardaniel, a terrifying angel of vast proportions whose mouth breathes fire. Moses is so terrified that he temporarily loses the power of speech and so is unable to use the protective formulas he has been taught, but God intervenes and orders Hardaniel to let Moses pass. Another gate and another keeper, an angel named Sandalfon, appears, if anything more frightening in aspect than Hardaniel; God places Himself between the gatekeeper and Moses and Moses passes safely through the gate and over the River of Fire which stretches between him and the audience chamber in which the Throne of Glory stands. Moses enters the Palace and comes ultimately to the Audience Chamber where the words of revelation will be spoken. Moses is in the Inner Palace, but not yet fully in God's Presence. There are further veils, not to be parted. Though he hears God's voice and sees wonders normally denied to mortals, there is no way for even Moses to penetrate the ultimate mystery (Ginsberg 6:46, n. 247).

The imagery which describes Moses' ascension parallels that of various non-Jewish manuals of the time which describe the soul's ascent during mystical exercises. These texts, which were common in gnostic and early Christian circles, held that communion with God required spiritual and ascetic preparation, ablutions, fasting, the discipline of daily prayer and the practice of vigils, until finally the mystic feels his soul drawn upward toward God's Presence and is rewarded by a sense of being enveloped by God's spirit. The imagery of heavenly gates guarded by sentry angels suggests not only that the mystical experience requires a person to leave the world of familiar sights and sounds for a dangerous and alien world, but that the dangers of the mystical experience intensify the nearer one comes to God. The mystic courts madness, if not death, when he opens his soul to the immediate and the irrational. Gautama fought these forces under the Bo tree. The modern notion that all a person has to do to find God is to open his heart finds no confirmation in the mystical literature or, for that matter, in actual experience. Those who find God easily on a beautiful sunlit afternoon are describing an aesthetic, not a religious, experience. Communion with God is dangerous and not for everyone. Psychologically, the most understandable detail of the Sinai scenario as presented in the Torah text is Israel's desperate plea when God begins to speak: "Speak you [Moses] with us, and we will hear; but let not God speak with us, lest we die" (Exod. 20:16). Most humans prefer to stay off the mountain when the thunder peals and the slopes begin to tremble.

The ascension stories sometimes introduce a promethean element into the Sinai episode. The Torah understands the act of revelation as a gift from God: God intends Israel to have the Instructions, and Moses is simply the conduit of the message. Now enters the idea that the Heavens guard their knowledge from man, that the angels are jealous of their prerogatives. Some who told the story described a debate between Moses and the angels. The angels ask God to withhold the Torah from Moses because mankind could not be trusted to use wisely the powers which would become theirs. They challenge Moses to debate the point with them. Moses at first fears to debate the angels, but God encourages him and tells him to take hold of the Throne of Glory—the familiar image of a desperate man who finds sanctuary at shrine or chapel altar. Protected in this way, Moses presents his arguments diplomatically and persuasively: the angels had no need of the Torah, he argues, for they could not sin, while man, because of his complex nature, needs guidance and instruction in order to know what he must do to avoid sin. The angels relent (Ginsberg 3:113 ff). Another *aggadah* takes the image of the angels' challenge even further and describes a Moses so apprehensive that the debate would go against him that he simply snatches the Torah from the angels and makes off with it (Ginsberg 6:47, n. 248). Moses begins to be described not only as the Torah's messenger but as a savior: had it not been for Moses' knowledge or merit or quick thinking, Israel might not possess the Torah, and without the Torah man would have remained in an unredeemed state. Much as Paul had denied that salvation was possible before the Christ's atoning death, these *aggadot* suggest that the redemptive way opened fully to man for the first time at Sinai and that it was in some measure thanks to Moses that such Instruction, and therefore the possibility of salvation, exist.

The Moses who stayed on the mountain top used his ears more than his eyes. The Moses who ascends into the Heavens learns from what he sees, as well as from what he hears. Rabbinic *aggadah* often enlarges on what Moses saw in Heaven, detailing what he learned about the nature of God and the operation of Heaven. Once there he makes good use of his forty-day excursion and is given a guided tour of the sights: the Palace, its gates and garden, the Throne of Glory, the courtier angels and the angelic chorus. Metatron, the Angel of the Presence, is often pictured as Moses' Vergil, and hosts of angels are delegated to be his guard of honor. Moses is escorted through the various levels of Heaven and

Hell and shown the mysteries and wonders of each. The wonders vary with every recitation. Generally, the description concludes with Moses offering a prayer to God to save Israel from Hell, to which God replies, each man will get his deserts; and with another prayer to make Israel worthy of Heaven, to which God replies, the reward is certain to those who obey the Torah. Moses is also shown the reward that is laid up for the pious in the World to Come and the reward laid up for Israel in messianic times (Ginsberg 6:49, n. 255).

In medieval literature Moses himself occasionally acts as a guide to the Heavens. Some years ago Moses Gaster published a *Revelation of Moses* based on the medieval *Midrash, Gedulat Moshe*. At the Burning Bush Moses accepts his commission, and as a sign of His pleasure God commands Metatron, the Angel of the Presence, to bring Moses to Him. Metatron objects: man does not belong in Heaven, the angels are of fire and Moses is of flesh and blood. God has a simple solution. He changes Moses' body into fire and in this form Moses is carried up to Heaven. Moses is shown the windows through which man's petitions pass, hears the heavenly choir singing the praises of God, notices rain-bearing angels, angels of fertility, angels who govern the planets and stars, angels of wrath and anger, the Angel of Death, and many others. Having introduced Moses to the angel who teaches man wisdom, as well as the angel who brings death, God invites him to visit the two places that He has created: one for the righteous and the other for the sinners, Paradise and Hell. From here on the *Revelation of Moses* is pure Dante. Moses sees men hung by their tongues because they gossiped, hung by their genitals because they committed adultery, hung by their feet because they had profaned the Sabbath or despised the Lord or persecuted orphans.

The vision of Paradise is far pleasanter: he sees thrones ready for the patriarchs, a throne of pearls for scholars, a throne of precious stones for pious men, of rubies for the just, and of gold for the men of legend, even a throne of copper for a wicked man with a good son. Moses' visit confirms all the grimmest fears and most buoyant expectations of the medieval Jew.

Presumedly in the course of his heavenly visits Moses sees and learns how the Heavens are constituted and the secrets of God's governance of the universe. Since he has come as close to God as any mortal can, he has also, again presumedly, learned a good deal about God's actual Presence. The rabbis distinguished *Mattan Torah*, the gift of Divine Instruction, from *Gilluy Shekinah*, the self-disclosure of God's Immanence, and taught that both occurred at Sinai. After Sinai there would be no other *Mattan Torah*, but the *Gilluy Shekinah* which Moses experienced was a moment of communion which other mystics could hope to achieve. During Talmudic times mystical writings began to circulate which have come to be called the *Hechalot*, or Palace Literature. Unfortunately, only fragments survive, describing long, solitary vigils during which, through fasting and incantation, a mystic achieves the feeling that he is rising to the Heavens, where he faces the same dangerous gatekeepers Moses faced, uses the same secret knowledge to pass safely through, and finally senses that he is in God's Presence. The man whose life was devoted to the nation's redemption becomes for those of a mystic bent the ultimate spiritual master whose life of prayer and religious discipline shows the way.

The centuries which preceded the destruction of the Temple were a period of intense and varied religious activity, during which Moses' role in the Sinai drama was repeatedly enlarged. Of all the new scenes written for him none would prove to be more significant, for it became the lynch pin of rabbinic Judaism, than the idea that during the famous forty days Moses received not only the familiar Torah scroll, which becomes known as the *Torah she'biktav*, the Written Torah, but also a vast oral deposit, the *Torah she be'al peh*, the Oral Torah. Ultimately this Oral Torah gathered to itself the sum and substance of all that wisdom and all those disciplines which the rabbis affirmed as sacred; to them the *Torah she be'al peh* was a second part of the body of Instruction authorized by God and transmitted to Israel through Moses at Sinai.

It is hard to say precisely how the *Torah she be'al peh* was organized or even to describe its contents. Even after the concept became a central convention of rabbinic culture, no one ever published a canonized text. In postexilic times, the community's sense of tradition assumed that, besides the Torah scroll, there were a number of ancient rules which had not been included in the Written Torah, but were part of Moses' message and obligatory. The editorial process which brought the Written Torah into being had not required that all other Instructions be cast out, any more than the publication of the Constitution eliminated English common law from the American legal system. Such rules came to be know as *Torah l'Moshe Mi-Sinai*, "laws given to Moses at Mount Sinai." As an example, we read that "Nahum the scribe said, 'I have received a tradition from R. Measha who received it from the prophets as a rule given to Moses from Sinai . . .' " (M. Peah 2:6). Other rules were prefaced by the formula, *be'emet amru*, which was accepted as a sign that this Instruction "is a matter of undisputed Mosaic origin" (j. Kil. 2:2).

The Pharisees taught that Moses had been informed on Sinai of an oral tradition which he memorized and subsequently taught to Joshua and the tribal elders, who faithfully passed this Oral Torah to an unbroken chain of competent teachers who made it the curriculum of the rabbinic schools and the new and enlarged constitution of Jewish life. As the spiritual heirs of the long-lived passion to unify all Instruction under the authority of Sinai, the rabbis readily and easily came to feel that the entire body of rules and teachings they venerated had always been part of the original revelation.

It was a bold and dramatic idea, and it did not go unchallenged. From the Sadducees of the first century to the Karaites of the ninth and tenth to liberal Jews of recent times, there were always those who dismissed this second revelation as a pious conceit. A critical definition of the Oral Torah would not, could not, list a specific text or group of texts; it would probably say no more than that *Torah she be'al peh* designates that undefined body of teachings, disciplines, and procedures which the rabbis "knew" to be Torah. Today we simply say that much of what went into the Oral Torah was not revelation at all, but the special teachings and disciplines and learning which had developed during postexilic centuries among scribes, sages, and sectarian priests of Judea—the spiritual ancestors whom the rabbis venerated—and that these became Torah because it was natural for Jews to ascribe to the Sinai revelation whatever they accepted as basic Judaism.

As the Torah grew, some Jews became increasingly conscious of the enormity of the commitment Israel had made at Sinai. A psychologically perceptive *Midrash* suggests that Israel did not willingly accept the Torah—few voluntarily accept additional duties and responsibilities and a generation of unruly ex-slaves was not likely to be the exception to the rule. But God was determined that Israel should accept, so He lifted up the mountain and held it over the peoples' heads warning them: "If you agree to the Covenant, well and good; if not, you will find your grave under this mountain." Another sage suggests that God had had to resort to threats only when the Written Torah was enlarged on: "Israel was willing to accept the Written Torah but not the unwritten" (Ginsberg 6:36, n. 202).

The Oral Torah was a conceptual way of binding the old-and-published and the old-and-not-published into a new sacred unity. It provided a conceptual basis for the practices by which the Pharisees and the rabbis reshaped Judaism. "The greater part of the Torah was given orally and only the minor part in writing" (b. Git. 6ob). The assumption that all was revealed to Moses on Sinai turns his stay there into a busy, even hectic period. Anyone who has tried to memorize quickly a sizable body of material must wonder how Moses could have heard, much less absorbed or written down, all the material God is supposed to have revealed to him during those fateful forty days. A medieval popularization imagines that God put Moses through a carefully designed course which included all the great texts of the Judaic curriculum. "When God began to give Torah he recited it to Moses in a systematic way, first the Bible, then *Mishnah*, then *Aggada* and then Talmud. . . . Even what an attentive pupil will ask his teacher" (Tan., Ki Tissa 17). Obviously, what God wills He can accomplish, but there were traditions that it had not been easy for Moses. According to R. Yohanan (second century), during the time that Moses was on Mount Sinai he memorized blocks of Torah each day and his overworked brain forgot parts of it each night until God ended his misery by granting Moses a flawless memory as a special gift (j. Horayot 3:8).

One consequence of this new concept of an oral revelation passed down through a chain of scholarly and trustworthy transmitters is the transformation of Joshua from his Biblical image of grizzled soldier and life-long military leader to his rabbinic image as an able, eager, and diligent graduate student who never spoke unless spoken to and who became a sage by modeling his behavior after his master. The sages sensed the enormous burden that mastery of the Oral Law imposed on Moses; they could not admit that his memory was unequal to the task—the old issue of the infallibility of their Torah traditions—yet they could allow themselves to suggest that it all was a bit too much for Joshua. An *aggadah* reports that before he died Moses asked his star pupil if he had his studies in hand; if not, Moses was prepared to review the material with him. Joshua demurred—so overconfident, even cocky, that he passed up a chance for review, which no conscientious student should ever do—and consequently forgot several hundred minor details, a lapse which explained those issues which the sages could not resolve because they had no Instruction to follow (Ginsberg 6:170, n. 7).

In theory, the Oral and Written Torahs were part of a seamless whole, but in practice the Oral Torah—that is, all that came to be considered Torah—became the controlling partner, fixing the curriculum of the schools, as well as the disciplines of Jewish life. In Talmudic times neither the synagogues nor the schools had Bible classes. Both institutions had Talmud seminars. Before long, the received Written text was swamped by the extent of the Oral. The Palestinian Talmud quotes Samuel b. Nahman (third century) who says unabashedly that the Oral Law is the controlling factor in decision making, "An Oral Torah has been proclaimed and a Written Torah has been proclaimed. We cannot tell which category is more precious; but since it is written, 'in accordance [al pi; literally, by the mouth of] with these commandments I make a covenant with you and with Israel' (Exod. 34:27), we infer that the oral laws are the more precious" (j. Peah 2:6). The rabbis insisted that the Torah was one, yet they acknowledged that what they now taught as Torah appeared in many ways to be different from the old. One story implicitly concedes that even Moses might not recognize the laws he had mediated. "Moses went [to the academy of Akiba] and sat in the back. Not being able to follow their arguments, he was ill at ease, but when they came to a certain subject and the students said to the master, 'Where is your authority' and the latter replied, 'It is a law given to Moses on Sinai,' Moses was comforted" (b. Men. 29b). Several centuries earlier Hillel had recognized that the acceptance of the rabbinic rule as Torah required an act of faith (ARN 15:24a).

Jewish apologetes like to emphasize that normative Judaism had neither reserved doctrine nor gnosis. Unlike most other classic religious texts, the Torah does not present itself as a shrine text only for priests' eyes or as a doctrine reserved for initiates. According to the accepted tradition the Ten Instructions—some said only the First Instruction—had been spoken for all to hear and the rest of the Instructions had been repeated publicly by Moses. In the synagogue the

Torah was and is read through annually in every congregation. In this respect the Torah scroll is rare among ancient religious documents, many of which were coded in sacred glyphs or written in an archaic script which only the priests could interpret. Knowledge is power, and control of religious knowledge assured a priest group its privileges.

Although the schoolmen tried to make the masses conscious of the *halacha* which they taught as Torah, they did not continue this open book policy. Throughout the rabbinic period the rabbis openly acknowledge the existence of a body of esoteric knowledge which is to be shared with only a few trusted disciples. They included in the Oral Torah not only law but a variety of subjects which were not to be disseminated publicly: metaphysics, *Ma'aseh bereshit*, theosophy, *Ma'aseh Merkavah*; messianic signs; mystical doctrine; and much else. There are innumerable warnings in rabbinic literature not to teach those matters to the masses or to young students, youth often being defined as anyone under thirty, or even to advanced students whose reliability was in doubt. Part of the mystique through which the scholar class maintained suasive authority in the community was the claim that it knew what the masses did not know. Moses was most useful to the rabbis as the founder-teacher of a many-faceted tradition which was oral, reserved, taught only by the ordained to those worthy of being ordained, and held to involve powerful secrets whose control gave the rabbis power and privilege.

The emphasis on an unpublished Torah was not purely self-serving. Disturbed by Christianity's appropriation of the Torah and misuse of it, the rabbis defended their division of Torah into *nigleh*, an open and fully available portion, and *nistar*, the reserved portion, as a means of keeping Torah out of the wrong hands. The *aggadah*, as always, personalized the argument. When Moses receives the whole Torah, the Written and the Oral, and is told by God to teach it to Israel, he is afraid that he might not be equal to the task and asks God to write it all down so Israel might have a true copy. God demurs, saying, "I know that in the future the nations will need the Torah scroll and translate it into Greek and claim that 'we are the true Israel.' Then I shall say to them, "You are not the true Israel, my children are those who possess the secret tradition' " (Ginsberg 6:6o, n. 3o8).

That hodgepodge of anecdotal materials, *aggadah*, peviously discussed, was gathered into the Oral Torah. Some are theological in import, some theosophic, some deal with relationships between God and various personages, many concern the lives of the people who appear in the Bible. Many of these anecdotes describe in dramatic and anthropomorphic terms God's activities, or the comings and goings of angels, demons, and a number of specially endowed immortals. Material of this kind had circulated for centuries. What is new in Talmudic times is that these stories came to be seen as elements of the Oral Torah and hence as part of the revelation. In effect, they acquire the status of unquestioned fact. All that the *aggadah* reports about Moses becomes part of Moses' accepted biography.

Had anyone looked at it this way, he would have seen Moses receiving a revelation which included all manner of new facts about himself; and, since the Oral Torah was considered interpretively controlling, in effect a new Moses emerged, a supernaturally endowed man who is as close to divine as a monotheistic tradition can tolerate. I will attempt to describe the life and activities of the new Moses—his biography as the world's holiest man—in the next chapter. Here it needs simply to be emphasized that this new biography was believed by the sages, as well as by the masses.

What began as a text which could be inscribed on two stone tablets became a sizable book to which was added an immense and ever-spreading Oral Torah. The rabbis described the Oral Torah as an ocean. The vision of Sinai changed as the community's perception of the content and size of the revelation changed. The power of the myth that "everything was said at Sinai," the compelling need for a Judaism, not Judaisms, cannot be exaggerated. Why did the community readily accept even the most dramatic of these additions? The answer is that they desperately needed to. The concept of the Oral Torah was formalized in the tragic first and second centuries when the Jewish world suffered a rapid-fire series of cataclysmic defeats: the destruction of the Temple and the suppression by Rome of the Judean rebellion of 68–73; the defeat of Jewish uprisings in Cyreneica, Cyprus, and Egypt in the early second century (114–17); and the crowning disaster of the Bar Kochba revolt of 132–35. The all-encompassing disciplines of the Oral Torah as exemplified in the Pharisaic brotherhoods and as taught in the rabbinic schools provided the tight discipline and rich wisdom required by a distraught and confused community. The Oral Torah proved to be a life-saving Torah. The practical success of an idea can always silence its critics, but it should not blind us to the dramatic changes which had taken place in Jewish self-consciousness.

# CHAPTER
# VI

## Moshe Rabbenu

**R**ABBINIC JUDAISM accepts the notion of a one-time and all-embracing revelation, rejects the possibility of any future revelation and, consequently, values fidelity more than creativity. To the constant frustration of liberal rabbis who want to summon their congregations to rethink and reexamine the tradition even as they seriously invest themselves in it, the literature's only idiom for Jewish commitment is *teshuvah* (literally, repentance), specifically defined as return to Torah standards in act and belief.

To cut a vertical slice into the Jewish past and study a single theme, as we have been doing, is to recognize that the image of a one-time, all-embracing Torah is one of those compelling ideas through which a group expresses its understanding of the essential structure of reality, an idea so compelling that the group does not feel challenged by all or any "evidence" to the contrary. In short, a myth. To analyze the treatment of Moses during the Talmudic period, roughly the first seven centuries of this era, is to recognize that he acquires an entirely new personality, that new incidents are added to his life, and that he is given a new name and a new persona; and to find no indication that anyone of the time expressed surprise at this significant transformation. God's man, the *ish-elohim*, is now *Moshe Rabbenu*, Moses our rabbi. In the Bible Moses is God's faithful servant. *Moshe Rabbenu* serves God and Israel's deepest emotional needs. He is a hybrid, part man, part divine, part a majestic figure from the past, part an ever-present protector.

The term, *Rabbenu*, needs some clarification for those who, on the basis of friendship with a rabbi, assume that *Rabbenu* describes Moses as a synagogue professional who conducts services, officiates at weddings and funerals, and counsels people who are having trouble taking hold of their lives. Nor is *Moshe Rabbenu* simply an honorific title for the prophet of the Torah, affirming his mastery of the learning which the Talmud sages considered Torah. *Rabbenu* comes from the noun, *rav*, which in Biblical Hebrew means "great." Its basic meaning is "the one whose authority we recognize." In the decades after the destruction of the Temple, the title *rav*, rabbi, was adopted by the sages who were heirs of the Pharisaic tradition to reflect and strengthen the authority they claimed over the community's religious life. When these same sages began to call Moses *Rabbenu* they were in effect creating him after their own image so they could ascribe to themselves Moses' authority in Torah matters and, at the same time, claim that Moses' power, if not his person, was still present and available.

In Talmudic times the role of rabbi involved a range of religious activities which included, but went far beyond, Torah interpretation and judicial service. The rabbis of Palestine and the *ravs* of Persia knew themselves to be, and were known as, religious virtuosos whose Torah learning equipped them with the power to bless and to curse, to interpret dreams, to predict events, to heal the sick, to exorcise evil spirits, to remove the evil eye, and even to revive the dead. Many of these men also enjoyed some fame as astronomers and masters of the occult, clairvoyants, writers of amulets, rainmakers, and intercessors. Such magical powers cast no doubt on a rabbi's learning or moral reputation. Indeed, his magical power grew out of his learning and the merit he built up through a discipline of piety. We spoke in the last chapter of the new idea that Sinai's revelation included a reserved Instruction, as well as the Torah which was made public. The rabbis claimed to possess this reserved knowledge and through it the authority to govern and the ability to perform wonders. *Moshe Rabbenu* is the father and prototype of the learned and powerful holy men who, during the traumatic centuries which followed the destruction of the Temple (70 C.E.) and the abrupt end of effective priestly power, became feared and revered religious leaders. Gradually they won the community's allegiance to their conception of Torah and their authority to enforce the Torah way. *Moshe Rabbenu* is learned in the *halacha* and armed with all kinds of secret knowledge which allow him to do what ordinary mortals cannot do. He is a charismatic in the original sense of the word—a man endowed with divine powers. And, as we will discover, because he is Moses, an original, he becomes more than the ultimate charismatic; he somehow participates in divinity.

A rabbinic account of the murder of the Egyptian taskmaster illustrates the type of special powers associated with *Moshe Rabbenu*. He had the gift of clairvoyance, knew the many crimes this particular Egyptian had committed; and, with the gift of second sight, saw the future and knew that if this thorough-going villain lived, he would sire an endless line of villains. *Moshe Rabbenu* had only to speak the Secret Name of God and the taskmaster fell in his tracks (Exod. R 1:29). We are trained to dismiss such scenarios as quaint legends which testify to the credulities of the times, and they are; but it must be emphasized that such *aggadot* were believed by the sages, as well as the masses. They were accepted as part of the Oral Torah which Moses had received at Sinai.

The term *aggadah* needs more precise analysis than we have given it so far. The usual definition derives the noun *aggadah* from a root which means *to tell* and describes *aggadah* as the nonlegal material in Talmudic literature—the sermonic, speculative, theological, historical, mystical, and esoteric anecdotes, vignettes, and comments of the Oral Torah. Most definitions add that the *aggadah* was valued as imaginative and suggestive literature rather than as reliable fact. There is a well-known rabbinic principle of interpretation, "we do not draw authoritative legal conclusions from the *aggadot*" (j. Peah 2:6). The main reasons for this diffidence about the *aggadah* were its addiction to imagery that is unabashedly anthropomorphic ("God cries when Israel goes into exile"; "God puts on *tallit* every morning"); its citation of incredible stories about Biblical personages (Moses walked and talked when he was only a day old, refused to submit to the Angel of Death) and use of stories which contradict established practice, such as the *aggadah* that Hezekiah suppressed a Book of Remedies, despite the rabbis' encouragement of medical treatment. For all these reasons many religious leaders during the Muslim period encouraged Jews not to treat *aggadah* as if it were Torah.

This had not been the attitude of most of the Talmudic sages who had accepted *aggadah* as part of the Torah. "R. Joshua b. Levi taught, 'Scripture, *Mishnah*, Talmud and *Aggadah*, even what a senior disciple is due to teach in the presence of his master, was already stated to Moses at Sinai' " (j. Peah 2:6). Of course, in Talmudic times, not everyone believed every detail of every *aggadah*. Some *aggadot*, in fact, contradicted each other and different schools had inherited different *aggadic* traditions. But the rabbis of the Talmudic era were generally prepared to treat *aggadah* material as reliable, and there is little doubt that the conventional *aggadic* image of *Moshe Rabbenu* as the incomparable charismatic and divine man was widely accepted. The *aggadah* consists of innumerable discrete traditions and reports of specific incidents, and there is no comprehensive biography of Moses based on the *aggadah*. We can, however, reconstruct the *aggadah's* approach to *Moshe Rabbenu*; it emphasizes his charisma, his supernatural powers and activities, and his learning.

I find it useful to distinguish rabbinism and rabbinic Judaism. Rabbinic Judaism is that long-lived, many-sided tradition which began with the Pharisees and continues even today wherever orthordox Judaism thrives. Rabbinic Judaism is based on the authority of a twofold revelation, the Written and the Oral Torahs. Over the centuries it has commanded the allegiance of a variety of communities which have been *halachic* in practice but distinctly different in their institutional forms and their approach toward such issues as messianism and the religious life. Rabbinism is a particular early modulation of rabbinic Judaism which emphasized the authority of the rabbi as holy man. Rabbinic Judaism taught that the rabbi's knowledge of Torah empowered him to organize the community. He understood what God willed. Rabbinism went several steps further. It claimed that the rabbi's mastery of the Oral Torah qualified him to be a "living Torah" and to set a personal example in matters of religious discipline, manners, and morals for his disciples (students in Talmudic times left home and family to live with the Master, in fellowships not unlike monastic communities, and were expected to pattern their lives after the model whose example was daily before them) and for the larger community. His knowledge of the Oral Law included mastery of an esoteric tradition which gave him the power to perform his "magic." Rabbinism's rabbi becomes the "living Torah" Philo believed Moses to be and the wonder worker Artapanus described Moses to be. Rabbis in every century wrote amulets and recited prayers for the sick, but rabbinism actively propagated the ideas which made the rabbi-holy man central to the community's religious life. In that sense rabbinism set a very special mood. My favorite illustration of rabbinism is the argument by some Babylonian rabbis that they should be excused from certain taxes used to maintain the city's walls because they were already invulnerable to enemy action.

Rabbinism's popularity faded during the second half of the first millennium, and rabbinic Judaism, the tradition we call orthodoxy, then achieved its classic form by removing the myth of the Torah master as holy man from the center of the tradition and significantly diminishing the authority of the *aggadah*. But even as rabbinism faded, most Jews continued to know Moses as *Moshe Rabbenu*, the charismatic figure and the most divine of mortals who had been the creation of and role model for the first generations of rabbis.

Beginning in the eighth century, largely under influences spread by the aggressive thrust of Islamic culture into the world Jews inhabited, the rabbis made a determined effort to desacralize the *aggadah*. They did so for many reasons. The personification of God, which had seemed unexceptional as long as the Jewish communities of Persia and the Near East were under the influence of traditions with colorful and complex cosmic myths like the Byzantine Christian tradition and Sasanid Persia's Mazdaism, began to seem an almost pagan idea when viewed from the unitarian perspective of Islam. At the same time, and perhaps also precipitated by the spread of Islam, a major challenge to rabbinic authority arose within the Jewish community. The Karaites, sectarian Jews who stubbornly labeled Oral Torah a rabbinic invention and dismissed it, found the anthropomorphisms and miracle stories of the *aggadah* wonderful grist for their argument that the Orah Torah was a blasphemous rabbinic invention that led Jews away from the monotheism of Scripture. The pressures generated by these internal and external challenges forced the Geonim, the heads of the national rabbinic academies in Baghdad, in the late tenth and early eleventh century to deal officially with the problem of the *aggadah*. What they tried to do was to desanctify *aggadah*, to deny it the authority of Torah it had so long enjoyed. "*Aggadic* sayings are not like authentic tradition, rather, each sage expounded as it occurred to him, as if to say, 'perhaps' or 'one might say,' and not as something definite; therefore, we do not rely on them" (Hai Gaon, *Hagigah u-mashkin* 2:59).

Theoretically, the desacralization of the *aggadah* freed the rabbis from having to defend embarrassing doctrines, but it did not stop Muslim, Christian, and Karaite polemicists from citing anthropomorphic and extravagant *aggadot* as proof of Jewish backwardness, theological error, or duplicity. Nor did it remove the *aggadic* inheritance from people's minds and hearts. *Moshe Rabbenu* remained *Moshe Rabbenu*. Few Jews knew where Torah ended and *aggadah* began.

*Moshe Rabbenu* appears in the three divisions of literature—Targum, Talmud, and *Midrash*—which were destined to become the core curriculum of rabbinic education and to remain so for as long as Jewish education retained its special curriculum. Targum means *translation*. It became custom in the early synagogue to follow the public chanting of the Torah portion with a line-by-line or paragraph-by-paragraph translation or paraphrase of the reading into Aramaic. This translation was called Targum. Rav, one of the founders of the Babylonian Talmud tradition, explained that the practice had been instituted by Ezra in the fifth century B.C.E. to inform those who did not understand Hebrew, particularly women and children, of the Torah's meaning. Recent studies have cast doubt on this explanation. It now appears that although classic Hebrew was no longer spoken or fully understood in Greco-Roman Palestine, a street Hebrew was commonly used; and at the time of the Targum's emergence many, if not most, of the unschooled would have understood a Hebrew reading more readily than an Aramaic paraphrase. The origin of an Aramaic paraphrase was apparently an attempt to replicate a practice of the Persian bureaucracy which required that all significant public and business documents in any language be translated into Aramaic. Targum met that requirement and in so doing declared the Torah's text to be significant. The Targum also provided the rabbis a way to make sure that the Written Torah was understood as they interpreted it. The rabbis were keenly aware that the devil and heretics could quote a text to their own purposes. "If one interprets a text literally he is a liar. If he adds to the text he is a blasphemer and libeler. What then is meant by interpretation? Our authorized interpretation" (b. Kid. 49a).

Beginning in late Persian or early Greco-Roman times, various traditions of Targum began to develop and one, known as *Targum Onkelos,* mistakenly named after a famous second-century proselyte-translator, Aquila, who evidently had nothing to do with it, came to be accepted for synagogue use. It is a spare and academic rendering, rather consciously literal except in its determination to eliminate all anthropomorphisms. Parts of three far more expansive Targumim have survived, all of Palestinian origin: *Pseudo Jonathan* or *Targum Yerushalmi I,* the *Fragmentary Targum* or *Targum Yerushalmi II,* and *Neofiti.* It is primarily in these three texts that we find *aggadic* elements. The versions of these traditions that survive show evidence of having been edited in Geonic or early medieval times, but as is usually the case with rabbinic material, much of it is much older.

Talmud is a general term for the "learning" of the early rabbis. Talmud consists of two distinct parts: a core of texts, mostly legal in nature, which were edited early in the third century C.E. into a legal chapbook, called *Mishnah;* and a gloss of notes, elaborations, case citations, legal decisions, and historical anecdotes on issues raised by generations of schoolmen and jurists during their discussion and study of *Mishnah,* called *Gemara.* Ultimately, there were two published compendia: the Palestinian, or Jerusalem, Talmud comprising notes from the discussions in the Galilean schools down to the early fifth century, and the better-known Babylonian Talmud containing records of discussions held in the academies of Sasanid Persia down to the early sixth century. There is little *aggadah* in the *Mishnah* and a great deal in the *Gemara.*

*Midrash,* which comes from a root meaning to press a point or to examine thoroughly, is the careful and many-sided analysis of the meaning of Biblical texts. Various collections of *Midrash* appeared over the centuries in Palestine, most contain *aggadot* cited in the Targum and the Talmud, plus *aggadot* not cited elsewhere. *Midrash* is commentary. The *aggadot* in the *Midrash* collections are always somehow related to a Biblical text, and the assumption was that *Midrash* presents ideas read out of Scripture. In fact, the process was often a reversal, an unself-conscious reading into the text of folklore, conventional wisdom, or the better-known *aggadot.*

Neither Targum, Talmud, nor *Midrash* present an official, or even a continuous, biography of Moses. The Moses material is scattered through all of them. Apparently, there was no perceived benefit in writing a biography, though behind the various citations and incidents one senses a broadly known and accepted story, a consensus biography built up out of long-circulating story elements. A sage quotes the tradition he or his school has received about a particular incident. Another sage chooses an incident from this consensus biography to illustrate a sermonic point or a particular understanding of a Torah text. A particular incident in *Moshe Rabbenu's* life, just like that of an individual rabbi, could provide a concrete example of commendable behavior, but emulation falls many levels short of adoration. To understand how the rabbis Judaism could cherish *aggadot* which describe Moses performing incredible miracles or acting as court-appointed intercessor in Heaven and not feel that they had crossed the line into idolatry, it is useful to remember that their definition of idolatry did not require the denial of all heavenly beings beside God. The Hebrew term for idolatry, *Avodah Zara*, literally means strange or unacceptable worship. In the minds of the sages of the Talmudic period, there was nothing unacceptable about demons or intercessors, as long as religious worship was focused on God alone.

With these preliminaries in mind, here are the opening scenes in the life of *Moshe Rabbenu* as they were known to a Jew of the Talmudic age and to most Jews for the next fifteen hundred years. Jochebed and Amram, Levites of rank, remarry. Their daughter, Miriam, prophesies greatness for the unborn child. Jochebed is elderly, but God renews her youth, her beauty, and her ovaries, and she conceives. Moses is a six-month-and-one-day baby. Every Hebrew pregnancy had to be registered so male infants could be immediately killed, but the early birth gave Jochebed time to arrange Moses' escape. Moses is put in the bullrush cradle as her due date approaches. Miriam watches, not out of fear for his life, for Moses' greatness has already been prophesied, but to see how God will handle the situation. Pharaoh's daughter is not at the river's edge by chance. God had afflicted her with a disconcerting itch, and she sought relief in the cooling water. The itch ceases the minute she touches Moses' cradle. The young Moses refuses Egyptian wet nurses and is nursed by his mother. Jochebed is not one to waste time, so between feedings she teaches Moses the history and tradition of his people. This was possible since Moses was a precocious lad who was walking and talking when he was one day old.

As a youth Moses sees the anguish of the slaves. His anger rises at the acts of the brutal taskmaster, but he does not act impulsively. Before he strikes he uses his special powers of foresight to determine that no proselyte or righteous person is destined to appear among this Egyptian's descendants. When he strikes he rids the world of not only a no-good but a never-will-be-good. The two fighting Hebrews who threaten to report Moses are no other than Dathan and Abiram, the well-known rebels of the wilderness years, quislings who had prospered in Egypt by working as spies for Pharaoh. Moses is apprehended, charged, tried, convicted, and sentenced to death; but the executioner cannot lift his sword to carry out the death penalty, and in the confusion Moses escapes to the Sinai where he befriends the daughters of the local sheik and is brought to their home. When Jethro learns that Moses stands convicted of killing an Egyptian officer, he fears Pharaoh's anger should it be discovered that he has harbored a criminal, so he casts Moses into a pit. Moses remains immured for ten years, fed all the while by Zipporah, who has taken a great liking to him. When he is finally freed, he marries his benefactress.

A few days after his nuptials, Moses wanders into the sheik's garden seeking a place for prayer. He comes upon a miraculous sapphire rod fixed into a tree engraved with the Tetragrammaton, the inexpressible Name of God. He is told that no one has been able to remove it. Moses reaches out, and the rod comes loose in his hand, the very rod he will later use to split the sea and bring water from the rock. Some time later Moses takes the sheik's flocks to the mountain of revelation. An angel, Zagzagel, calls to him from a bush that burns with fire but is fresh to the touch. Moses answers, using the formal language usually reserved for Temple ritual, and after some talk, which includes the revelation of the power of God's special Name, God commissions Moses as His agent for the release of the slaves. Ever conscious of the obligations of family and hospitality, Moses formally requests of Jethro permission to return to Egypt. It is granted. On the way he and his family stop at an inn. Their sleep is interrupted by an angel who seeks to kill Moses. His second son had not been circumcised. The fault was not Moses'; Jethro had forbidden the rite. Zipporah acts quickly. She circumcises the boy, the blood is an atonement for Moses' sin, and God's ambassador moves on to Egypt.

How came these stories into being? Most had certainly been in circulation for a long time; some came from the sages' detailed examination of the Torah text, others from the embellishments by storytellers of Second Temple times. The Torah was God's Words, and Jews universally assumed it contained no errors. Everything fit. Nothing was redundant. There were no loose threads or textual inconsistencies, and anything that hinted of either was quickly made orderly and smooth, no matter how complicated the reweaving of a story's elements might be. As an example, take the unexpected reference to the remarriage of Amram and Jochebed. Since the Torah gives no indication that Amram and Jochebed had ever separated, how did such a notion ever develop? The Torah introduces Moses' parents in this way: "A certain man of the house of Levi went and married a Levite woman. She conceived and bore a son" (Exod. 2:1–2). The text seems to tell us that Moses is the first-born of this union, but we quickly come upon his sister who watches over the cradle as it floats on the Nile. Certainly, she was older than her infant brother. The ceremony the text refers to must, therefore, have been a remarriage. Why had Amram and Jochebed separated? Because they did not wish to bring a son into a world where he would face immediate death. And, since Amram was the nation's acknowledged chief, all Hebrew couples had followed their lead and separated. Why had they remarried? What had changed their minds? Their daughter. Miriam had told her father: "You are worse than Pharaoh. He proposes to kill all Hebrew males. You are denying all Hebrew children their chance for life in this world and in the World to Come." As an aside, I began to read this imaginative dialogue, in which Moses' birth becomes a radical affirmation of life, with greater appreciation after I came across the heartbreaking diaries of European Jews trapped by the Nazis who had to wrestle with just this question of bringing children into a doomed world.

That whole chapter in the Moses story grew out of a single Torah sentence which consists of twelve Hebrew words. There was still more in the sentence for the serious and imaginative commentator to work on. Read literally, the phrase "a daughter of Levi" would indicate that Jochebed was actually "Levi's daughter," that is, the daughter of one of the brothers who had come to Egypt with Joseph centuries before. If this were the case, Jochebed was so long past the age of childbearing that a new miracle is required. Her rejuvenation becomes a "fact" of *Moshe Rabbenu's* story. Judaism does not accept the concept of an immaculate conception, but the idea of a miraculous conception is no less a strain on credulity.

Other elements of Moses' early *aggadic* biography seem to have been taken over from the rich stock of situations which were part of every storyteller's repertoire. The imbedded magical rod which none can withdraw save the appointed hero would appear again in Europe as the Excalibur, King Arthur's sword. So is the theme of a child prophesying the coronation of a newborn. Over time stories which began as attention-catching embellishments of a recital of Moses' life or happy inspirations to build up excitement in an audience became credited traditions.

One of the most popular stories in West Asian folklore presents a sorcerer who informs the king that a child has been born who will threaten his throne. Having done so, the sorcerer instructs the king how to organize tests to discover the dangerous child so he can be eliminated. The drama of the story centers on the tests even though the audience knows that the child will escape and ultimately unthrone the king. A version of this story became part of the *aggadic* biography of *Moshe Rabbenu*. A court sorcerer apprised Pharaoh of such a dangerous child and suspicion immediately focused on the child Moses. Many in the palace remembered that one day the king had playfully put the crown of Egypt on Moses' head and that Moses had reached up and thrown the crown to the ground. Loath to kill his daughter's beloved son, Pharaoh resolved on a test. A jewel and a hot coal were placed in front of Moses. If the child picked up the jewel it would prove that he had acted out of calculation and he would be put to death; if the coal, he was still an innocent and the crown incident could be dismissed. God guided Moses' hand to the coal.

The story comes directly out of the deposit of well-known folk tales, but the detail of the hot coal is a tribute to the ingenuity of some ancient storyteller who remembered that Moses was said to have a speech impediment and set out to explain how this misfortune had come upon him. When Jochebed first saw her son she pronounced him goodly to look at, flawless; yet, at his commissioning, Moses protests that his speech is flawed. Obviously, between age three months and adulthood some accident had to account for Moses' physical disability, and the hot coal explained it all. The infant had put the ember in his mouth. Later this scene was embroidered in various ways. Who is this anonymous court sorcerer who warns Pharaoh of the child? The *aggadah* identifies him as Balaam, the gentile prophet who, according to the Book of Numbers, is hired by the king of Moab, Balak, to curse Israel. Why Balaam? Balaam is the only gentile prophet mentioned in Scripture who is conceded to have genuine prophetic powers; and in the *aggadah* the court sorcerer speaks truly. Moses did threaten Pharaoh and Egypt. How did this non-Egyptian prophet get to Pharaoh's court? The Torah never mentions Balaam in the employ of Pharaoh. A rabbinic version of Moses' military career as general of the Egyptian Expeditionary Forces (which was discussed in chapter II) describes Balaam as the sorcerer in charge of the defenses of the Nubian capital. When Moses captures the city, Balaam flees north with his two sons to Pharaoh's court where he is given the position of chief sorcerer. Storytelling, like street theater, prefers figures which evoke predictable responses and so enhance the storyteller's point: Balaam was the stock prophet in the enemy camp. Nor do time and place impose the familiar constraints on *aggadah*. In a world where the miraculous and the supernatural are the normal conditions of life, there should be no surprise that Moses pulls an imbedded sword out of a rock or Balaam escapes from a besieged city. In *aggadah* the actors enjoy supernatural power.

Even minor details in the story of *Moshe Rabbenu's* early life can carry some thematic weight. The princess's itch is a little thing, but it underscores God's providential control of events. Normally a princess would bathe in the palace pool rather than the Nile. She had to be at the Nile that day in order to rescue the baby Moses. That Pharaoh's daughter is healed when she touches the cradle proves that blessings accrue to those who help carry out God's plans and that good deeds are rewarded. That Jochebed taught, as well as nursed, the lad explains the otherwise inexplicable anger at the Hebrews' enslavement of a young Egyptian prince raised in a world inured to slavery and further suggests the moral value of a good religious education. Moses' gift of foresight removes from him the stigma of murder; it is not considered murder to take the life of a hardened criminal, particularly if society loses nothing by his death. The appearance of Dathan and Abiram as the two quarreling Hebrew slaves is an example of Biblical figures reappearing in other roles for which their well-established personalities fit them. The rod is the Excalibur in a Biblical tree trunk, but note that Moses' weapon is a magical staff, not a magical sword. Moses is Merlin, not Arthur. The revelation of God's Name at the Bush reflects the popular belief that knowledge of God's secret Name is a powerful weapon. The scene at the inn exonerates Moses of failing to circumcise his son by placing the blame on the pagan Jethro while, not incidentally, suggesting that the drop of blood from Moses' son is the basis of the *halachic* requirement that a drop of blood be drawn at a circumcision.

*Moshe Rabbenu* does what holy men do, that is, he lives apart from other men, outside the camp. He remains celibate during his public career. He fasts regularly and is care-

ful to remain in a condition of ritual purity. He possesses secret knowledge which he teaches privately to a chosen successor. He has the power of healing, shielding, and foresight.
He can curse and bless. He draws a circle around himself
when he intercedes with God. He brews magic potions.
Moses takes up the fragments of the shattered tablets of the
law which he had hurled to the ground in anger over the
Golden Calf and grinds them into a fine powder which he
mixes with the camp's water supply. In this way he identifies the ringleaders of the idolatry: shortly after they drink,
an incriminating brand appears on their foreheads. He possesses second and third sight. When he ascends Mount
Nebo to gain a glimpse of the Holy Land he is forbidden to
enter, he sees through the Judean hills to the valleys beyond,
what is happening that day and all that would happen to Israel until End Time. His presence is that of a holy man. The
special penumbra of light which glows around Moses on his
descent from Sinai did not dim for the forty years of his
public career. He dresses in a distinctive way and walks
about the camp with the crystalline rod in one hand and the
crystalline Tablets of Instructions in the other (*Pseudo Jonathan*).

*Moshe Rabbenu* is equipped with supernatural powers
through his possession of the miraculous rod and the secret
of God's Name. In the Torah the rod is depicted as an ordinary shepherd's crook which God invests with power at the
Bush. In the *aggadah* the rod is a well-known power-laden
instrument made, some say, between sunset and the onset of
darkness at the end of the sixth day of creation, a particularly mysterious and potent time, and of the same substance,
crystal clear sapphire, as God's Throne of Glory (*M. Avot*
5:6). The difference between the Bible's sense of Moses and

that of a fourth- or fifth-century Palestinian Jew can be appreciated by placing Exodus 14:21 as it appears in the received text side by side with its paraphrase:

Text: Then Moses held out his arm over the sea and the Lord drove back the sea with a strong east wind all that night. . . .

Targum: Then Moses held out his arm over the sea, with the great and glorious staff which had been created at the beginning, and upon which there was inscribed and set forth the great and glorious Name, the ten signs which had smitten the Egyptians, the three fathers of the world, the six mothers and the twelve tribes . . . [*Pseudo Jonathan*].

Moses' knowledge of God's Names allows him safe passage into Heaven. His evocation of The Name in his final blessing of the tribes (Deut. 33) guarantees that the blessing's promises will come to pass. Moses' knowledge of The Name is a significant element of the secret Torah he controls and passes on to Joshua, through whom the esoteric tradition ultimately comes down to the rabbis, whose success as healers, rainmakers, and amulet writers depends on their competent handling of the secrets. That, at least, was the way it was told in the schools of the time. "Rabbi Judah said in Rab's name, 'The forty-two lettered Name is entrusted only to him who is pious, meek, middle-aged, free from bad temper, sober, and not arrogant. He who knows it is not to use it lightly, observes the rules of purity, is beloved above and well-known below, his fear lies on mankind, and he inherits this world and the future world' " (b. Kid. 71a).

The origin of Jewish name magic and details of its techniques cannot be recovered. Those who knew the names were bound to secrecy, and what they knew or thought they knew has long sing been lost. One rabbi reports, "The proper pronunciation of the Tetragrammaton [YHVH] is confided by the sages to their disciples once in seven years ... Rava thought to lecture on it in public; a certain old man (Elijah?) said to him, *le'alem* to be kept secret' " (b. Pes. 50a). The old man's response requires a word of explanation. After God has revealed His Name to Moses at the Burning Bush He says: "This shall be My Name forever [*le-olam*]" (Exod. 3:15). In the text *le-olam* is written defectively, without a *vav*, and in this form can be pronounced *le-alem*, giving the old man's reading: "This My Name shall be concealed." Because the secret Name of God was engraved on it, the rod had powers over angelic adversaries, as well as over Pharaoh and Egypt. There was a tradition that *Moshe Rabbenu* had used the rod as a dueling sword against the Angel of Death and so put him to flight (Deut. R. 11:10). Though no synagogue ever had a reliquary containing pieces of the true rod, it is clear that the rod served imaginatively as Judaism's answer to Christian legends about the power of the Cross. There were several traditions about the rod's fate. Some said that after Moses' death God took the rod and placed it in His Palace where it witnesses to His promise to Moses that Israel would ultimately be redeemed; others that Moses holds the rod as his scepter as he serves in God's Palace. The *aggadah* imagines Joshua invested with most of Moses' powers but insists that the rod was not given to him. Moses' leadership dealt with ultimate redemption, while subsequent leaders faced the political and survival problems of their times.

The magical powers of Moses' rod was a well-established and popular image among Hellenistic Jews. The rabbis repeated some of these legends, but they associated the magic less with the rod than with the Name of God inscribed on it. They were much more interested in Moses' knowledge of the powers of God's Name since they claimed to have received that knowledge. A rabbi's routine activities included writing God's Name on protective amulets and speaking The Name in blessings and curses. Some rabbis even claimed to be able to create animals with the knowledge they possessed of the powers of The Name.

The Torah does not suggest that Moses was to keep God's special Name secret. Quite the contrary. Moses asks for and is given The Name in order to tell the Hebrew slaves the Name of God Who has commissioned him (Exod. 3). The *aggadah* interprets the commissioning scene at the Burning Bush as God's Revelation to *Moshe Rabbenu* of a Name he was to keep secret, and Moses keeps it secret until the end of his life when he imparts it with similar restrictions to Joshua. There are innumerable *aggadic* references to Moses' effective use of The Name. "Moses wrote The Name on a tablet of gold in order to raise Joseph's coffin from the Nile into which it had been sunk" (Mek. Va-yehi-Intro). "By uttering The Name, Moses slew the Egyptian taskmaster" (Lev. R. 32:4). "Moses wrote this name on the wooden rod which he cast into the bitter waters of Marah, an act which made these brackish waters sweet" (Rashi to Exod. 15:25). By speaking The Name Moses delayed the Angel of Death who had come to claim his soul.

The rabbis used the power of The Name to perform the public acts expected of holy men and to overcome the dangers which threaten those who would ascend the Heavens to draw close to God. It was his knowledge of The Name which allowed Moses to pass safely by the fierce angelic gatekeepers of Heaven. Since the gates of Heaven are barred to uninitiates, a rabbi could hope to climb the ladder of devotion, enter Heaven, and draw close to God in mystic communion only after he possessed this knowledge. The Talmudic tradition is a mandarin tradition which did not encourage the idea that an uninformed Jew should undertake the vigils and attempt to climb the ladder of mystic experience.

The Torah's Moses is earthbound. *Moshe Rabbenu* was frequently involved with the *famalia shel ma'alah* and a familiar visitor in the Heavens. The Hellenistic tradition had lingered on Moses' first ascent at Sinai. The Talmudic tradition describes at some length two ascents to Heaven. Moses' second ascent came immediately after his death. When God announced; "The time is drawing near for you to die" (Deut. 31:14), the *aggadah* insists that a titanic struggle began. Moses pleads with God for a delay sufficient for him to enter and visit the Promised Land. He cites his years of faithful service. God does not relent. Moses argues further; by forcing him to die God maligns him in the eyes of future generations, for there will be those who say he had died for his sins, though he had not sinned. God is not persuaded. Failing in this direct approach, Moses looks about for effective intercessors. He appeals to the Earth, the Heavens, the Sun, the Moon, the Planets, the Stars, Mount Sinai, the Great Sea, but none will help him. Moses turns to those who might owe him favors: Eliezer, Phineas, Caleb; they pray for him but the angels intercept their prayers. The Angel of Death is dispatched, but he is unable to complete his familiar task. Some said he could not find Moses, others that Moses' powers stopped Death in his tracks. "When the Angel of Death stood before him, Moses said, "Where I dwell you are not allowed to stand, yet you say to me surrender your soul.' Thereupon Moses rebukes the Death and he left reprimanded" (Sifre Deut. 306). To delay death Moses starts to study Torah. It was widely believed that Death had no power over one engaged in Torah study; the literature contains more than one story of an aging and suffering sage who finally asks his pupils to cease their studies so that he may die. God sends the Archangel Michael. Moses refuses to give up his soul even to this friendly angel, and he has sufficient power not to be overcome. Finally, God Himself descends, accompanied by three archangels, and take Moses' soul with a kiss. The angels look to the burial of his corpse, and two reliable witnesses, Joshua and Caleb, are allowed to watch the ascent of Moses' soul to Heaven (Deut. R. 11:10). In its description of Moses the *aggadah* seems at times to cross the unseen line between eulogy and apotheosis, but, ultimately, the line is drawn. For all his talents and powers *Moshe Rabbenu* was neither the son of God nor a savior. He ascended to Heaven after dying, but his death was not an atonement for the world's sins.

Byzantine monks and Persian magi practiced all manner of austerities in the hope of transcending their physical existence, experiencing communion with God, and achieving immortality. The path of mystical illumination was well known to the rabbis, who called it the Work of the Chariot, *Ma'aseh Merkavah*, since much of the language they used to describe the mystical ascent was based on the imagery of the opening chapters of Ezekiel. Their reserved Torah included, along with the Names of God and certain useful information about the mystic way, cosmological secrets, *Ma'aseh bereshit*, traditions about the dimensions and presence of God, *Shiur Komah*, and information about the coming of the messiah and the nature of the messianic age. In all these areas *Moshe Rabbenu* was the first to know, master of those who know, and the model for all those who want to know.

It is interesting to speculate on the shift in religious interest which caused the transformation of the Torah's Moses into *Moshe Rabbenu*. Moses had been the agent of Israel's first redemption and the prototype of the prophet who would announce or be God's agent for the final redemption. The focus of Moses' work was national and political. *Moshe Rabbenu's* life centers on his commissioning and his two ascents; at the Bush he gains the secret lore, on his first ascent redemptive knowledge and spiritual illumination, and on his second immortality. *Moshe Rabbenu's* work centers on personal salvation. I do not suggest that the Exodus and Sinai disappear. Not at all. The Talmudic age simply spread a myth of personal salvation alongside the older myth of national redemption.

Moses was a man. *Moshe Rabbenu* is a man and a semidivine being. He could go where other mortals could not, and even the Angel of Death is helpless before his power. Throughout the ages he acts as a courtier in God's Palace, always prepared to intercede with God on behalf of his people. In one popular version of the Purim story, Satan adds his power to Haman's in order to annihilate Persia's Jews. Deeply disturbed, Elijah appeals to the patriarchs and to Moses to intercede, "How long, fathers of the world, will you be sunk in sleep and not behold the distress into which your descendants are plunged?" The patriarchs are not much help, but Moses tells Elijah, "Go and tell Mordecai so that he may stand and pray there and I will stand and pray here and together we will seek mercy from God"

(Esther R. 7:13). Given his special powers and nature, and the universal belief that Moses was Israel's best friend in Heaven, it is all the more remarkable that *Moshe Rabbenu* did not become an object of worship and that the rabbis did not develop an elaborate liturgy which addressed Moses as Israel's special intercessor.

Our knowledge of synagogue practice and popular prayer during the Talmudic period is admittedly limited; still, the absence of even indirect evidence linking Moses to the prayer formulae is striking, particularly since it is certain that prayers are addressed to God through various friendly ministering angels—Michael, Gabriel, Metatron (j. Ber. 9:1)—despite rabbinic disapproval. The patriarchs, too, had a place in the liturgy; prayers were addressed to "the God of Abraham, Isaac, and Jacob," apparently in the belief that the merit of the Fathers, *Zechut Avot*, would add weight to these petitions. But there is no reference in the prayers which have come down to us of any addressed to the God of Moses. The absence of any mention of Moses in the liturgy was obviously deliberate, to point up the fundamental purpose of public worship: to praise and supplicate God to hasten redemption. The merit of Moses was not summoned in Talmudic liturgy for the same reason that his name did not appear in the liturgy of Biblical times, to make the point that Israel had been redeemed and will be redeemed by God. In no other area of religious life is Judaism's commitment to monotheism clearer.

With minor variations of shading and emphasis *Moshe Rabbenu* lived in the Jewish spirit for at least eighteen hundred years, and he can still be found alive and well in some of the more orthodox day schools and yeshivot. I will illustrate this fact and fill in the portrait with illustrations from the work of the most influential and popular of all medieval Bible commentators, the famous French Talmud scholar Solomon b. Isaac, Rashi (1040–1105). Though he lived long after the Geonim had expressed their reservations about the *aggadah*, Rashi's commentary presents an image of Moses as a charismatic, almost divine man. Since Rashi consciously set out to present a consensus tradition, it is safe to assume that this image of Moses was the popular image in his day. Indeed, since Rashi's commentary became the text every Jewish school boy was started on—and few went much farther—this assessment of *Moshe Rabbenu* was remarkably long-lived, and survived almost to our day.

Rashi proposes to present with clarity, brevity, and precision what he considers the simple meaning of the Torah text, *peshat*, a term which meant for him the accepted interpretation of the rabbinic tradition. He reports as "fact" that Moses was born on the seventh of Adar in the three hundred and twentieth year of the Israelite sojourn in Egypt, that he was a six-month-and-one-day baby. When there were conflicting traditions or some questions about a date, Rashi examines the issue thoroughly and presents the consensus tradition in full. One example: the Torah stated that the tribes ate manna "for forty years." A close reading of the text would seem to indicate that manna appeared for the first time on the sixteenth of Iyar in the first year of the Exodus and ceased on the fifteenth of Nisan in the fortieth year which would leave the count thirty days shy of forty full years. Rashi quotes the full Talmudic explanation: the unleavened bread baked in haste before the Israelites had fled Egypt tasted like manna, and so the period during which these cakes were eaten were included in the number of manna days (Rashi to Exod. 16:35).

The passion for detail is omnipresent. Rashi lists the exact distance between encampments and precisely where each of the twelve tribes pitched their tents. He provides the names of characters the Torah leaves anonymous. The Hebrews who accosted Moses the day after he killed the overseer were Dathan and Abiram, the very same men who years later showed their ugly nature as rebels against Moses' authority. The taskmaster whom Moses murdered was not just another overseer but an uncompromising villain. Rashi even provides the taskmaster's criminal record, including convictions for assault and battery and adultery. Rashi bases his information on an *aggadah* which identified an anonymous Egyptian (Lev. 24:10 ff) as the father of a young man who blasphemed God while the Israelites were at Kadesh Barnea and was put to death for his sins. According to this *aggadah*, the infamous taskmaster had fathered this illegitimate son with Shelomit, a beautiful but silly Israelite woman who didn't know enough not to talk with strangers. She had been led into an affair with the taskmaster while her husband was slaving away. Rashi even reports that the beating of a Hebrew slave which Prince Moses had interrupted involved the unfortunate husband and the taskmaster-lover.

Asceticism played a much larger role in Talmudic and medieval Judaism than some modern apologetes acknowledge. *Moshe Rabbenu* is the creation of a culture in which the sexes lived largely unto themselves. Men and women, even husbands and wives, rarely talked with each other. After crossing the Reed Sea Moses sang his hymn of praise and deliverance with and for the men and only then did Miriam take up a timbrel and sing with and for the women (Rashi to Exod. 15:21). Romance had no place in *Moshe Rabbenu's* world. Rashi was deaf and blind to the romantic element in the story of Moses helping the daughters of Jethro defend themselves against the local bullies and meeting Zipporah. He believed that Jethro had taken into account Moses' family connections and that Jethro's decision to marry his daughter to Moses was a calculated plan to align his house with a man of distinguished connections (Rashi to Exod. 2:20). *Moshe Rabbenu* marries only to have children and remains celibate during his entire public career, all forty years of it, in order to remain in the state of purity required of one who visits with God.

*Moshe Rabbenu* is well born, a gentleman of wealth who bears himself with the unself-conscious dignity of one born to privilege. As a true aristocrat, *Moshe Rabbenu* knows when to stand on ceremony and when to set protocol aside. People rose as he passed and remained standing until he was out of sight, as was expected when the liege lord processed (Rashi to Exod. 33:8). God had instructed *Moshe Rabbenu* to hire trumpeters to announce his passages through the camp (Num. 10:1). Yet, when Jethro arrives in the Israelite camp *Moshe Rabbenu*, though of superior rank, takes the initiative in welcoming him (Rashi to Exod. 18:7). Moses' best-known virtue, humility, is not the self-effacement of a saint but a royal restraint which keeps him from abusing his station or privilege. His major vice is anger, that quick flash of impatience which often accompanies power. In Rashi the legends of Harun Al-Rashid and Charlemagne echo around *Moshe Rabbenu*, just as in the Talmud and *Midrash* they pick up reverberations of Alexander and Caesar.

*Moshe Rabbenu* exhibits many of the accoutrements and all the attitudes of royal power, but these represent only one side of God's man. The king is also a Talmudic scholar. Each day when God greets *Moshe Rabbenu* He teaches him a particular section of law, the text and all that was subsumed into it. After each session God pauses to allow Moses to absorb what he had heard. *Moshe Rabbenu* repeats each rule two or three times until he has memorized it and then interprets the rule to God to be sure he understands its implications. Aaron enters the Tent of Meeting. *Moshe Rabbenu* instructs him and hears his recitation. Aaron takes his seat and his sons enter. *Moshe Rabbenu* repeats the lesson. They take their seats. The elders enter and the lesson is repeated for them. Finally, the people enter and are instructed. The emphasis is on the leaders gaining absolute mastery of the Torah, clear and certain knowledge. In his teaching *Moshe Rabbenu* proceeds through the law systematically, a section of Torah at a time or, when need be, a single *halacha* and all its implications. Before each festival he teaches Israel its appropriate forms and laws. *Moshe Rabbenu* is able to teach the law in seventy languages. It is also reported that he taught like a Roman rhetor, whispering the teaching to an aide who then spoke the teaching loudly.

Verisimilitude is one thing, history quite another. Rashi was not an historian. He did not make a serious attempt to place people and events in an understandable perspective or to discover meaningful connections between time-related events. History seeks to understand how and why events occur as they do. The rabbis acknowledge only one cause, God, and though some philosophically minded sages knew about natural law, ultimately it was the will of God rather than the interaction of men, economics, culture, and political institutions which explained the how and why of everything. The rabbinic Jew lived in the swirl of the real world and did not deny it; but, at the same time, he drew little en-

couragement or pride from it. He was in *galut,* limbo, a
dreary weariness between a glorious past and a glorious future. His indifference to the passage of time was not primarily the result of the trauma of national disaster, although
the numbing pain of defeat certainly deadened Jewish interest in the game of power. Rather, it was an emotional
numbness born of impotence, an awareness that he was a
political prisoner serving an indefinite sentence. History
deals with power and change and is a function of a society's
sense of expectancy. Confined for life, a prisoner has no reason to keep records since no day has any particular distinction. In his cell memories of the days before his incarceration take on added poignancy, and his mind dwells on the
possibility of a miraculous escape or unexpected pardon. In
*galut* each Jew was born into chains, as was his father before
him. But his imagination could not be shackled. Time was a
flexible category in which what had been, what is, and what
will be merged into each other. The Torah says that Moses
returned to Egypt from Midian mounted on an ass. Rashi
was sure that this was the same animal on which Abraham
had traveled to Mount Moriah and that the King Messiah
will ride on the day of his triumphal entry into Jerusalem
(Rashi to Exod. 4:20). On Mount Nebo God showed Moses
not only all of the Promised Land as the Torah indicated
but its future history, including the conquest, the exile, the
messianic age, and the resurrection of the dead.

*Moshe Rabbenu* is a mortal. He is born, he marries, he
has children, but he never ages. His body is as vigorous and
his mind as sturdy on the day of his death as in the first flush
of his maturity (Rashi to Deut. 31:1). He dies. Inconsistent
as it may seem *Moshe Rabbenu* is also an immortal. Rashi
interprets the line, "Moses was one hundred and twenty

years old when he died; his eyes were undimmed and his vigor unabated" (Deut. 34:7), to mean "Even *after* he died his eye was not dimmed nor his natural force abated." *Moshe Rabbenu* is for Rashi, as for the Talmudic sages, a semidivine being. Before his birth Miriam prophesied that her mother would bear a child who would deliver Israel (Rashi to Exod. 15:20). At his birth preternatural light filled the room. During all the years following the theophany on Sinai a nimbus of light played about his head (Rashi to Exod. 34:29), and his halo was different in kind from that of other holy men. "Moses' face had the brightness of the sun, Joshua's the pale light of the moon" (Rashi to Num. 27:20). After death his body was not subject to decomposition (Rashi to Deut. 34:7), and his grave had been prepared for his body before Creation (Rashi to Deut. 34:6).

Rashi repeats the *aggadah* that *Moshe Rabbenu* was charged, tried, and sentenced to death for the taskmaster's murder. In presenting the details of Moses nick-of-time escape Rashi does not choose among three popular versions but presents all of them: there was so much tumult in the court room that the executioner did not hear the court's decision; the jailers were put into a trance and did not see *Moshe Rabbenu* make his escape; when Moses was brought to the killing ground the executioner could not raise his sword. Whichever version one accepts, the theological implications remain the same—God protects the faithful—and the image of *Moshe Rabbenu* is the same—he has powers denied to ordinary mortals.

As a magician *Moshe Rabbenu* is Merlin, a royal wizard and powerful chief, not a gypsy trickster; and as a prophet he is a respected elder dressed in purple linen, not a sideshow clairvoyant dressed in clown's costume. There is no indication of ecstasy nor automatic speech. He is always in full control of his senses. Though dressed as prophet, *Moshe Rabbenu* is an ascetic and celibate. When Zipporah hears that other prophets have appeared in the camp, she goes to console their wives on the loss of their husbands.

In the Talmudic world miracle and magic are two sides of a single coin: the difference is that God initiates a miracle, and a wizard performs magic. God Himself teaches *Moshe Rabbenu* the formulae by which to "awaken God's attribute of Mercy," that is, the art of intercessory prayer which required, besides speaking God's powerful Name, wrapping himself in a *tallit* and repeating the text of the Thirteen Attributes (Rashi to Exod. 34:607). Even the Angel of Death contributes to *Moshe Rabbenu's* education by teaching him that incense overcomes plague (Rashi to Num. 17:11). The Talmud's portrait is inconsistent. Generally *Moshe Rabbenu* is the agent of God's power. In other situations he is a magician who displays his powers. Clearly theological caution did not always prevail over credulity.

The simple story of the baby Moses in his cradle in the bullrushes became a tale dark and magical. The princess's handmaidens are evil spirits who try every way possible to distract their mistress. They fail. The cradle is floating in midstream, far out of reach, but the princess's arm magically extends until she is able to reach the basket and bring it to shore. A battle against Midian is described as an aerial dogfight: The wizard, Balaam, causes the Midianite host to fly, but Israel's zealous priest, Phineas, thwarts the attack by holding up a powerful amulet which causes Balaam's air force to crash to the ground (Rashi to Num. 31:6). When the Amonites attack, their guardian angel is cast down from Heaven, and *Moshe Rabbenu*, to protect Israel, tramples on his neck (Rashi to Deut. 2:29). The manufacture of the Golden Calf is something of a puzzle since the Torah does not describe anyone making a mold into which hot metal could be poured. One *aggadah* suggests that some magicians from the mixed multitude who accompanied the Israelites shaped the calf with their black art. A much more complicated *aggadah* suggests that *Moshe Rabbenu* was, unintentionally, the sorcerer. To raise the patriarch Joseph's casket from the Nile, in accordance with Joseph's deathbed wish that his body be returned to Canaan for burial, Moses had prepared silver amulets. One of these amulets, inscribed "Rise ox, rise ox," had not been needed and this power-laden piece had come into the possession of one Micah, a ringleader of the camp rebellion. When Micah tossed it into the vat of molten gold it brought forth a calf. Rashi, who quotes both traditions, would not have gone to the stake for either, but he is a medieval man living in a medieval environment full of wizards, witches, and wonders, and he readily accepts *Moshe Rabbenu* as the chief wonder-worker of them all.

Despite his special nature and special powers, *Moshe Rabbenu* exhibits his full share of failings. *Moshe Rabbenu* is mortal and immortal, holy man and sinner. Angry and frustrated at the obtuseness of the people, he strikes the rock at Meribah though God had ordered him "simply hold your rod over it" (Rashi to Num. 20:11). Moral: a leader must always control himself. Vain about his capacities, Moses assumes that he is able to adjudicate all cases submitted to him, but he does not know the law applicable to a number of cases (Rashi to Num. 27:4). Moral: even the wisest of men has his limits. At Rephidim Moses is fearful and anxious lest the tribes begin to stone him (Rashi to Exod. 17:5).

Moral: even heroes can be intimidated. Moses had sinned. His death was the ultimate proof of his sin in a world which believed that death comes to a person only because of his sins. *Moshe Rabbenu* is part man, part divine; part prophet, part magician; mortal yet immortal. "When Moses went up on high, he was very much a man; but when he came down below, he was like unto God" (PRK Sup. 1, 9). The Heavenly Court once excommunicated Moses because, without permission, he had allowed the *asafsuf,* the riffraff, to join the Exodus and it was they who were responsible for the incident of the Golden Calf (Rashi to Exod. 32:7).

Despite his flaws *Moshe Rabbenu* is a worthy role model. Moses' life "can teach you manners" (Rashi to Exod. 19:8). Moses' concern for his elder brother's rights; his care for his flock, particularly the fact that he pastured them far from private property; his deference to his father-in-law; his attention to the burial of his sister and brother; his daily work as teacher; his love of Israel—all are cited as examples of virtue.

The death of Moses had been a great loss to Israel. The measure of Israel's loss was that his special powers to shield the people against their enemies died with him. Joshua is a fine man, a good scholar, and a capable leader; but he lacks all those special qualities which made Moses *Moshe Rabbenu.* Lest the nation despair, *Moshe Rabbenu* is made to live on in Heaven ready, willing, and able to protect Israel from her enemies. *Moshe Rabbenu* suggests a tradition eager for a protector and savior but which ultimately will not bend its theology sufficiently to accommodate that need.

# CHAPTER
# VII

# Moses
# and Mohammed

IN THE CENTURIES following the destruction of the Temple most Jews lived within host cultures whose religious approaches were fundamentally different from their own. Christianity promised salvation to individuals on the basis of faith in a divine savior. The Zoroastrian traditions of Persia centered on a cosmic myth of unceasing struggle between the forces of Light and Darkness. Christianity and Mazdaism had venerated texts, the New Testament and the Avesta, but neither tradition prescribed their study as a requirement of piety. In both traditions a clerical hierarchy controlled worship and great powers were ascribed to wonder-working holy men, magi, and monks. Having become acquainted with *Moshe Rabbenu*, we can appreciate the degree to which Jews assimilated some of these attitudes; some, but not all. Any qualified layman could lead the synagogue worship service. The rabbis' home territory was the school, not the synagogue, and their lives were focused on the study of God's revelation rather than on a discipline of meditation and devotion.

The many conquests of the Arab armies during the seventh and eighth centuries and the mass conversions to Islam which followed their remarkable victories brought the Jewish communities of West Asia and the Mediterranean littoral under the influence of a host culture whose religious structures were similar to their own. Islam proclaimed the Quran to be a one-time and all-embracing revelation mediated through a single prophet-leader. The prophet did not put himself forward as a Perfect Man or a Divine Man but only as the vehicle whom God had chosen to mediate His message and to carry on His work. Mohammed did not claim to be a wonder-worker: "Miracles rest with God alone—I am only a man warning you." Worship in the mosque, like worship in the synagogue, could be led by any qualified male. Islam's religious leaders functioned in the schools of the *shariyah,* Muslim law, rather than at the mosque's pulpit. The imam was primarily a community leader and learned jurist, a man of affairs whose authority derived from his learning rather than his personal charisma and whose professional function was to see that his community abided by the terms of the *shariyah.*

Islam, like traditional Judaism, rests on the proposition that society should be organized according to God's Instructions which had been made known through a prophet. The faithful treasure the Quran, "God's great and long speech," as God's gift of truth to mankind—a truth which explained the mysteries of life; it is a way, the only way, which guarantees salvation. Islam teaches that life can be redeemed and immortality attained only through participation in the community of those blessed with God's rule, that

Heaven is reserved for the faithful, that right belief and righteous living are prerequisites for salvation. After Mohammed there would be no other prophets; there was nothing more for men to hear. The future needs of the community would be managed through careful interpretation of the Quran; and, as in Judaism, the art of commentary camouflaged change.

Islam teaches that God controls history but, unlike the Torah's treatment of Moses, the Quran shows no evidence of any editorial attempt to diminish Mohammed's significance as an actor in the political events of his time. Quite the contrary. Mohammed is described as a caliph-prophet who was a successful leader because he clearly understood God's Will. Unlike Moses, Mohammed prepares his troops for battle and sets out the strategy that they are to follow. In our Freudian age we study prophecy under the heading of abnormal psychology and/or religious experience. Muslim scholars studied prophecy as a phenomenon associated with leadership. Prophets like Mohammed and Moses were sent "by God for the improvement of mankind" (ibn Kammuna 15). A prophet's political success was held to be the ultimate test of the truth of his words, a comforting thought when your armies have just conquered half the world. "The True Prophet will institute a might and a sacred law among men so that the salvation of that age will there have its foundation" (Avicenna 9:6).

Islam numbers Moses among those "men of decision"— the list stretches back through Jesus to Elijah, Moses, Abraham, and Adam—who had brought God's Instructions and successfully governed their communities. Each is given a special title: Adam was the chosen one of God; Noah, the delivered of God; Abraham, the friend of God; Moses, the

confidante of God. These honorable titles appear often in
Muslim texts and even in the liturgy, but it is always made
clear that Mohammed was the last of the prophets and of a
rank far above all other "men of decision." Later Muslim
scholastics would insist that the label, prophet, which Mohammed used of himself, is an amphibolous term. Its conventional meaning—"there was no other prophet like
him"—is inadequate for Mohammed, but it was useful to
place him at the end of this line of "men of decision" in
order to connect the Arab nation with the traditions of the
major population groups who passed under its control,
thereby making conversion to Islam easier and more appeal-
ing.

The Quran treats Moses as a respected prophet, one of
the best, through whom God displayed His power and spoke
His Word, one who had been enlightened and instructed by
God Himself.

We also showed favors to Moses and Aaron and delivered them
both, along with their people, out of great distress. We aided
them so that it was they who were the conquerors. We gave to
both of them the book that makes clear and guided them both to
the straight path. We left with those of later times [the saying]
"peace be upon Moses and Aaron." Thus do We reward those
who do well. Truly, both of them were among Our servants, the
believers [37:114–122].

Incidents in Moses' life are mentioned in thirty-four chapters of the Quran. One sura describes Moses spending forty
days and nights with God, being given "the Book of the
Law and the distinction between Good and Evil" (2:50).
Another, Moses bringing down God's Words on tablets,
"an admonition concerning every matter and a decision in

every case" (7:142). But unlike the early Christians, neither the editors of the Quran nor later Muslim theologians show any particular interest in proving that their prophet had been predicted in the Torah. One Quran text has God tell Moses that good will be given "to those who shall follow the apostle, the illiterate prophet, whom they shall find written down with them in the Law and the Gospel" (7:157); but no serious attempt was made to certify Mohammed's career on the basis of Scriptural prophecy or to attach the patterns of Moses' life to Mohammed's. The older Scriptures had been useful, but they were filled with error and should not be relied on. Neither the Old Testament nor the New was ever bound by Muslims with the Quran into a single book entitled Holy Scriptures. Although Moses is quite visible in the Quran, he is just one, and not the most important, among a number of apostles.

Mohammed seems to have picked up his knowledge of the Jewish tradition from conversations with Jewish neighbors in Arabia and from whatever was known about Judaism among his fellow Arabs. His description of a Moses in the Quran suggests materials in both the Written Torah and the *aggadah*. He reports, for one example, that when Moses is saved by Pharaoh's wife, whom the Quran names Asiya, the infant refuses to suckle at the breast of a non-Hebrew. This detail, which appears also in the *aggadah*, explains why Moses is turned over to his mother as wet nurse and, not incidentally, emphasizes God's complete control of history and confirms the tradition dear to Muslims and Jews that to receive God's Word a prophet must be in a state of ritual purity. He may not have touched or tasted anything impure (b. Sotah 12b). The murder of the taskmaster represents both an identity crisis and a rash act of which Moses later repents, recognizing that he had been tempted to it by Satan. Moses flees to Midian, where he helps the daughters of the local sheik water their father's flock, is welcomed into the sheik's home, and marries one of his daughters in exchange for an undertaking to work a number of years in his service. Moses receives his commission at the Burning Bush, which is located not on Sinai but in the valley of Towa: it is night; Moses and his family are traveling; Moses sees a fire and, leaving his family, seeks it in order to bring back a brand with which to light his campfire. At the Bush God speaks to Moses: "Take off your shoes. This is the holy valley of Towa. You are chosen. Listen well. I am God, there is none else. Pray to Me. There will be a time—soon—of retribution for all. Let no one who is passionate turn you aside from this truth" (Quran 20:11 ff).

The Quran treats the Moses-Pharaoh confrontation as a conflict between an apostle of God and a wicked king. The issue is not whether the slaves will be allowed to leave but whether Moses can secure Pharaoh's repentance. Pharaoh has "burst all bounds" and Moses offers him religion, defined as correction from the Lord. When Moses bests Egypt's sorcerers at their own tricks, they acknowledge the superior power of God and convert and are summarily executed by Pharaoh, who remains deaf to good advice and blind to the display of God's power. The confrontation with Pharaoh and his chief minister, Haman, proves the obduracy of the powerful and the folly of the spiritually blind: Pharaoh demands a sign, Moses performs miracles (eight, rather than ten), still Pharaoh refuses to believe. In the end Pharaoh is drowned and denied life eternal (29:39).

One sura depicts Moses as a young man setting out on a voyage to discover the confluence of the seas. He takes along

a servant, something of a *schlemiel* who forgets to pack the
necessary provisions. Along the way they encounter a
prophet of Allah whom Moses asks to teach him wisdom.
The prophet agrees but stipulates that Moses must not
question anything that happens. Together they build a ship,
but when it is launched the prophet drills a hole in the bot-
tom. Later the prophet kills a young man in a town where
they had been offered hospitality; on another occasion he
holds up a broken-down fence which is about to collapse.
Ultimately, all is explained. The ship was owned by poor
men and was about to be captured by pirates who would
have sold the crew into slavery. The young man was destined for a criminal life and his death encouraged his parents
to have another child whose future would be more auspi-
cious. There was a treasure under the fence, the property of
orphans, which would never have been discovered had the
fence collapsed over the site (18:60–82). The lesson is clear:
trust the prophet-apostle even when his actions seem bizarre, for he sees what even a Moses does not see. Another
lesson is clear: a prophet of Allah sees far more clearly than
Moses.

Muslim commentators name Moses' travel guide, al-Khadir, the verdant one, and identify him with Elijah, perhaps
having learned from Jews that the story is a variant of a Talmudic anecdote. The Talmud reports that the sage Joshua
b. Levi traveled with the prophet Elijah to learn wisdom.
During this trip Elijah acted in bizarre, but ultimately ex-
plicable, ways. Whether or not al-Khadir was based on Elijah, there is a tendency, perhaps deliberate, in Muslim writing to magnify Elijah over Moses. According to Muslim
commentary, the children of Israel once asked Moses
whether there is anyone wiser than he. He answers no, but

God Himself contradicts him: "al-Khadir [Elijah] is wiser" (al-Bukhari 16:19). Emphasizing Elijah's superiority was a subtle and vivid way of denigrating the prophet whom Jews revered as the mediator of their Torah.

During the Middle Ages Muslim anthologists published a series of popular legend books and included some of the stories about Moses. Al-Thalibi's *Legends of the Prophets* (fourteenth century) includes a story which described how the maid-servants who had touched Moses' cradle were healed of various ailments. He also collected wonderful stories about Moses' rod. One reports that the famous rod, the sign of Moses' power, had been cut from a tree in Paradise and had been in the possession of Adam, Noah, and the patriarchs before an angel offered it to Moses. The rod shone in the darkness, provided water in times of drought, became a fruit-bearing tree when placed in the ground, and a double-headed, fire-breathing dragon when enemies threatened its possessor. One day, while Moses napped, seven assassins hired by Pharaoh sought to kill him; the rod dispatched them without disturbing Moses' sleep. In Islam, as in rabbinic Judaism, monotheism assimilated the world of angels and demons, and the miraculous legends with which credulity embellishes heroic careers. Mohammed claimed only to be God's prophet-apostle, but Muslim piety surrounded his life with a thousand wondrous tales.

The mainstream of Islam emphasized the way of learning rather than the mystical way and based religious authority on learning. There was a tradition that "the Prophet regarded any day as lost in which he did not increase in that knowledge that would draw him closer to his Lord" (al-Ghazzali p. 3). The state could not be properly organized without the help of men learned in the *shariyah*. *Shariyah* is religious law and its study inevitably entailed discussion of issues in theology and the psychology of religion which, in time, led to interest in the philosophy of religion and what is now called scholasticism, the reconciliation of philosophy and religion, of reason and revelation. Though Islamic scholasticism in its various manifestations was of interest only to small groups among the urban, literate classes, its approach was broadly known and made religious leaders sensitive to the difference between true belief and credulity. Efforts were made to separate what was doctrinally acceptable from the detritus of popular legend and innocent piety.

The heads of the major rabbinic schools situated in those large urban areas where the Muslim scholastic enterprise was most approved and pursued began to take an interest in applying the same concepts to Judaism. The first fruits of this effort have already been mentioned, the desacralization of the *aggadah*, whose vivid but thoroughly anthropomorphic images of God now seemed scandalous to those who insisted that Judaism's affirmation of monotheism required that its literature not propogate ideas which violated the commandment that God is not to be portrayed. One of these college presidents, Egyptian-born Saadiah b. Joseph, wrote a scholastic work, *The Book of Beliefs and Opinions*, in which he distinguishes between beliefs and opinions and provides scholastic arguments in support of Judaism's basic beliefs. In the course of the work he examines the Christian claim that Jesus' mission, like Moses', ought to be judged by his performance of miracles and judged superior since Jesus' miracles were more impressive. Saadiah countered the Christian argument by saying that Jews believe in Moses not solely because of the miracles he performed "but because he called upon us to do what is proper" (Saadiah, 3:8). The value of the message is the critical issue; the miracles are necessary but only confirmatory. Saadiah's Moses holds his own against *Moshe Rabbenu*. A *Midrash* popular among Jewish scholastics suggests that when God orders Moses to raise his staff over the Reed Sea, Moses remonstrates that if the sea were to part God would be violating His own pattern of creation. God responds by saying that at Creation He had stipulated that the sea would part (Exod. R. 21:6). The miracle was not that the sea parted but that God had told Moses it would and that Moses had announced that it would. Such a miracle is a sign pointing to the power that controls history and demonstrating the purposeful orderliness of the world—just that perception of the world which causes many moderns to deny miracles.

As in the West, so in Islam, the attempt to validate religious doctrine on the basis of philosophical argument proved to be an immensely important activity in the development of thought, but immensely unsettling to those who took their legends straight. In the popular culture, the prophet-caliph is seen as a semidivine prophet-mystic who, like *Moshe Rabbenu*, worked miracles on earth and continues to work miracles in Heaven.

As the caliphate declined, the philosophic circles tended to get smaller and more radical and to become the target of heresy hunters. Philosophy came to be seen as the cause of division in the religious community. The philosophers were accused of raising more doubts than they resolved. After the thirteenth century Muslim learning generally limited itself to the pragmatically useful *shariyah* or to mystical and theosophic speculation, and rather comfortably made its peace with the folk image of Mohammed as a miracle worker. There were numerous cults of saints and holy men. The

more learned joined the ascetic brotherhoods of medieval
Islam—generally called Sufis after the wool of the coarse
cloak the men customarily wore. Mohammed was pictured
as the first and incomparable Master of their brotherhood,
he whose spirit is free of error and passion, whose love of
God is wholly selfless, the most perfect of men who has left
behind all human limitations and become a saint, in effect, one with God. Being one with God, Mohammed
participates, according to these mystical theories, in God's
powers. For the Sufis nothing exists outside of God, so their
Mohammed was not only the historic figure of the Quran
but a heavenly figure who continues to radiate divine power.
Theirs was a world of fervent piety and esoteric mystical
speculation.

Islamic cultural patterns deeply affected the Jews who
lived in centers of Muslim culture. In the villages and
among the semieducated in the cities, *Moshe Rabbenu* remains wondrous in his miracles, the *aggadah* retains its authority, and no one really cares where doctrine ends and legend begins. Among the educated elites, for whom the value
of the Torah was that it was Torah, not that Moses, its messenger, was a semidivine man or a wonder-worker; *aggadah*
is no longer accepted uncritically and *Moshe Rabbenu* is
transformed into Israel's great caliph-prophet, the Jewish answer to Mohammed.

Reshaping Moses' biography to fit Islam's emphasis on
the prophet-caliph encouraged Jewish scholastics to refer to
Moses as a king. Talmudic literature, which had stressed
Moses in his role as a prophet–wonder worker, contains a
few stray references to Moses as a king. An *aggadah* about
Elisheva, Aaron's wife, lists five special blessings which
she enjoyed, one of which was that "her brother-in-law was

a king" (b. Zeb. 102a). A Talmudic sage explains that the Torah's description of Jethro as "Moses' father-in-law" was a way of honoring the sheik who had sheltered the exile and taught Moses much about the administration of justice, for "it is an honor to be father-in-law to a king" (Sifre Num. 10:29). These references to Moses as a king seem to derive from a variant reading of a difficult passage in Deuteronomy which is generally translated, "When Moses charged us with The Teaching ... Then He (God) was king in Jeshurun. When the heads of the people assembled the tribes of Israel together" (33:4–5), but which can be construed to read, "When Moses charged us with The Teaching—then he became king in Jeshurun." The first reading suggests that in accepting the Torah Israel acknowledges God as king. The second says that once the Torah was pronounced, Moses became Israel's king. But there is little evidence in the Talmudic literature that the rabbis gave much weight to the idea of Moses as king.

In Islamic times Moses' coronation is taken seriously. Lengthy comparisons are made between the royal administrations of Moses and David (Mid. Teh. 1:2). The basis of Korah's complaint/rebellion was that Moses had been crowned. Because he was of nobler rank Korah felt slighted and aggrieved (Num. R. 18:2). Targum *Pseudo Jonathan* interpolates into Deuteronomy 34:5 an assertion that Moses had been invested with four crowns: the crowns of Torah, of priestly service, of royal authority, and of the power of The Word. When Moses wonders why Bezalel, and not he, was commissioned to fashion the sacred vessels required for the sanctuary, one *aggadah* imagines God saying, "Moses, I have made you a king, it does not befit a king to do anything himself, he gives orders to others" (Exod. R. 40:2).

# Moses and Mohammed

Another sage explains God's command that Moses fashion "two trumpets of silver" (Num. 10:2) as an Instruction that Moses be paid the deference due a sovereign: "God said to Moses: 'I made you a king,' as it is said 'and he was a king in Jeshurun' (Deut. 33:5). Just as a king is preceded by trumpet blowing, so when you go out let them blow before you. Thus the command, 'fashion two trumpets of silver' " (Tan. Beha'aloteha 15). Joshua's commissioning is also described as a coronation: "Every Israelite came up in Joshua's honor and afterwards Moses commanded them to bring the golden throne and the pearl crown and the royal turban and the purple robe. And Moses stood and ordered the rows and the benches of the Sanhedrin and of the officers of the army and of the priests. And afterwards Moses went to Joshua and he dressed him and he put the crown on him and he seated him on the golden throne" (PM 272–78).

Because the Jewish community existed in the Muslim world only on sufferance, it became important to its self-esteem that Moses be seen as Mohammed was seen, as effectively exercising royal prerogatives. This image also reinforced their faith in the prophet who had brought the Torah. The idea that a leader like Moses proved his virtue by political success was, as we saw, a key concept in Hellenistic thought. It is a new theme in rabbinic literature and has no secure base in Torah. To the contrary, the Torah insists on Moses' indifference to royal office and its trappings and points out that he made no attempt to establish a dynasty.

The tendency to enthrone Moses prompted a conservative reaction by those who felt more closely bound to the text's evident meaning. Joshua b. Korha (second century C.E.) is cited as the authority for a fully developed *Midrash* which pointedly suggests that both Abraham and Moses had sought the high priesthood and the crown, but only Abraham had been granted his request. Commentators were intrigued by the linguistic and stylistic similarity of two texts whose highly stylized form cried out for exegesis: Genesis 22:1, Abraham's summons to the Akedah; and Exodus 3:4, Moses' summons at the Burning Bush. In both cases God repeats his salutation: "Abraham, Abraham," "Moses, Moses," and he who is summoned responds in courtly language, "*hineni.*" The commentators interpreted the double salutation as God's formal offer of the two crowns and the formal response as an acceptance: "I am ready for priesthood and the crown."

Joshua [b. Korha] said, on two occasions Moses compared himself to Abraham and it was of no avail to him. Abraham said *hineni,* "I am ready for priesthood and the crown" and he attained both [Ps. 110:4; Gen. 14:17]. Moses, too, said *hineni,* "I am ready for the priesthood and the crown," but God answered him *al tikrav halom,* "Do not approach here." *Tikrav* eliminates the priesthood [the verb *karav* comes from the same root used to designate the offering of sacrifice, so *al tikrav* could mean "do not offer sacrifice]. *Halom* eliminates the crown on the basis of 2 Samuel 7:18 "David the king went in and sat before God and said, 'Who am I, O Lord, that you have brought me this far [*halom*]' " [Deut. R. 2:7].

The answer Moses receives, *al tikrav halom,* is given the inflated reading, "Do not expect either the priestly or royal office."

The need to claim that "my prophet is better than your prophet" led Jews to reemphasize Moses' activities as a scribe. A frequent Muslim challenge to the authority of the Torah was that the Torah was not a true copy of the teaching Moses had received. Fully developed, the argument ran this way: because Israelite society had not had the benefit of the professional memorizers who played so important a role in the Arab milieu, priests of the Jerusalem Temple had been made responsible for memorizing the Torah, each assigned a single chapter. Many of those priests had been killed during the Babylonian invasions of the sixth century B.C.E., and more had disappeared during the Exile. When Ezra tried to write out a Torah scroll there were inevitable gaps and misquotations; so he had added uncertain material to the text and omitted much that should have been in it. As a consequence, the Torah "is in truth a book by Ezra, not a divine book" (Ibn Kammuna 49). In response Jews again began to use an old but rarely cited title of Moses, *Safrah Rabbah b'Yisroel*, Israel's greatest scribe (Onkelos to Deut. 33:21). When the Talmud describes Moses as a teacher, the image suggests lectures and recitations from memory as well as pen and parchment. Now the image shifts. Moses' work as God's secretary is emphasized. He had inscribed not one but thirteen identical scrolls, one for each tribe and a master copy which was kept in The Temple in case questions arose. Maimonides is careful to say that "Moses was like a scribe writing down from dictation" (CM San. 10:7), and the thirteenth-century Torah commentator and kabbalist, Nahmanides, said it this way, "Moses our teacher *wrote* this book of Genesis together with the whole Torah from the mouth of the Holy One, blessed be He" (Nah. introduction to Gen).

Competitive bragging is not the world's most noble enterprise, but it did encourage a few thoughtful men in both faiths to examine the nature of prophetic consciousness. Could a person prepare himself to be a prophet and, if so, how? Did a prophet have to be a pious and learned man, or was prophecy an unexpected gift? What part of the mind was involved in the prophetic experience? Were there objective criteria by which a prophet's message might be judged? Must miracles accompany prophecy as proof that the words came from God?

All agreed that there were levels of prophecy. Some prophets saw visions, others heard words; some understood what they heard, others did not. According to Muslim teaching Mohammed was the only prophet to hear God's words without distortion. The conventional Muslim view was that Moses was not a false prophet who speaks lies but a true prophet of fine but limited prophetic capacity. Jewish apologetes reverse the argument. They emphasize Moses' uniqueness as a prophet. "The Torah says the Creator has never spoken *to anyone* without an intermediary except our teacher Moses" (Saadiah 2:10). The basis of this claim is the Torah text which describes God and Moses speaking to each other "face to face" (Deut. 34:10). The Quran states that the Angel Gabriel had dictated the book, portion by portion, to Mohammed as he lay in bed at night and that Mohammed later repeated to secretaries what he had heard. Jews claimed that the Torah had been given to Moses by God without the interposition of an intermediary and that Moses himself had written it down. It seemed to them self evident that the Torah was a more accurate manifestation of God's speech. Maimonides had Mohammed in mind when he cited four features which distinguished Moses' prophecy from that of all other prophets: only Moses was addressed immediately and not through intermediaries; prophecy came to all others in sleep or in a daytime trance, only Moses was addressed in the daytime and while standing on his feet; only Moses had no fear during the prophetic meeting; and, finally, Moses alone could speak with God whenever he wished, while all others had to wait without any assurance that God would again speak to them. No Gabriel. No night visions. No interruption of the revelation. Moses had spoken with God openly and easily, fully awake, as one person might with another. Prophecy came to him not infrequently but daily and without any sensory distortion (CM San. 10:7).

Prudence led Jews to code the Moses-Mohammed comparison in their polemic. Balaam was used as a stand-in for Mohammed. "Moses' prophecy exhibited three features which were absent from that of Balaam. When God spoke with Moses the latter stood on his feet. God spoke with Balaam only when he lay prone on the ground. With Moses God spoke face to face, but with Balaam He spoke in a vision and it was as if he heard the words of God. With Moses God spoke openly, but with Balaam He spoke only in parables" (Num. R. 14:20). Comparisons extended to the prophet's character, as well as to his endowment. Moses had never sought personal gain. Balaam had a wide streak of avarice and greed. He had been willing to curse a whole nation for a purse of gold. Jews never forgot that Mohammed had turned violently against their fellow Jews in the cities of the Hejaz when they refused to finance his mission.

In certain Jewish philosophic circles a brisk debate arose over the nature of the prophet's call. Did God choose anyone He willed or did God limit his choice to the spiritually enlightened? There is no indication in the Torah that Moses had prepared himself in any way to receive the voice which came from the Burning Bush, and some thinkers like Judah Ha Levi (1075–1141) stayed with this position and insisted that prophecy was a gift of God's grace. Ha Levi wrote that God deliberately chose Moses, by tradition already an elderly man of eighty and a shepherd, not a trained philosopher, to emphasize God's complete control of the prophetic event (Ha Levi 1:83). He also insisted that prophecy occurs only to pious Jews and only in the Holy Land, criteria which Mohammed, of course, did not meet.

A handful of thinkers deeply influenced by Aristotelian assumptions, Maimonides among them, argued that prophecy comes only to a superior person who has perfected his character, disciplined his imaginative facilities, and fully developed his rational mind. To put it precisely, prophecy is an emanation of the divine being which is apprehended through the medium of a man who controls his actions and appetites and has fully prepared his rational facilities (*Guide* 2:37). God sometimes withholds prophecy from those who are prepared for it, but prophecy is seen as the culmination of schooling, and moral discipline, combined with natural endowment, an attainment rather than a bolt out of the blue. We are back in Philo's world, but now the terms are more precisely used, the body of philosophic truths is more clearly defined, and the way to enlightenment is seen as academic as well as contemplative. Maimonides describes Moses' youth as one of study and preparation, and his enlightenment as a result of diligent preparation. Both Ha Levi and Maimonides, incidentally, believed that Moses' ascent was intellectual, not an actual physical translation into the Heavens. For them Moses never left the mountain.

Ha Levi continued to see Moses as a man, as well as a prophet. His Moses was not above sin. In Maimonides' view Moses ultimately became incapable of sin. Maimonides sees prophecy as an attainment achieved by a few men of rare capacity who develop their minds until they are able to receive the knowledge which flows from God. Moses is the consummate philosopher who bcame the consummate prophet. To Maimonides

Moses was the Father of all the prophets before him and all who came after him were beneath him in rank. Moses was chosen by God from the whole of humankind. He comprehended more of God than any man in the past or the future ever comprehended or will comprehend. . . . There was no veil he did not pierce" [CM San. 10:7].

Maimonides describes Moses as one who had raised himself beyond the level of ordinary human beings and who had become, in effect, immortal and incapable of sin. He speaks of Moses as having attained "angelic rank" (ibid). Maimonides did not mean that Moses had become a white-robed winged creature. To Maimonides an angel was one of the animating intelligences who are responsible for the motion of the spheres. For Moses to attain angelic rank is for Moses to have so developed his mind and gained such control of his senses that he has become like these separate intelligences, one who "always did that which is good and only that which is good" (Guide 2:7). Ordinary folk held ordinary ideas about angels, far removed from Maimonides'. Yet, both Maimonides and a bazaar merchant knew Moses as one who had risen beyond all the limitations of mortality. In a strange way the most sophisticated analysis and the simplest piety led in the same direction.

Under Muslim influence rabbinic Jews during these centuries began to practice rituals which centered on the life of the prophet. Egyptian Jews made a yearly pilgrimage to the town of Dammuh, located several miles west of Fustat Misr among the ruins of the old Pharaonic capital of Memphis. A Synagogue of Moses, Kanisat Musa, was located there, which many claimed was built on the spot of Moses' ambassadorial residence during his mission to Pharaoh. This memorial shrine was kept up by contributions from all over Egypt, and formal ceremonies were held there on the seventh of Adar, the traditional day of Moses' death. The Cairo Genizah has yielded a document which lists regulations governing pilgrims on such visits. Benjamin of Tudela (late twelfth century) visited the shrine and reported that it included "a certain pillar made by magical means, the like of which is not seen anywhere else in the country." The existence of this Jewish Ka'abah suggests that Jews had been affected not only by the official Muslim requirement of pilgrimage but by the identification of a meteorite like the Black Stone with a holy place. It is doubtful that Jews worshipped this stone any more than pilgrims to Mecca worship the Black Stone—to do so would have been defined as idolatry by either religion—but their veneration was the next thing to worship. One is reminded of the anecdote told of the caliph Omar who on visiting the Ka'abah is reported to have said, "I know you are a stone that neither helps nor hurts, and if the messenger of Allah had not kissed you, I wouldn't kiss you." And then he kissed the stone.

Jews also began to pay attention to the anniversary of Moses' death. During the eighth and ninth centuries hymns and readings commemorating the death of Moses were introduced into synagogue liturgy. Originally, the practice seems to have been limited to the festival of Simhat Torah. Later such hymns, *piyyutim*, were introduced into the afternoon service of the Sabbath and into the service of the seventh of Adar. An *aggadic* tradition dated Moses' death to the afternoon of a seventh of Adar which fell on a Sabbath. The seventh of Adar was also observed as Moses' birthday, in line with a maxim of conventional piety that "the righteous die on the day of their birth." The life of a righteous man was believed to be symmetrical and harmonious in every way, so his *yahrzeit* was also his birthday. Muslim tradition taught that Mohammed had died on his birthday, the twelfth day of the month Rabi-al-awwal, a Monday.

Commemorative hymns memorializing the death of Moses were added to the liturgy. Researchers have collected almost a hundred such poems from the rites of synagogues where Palestinian and Sephardic customs prevailed. The hymns are essentially versified *Midrashim* based on the text of the required scriptural reading for the festival of Simchat Torah, Deuteronomy 33–34, Moses' valedictory blessing and eulogy. A special *Midrash* collection, *Midrash Petirat Moshe*, was edited based on these chapters, and Joshua 1, the designated *haftarah* of Simhat Torah. This Midrash was studied on the Festival and on the seventh of Adar which, incidentally, was treated as a fast day, a day of mourning.

The earliest of these hymns developed two themes: Moses' commissioning of Joshua as his successor and Moses' efforts to avoid the Angel of Death. Both themes raised important domestic issues and were central in the continuing religious debate with Muslim critics. The officers of the Jewish community had to defend themselves against sporadic challenges to their leadership. They did so by citing Moses' authorization of Joshua as the legitimate basis of their own authority. Theologians of every generation debated the question, How should a community leader be chosen and what were the limits, if any, of the authority he should exercise? The rabbis defended their prerogatives by emphasizing that Moses himself had chosen, instructed, and commissioned Joshua, who stood for all properly ordained leaders, and had defined Joshua's authority as the right to govern under the rules laid down in the Torah. The Jews proudly claimed that as a prophet-caliph Moses had succeeded where Mohammed had failed. Moses provided for the peaceful and effective transfer of power. A struggle over legitimacy, which was destined to split the Muslim world, had broken out immediately after Mohammed's death between the followers of Abu Bekr and the supporters of Ali, Mohammed's son-in-law.

The story of Moses' argument with Death was already well known in Talmudic times. Moses claimed that since he was a thoroughly righteous man, Death had no power over him, for "righteousness delivers from death." He dies, of course, but as these hymns delight to recount, when the Dark Angel arrives to take Moses' soul, Moses successfully defies him. In the end it is God, not the Angel of Death, who takes his soul. By way of contrast Muslim traditions picture Mohammed as sick, resigned and docile. Gabriel is supposed to have said to him, "Apostle of God, Death asks for permission to enter." The Angel of Death enters and asks, "Apostle of God, shall I strike at your life?" and Mohammed answers, "Fulfill, O Death, the command." To many Jews the contrast between Moses' defiance and Mohammed's passivity proved Moses' superiority. If pressed the rabbis had a proof text for this particular scenario. The text is the Torah portion read on Simhat Torah which begins: "This is the blessing with which Moses, the man of God, bade the Israelites farewell before he died." The concluding phrase, "before he died," would seem to be redundant. Moses could not have spoken this blessing after his death. It is possible to read the Hebrew "in the presence of Death"; to capitalize *death* in this way brings the Black Angel into the scene and allows an imaginative sage to create a situation in which Moses secures for Israel the promise of immortality.

R. Abin said that all of his life Moses had wished to bless Israel, but the Angel of Death (knowing that Moses' blessing of Israel would limit death's dominion) did not allow Moses to bestow the blessing. What did Moses finally do? He seized and bound the Angel of Death and, having cast him down at his feet, blessed Israel in the very presence of the Angel. . . . "And what blessing did he bestow on them?" "Save your people and bless your inheritance, shepherd them, carry them forever" (Ps. 28:9) [PRK Sup. 1:10].

The value of such a blessing might seem to be blunted by the fact that Moses ultimately loses his struggle and dies. The hymns therefore emphasize the special conditions which surround Moses' death—God Himself took his soul with a kiss and the three senior archangels bury his body— to suggest the distinction between death as extinction and death as a prelude to immortality. Death cannot obliterate Moses. He dies as his faithful followers die, not into the fearsome hands of the dark forces but into the care of God.

I cannot help but believe that these hymns and discussions helped Jews accept the inevitability of death; no one, not even Moses, is immune. "Moses led his people in justice and perfection/He strengthened them and gave them laws and wisdom/And when he died Israel spoke with sorrow/Moses died; who then shall not die?" (Weinberg 284).

Moreover, if Moses had to die no one need feel impugned by death, a feeling which was, unfortunately, all too common and taken far too seriously at the time by Jews who had been conditioned to believe that everyone died for his sins. These hymns probably had another psychological benefit. Even though God has told Moses that he will be welcomed in Heaven, the incomparable prophet doesn't want to die and is anxious, if not downright frightened, at the prospect of death. At the very least, those who had never been in Heaven and had no guarantee of entry—that is, everyone other than Moses—could appreciate and draw comfort from the fact that their fears were natural and human.

Such was the brilliance of the various small circles of intellectuals who stimulated the renaissance of Jewish letters during the eleventh and twelfth centuries that there is a tendency to forget that for all their philosophic sophistication they were medieval men. The scholar-poet-wanderer, Judah Al-Harizi (1170–1235), was a slightly younger contemporary of Maimonides, who corresponded with many in Maimonides' circle and translated from Arabic into Hebrew the philosopher's *Commentary on the Mishnah* and *The Guide of the Perplexed*. His own views on Moses are not known, but the fifteenth chapter of his *maqama*, or extended dialogue-novel, *The Tahkemoni*, is entitled "A Prayer of Moses, the man of God, that opens the gates on high to all who recite it," and purports to be a prayer whose recital guarantees results. Al-Harizi's work is designed as a report of conversations between two friends who report what they have seen and done in their lives. In this chapter one of the friends, Heman, tells of being shipwrecked and of losing all his possessions. When he returns home a comforter, Heber, visits him. Heber cannot offer Heman what he most needs, money; but he can give him "from what God has allotted to me . . . a prayer of Moses, the man of God, which will open for you the gates on high and bring you early deliverance." If Heman recites this prayer three times a day, addresses it properly to Moses, and behaves as a righteous man should, "God will open to you His good treasure, the Heavens, and will pour on you His blessing."

Al-Harizi himself may not have believed in the efficacy of this prayer—a *maqama* was a poetic fiction which offers a panorama of the life of the times—but there is no sarcasm or innuendo in his presentation; and if the author did not believe in Moses as a heavenly intercessor, he certainly knew many who did. The prayer begins with a request that the angels bring the worshipper's lavish praises of Moses to the place where he sits in God's court. Moses is God's faithful messenger, the incomparable prophet, the most humble yet most illustrious of men. "Moses is our master who brought us out of darkness to light." He caused us to inherit law and truth. He is from the best stock. All men find enlightenment in him. He ascended to Heaven with a fully prepared mind. The angels who preceded him sang as he approached, "open the gates so that the choicest of the chosen may enter." The ministering angels made Moses welcome. In Heaven he was taught every hidden secret. He spoke to God face to face; and when he returned to earth he carried back the crystalline tablets of Instruction. After the praise comes the petition:

O righteous one, foundation of the world, bring me up out of my snare through your entreaties. Peradventure, your righteous deeds which you have done beforehand in the land of the living will plead on my behalf for good and will bring me hastily out of the pit of grief. For I know that the living who in their lifetime were joined together with God, in their death will not be divided. Therefore, I lay hold of the skirts of your glory so that you may have compassion upon me. I will not let you go, except you bless me, and plead good on my behalf, for from you the celestial saints learned to intercede for good on behalf of debtors [*al-Harizi* 15].

A prayer to be quit of debt is hardly the stuff of spiritual exaltation, but it is altogether human. We recognize such praise of Moses as unique to the times, a profession of faith by one who believed in Moses as well as in God. In Biblical times the Torah was trusted because it was the Word of God; Moses was simply the chosen messenger. Now the character of the prophet is an important factor in substantiating the authority of the revelation. Two elements were significant in the Muslim creed, that Allah was God and that Mohammed was His prophet. Both elements are now significant in Judaism. God is One and Moses is His prophet:

He [Moses] is the Lord of all Creation and our lord who puts the fear of God upon our faces; who joins the Divine Radiance and us together; who makes us worthy to behold in the world to come the face of the living God; who gives us to eat of the fruit of the tree of life in the garden of Eden, of whom we said: "Under his shadow we shall live among the nations!" He lives, although his pure body be dead. He is revealed to the eye of thought, though his soul be hid. He is blessed by the mouth of Him Who dwells in the lofty heights. He is our lord, and the lord of all that is created: Moses, the man of God [al-Harizi 15].

An interesting document reveals another side of the sophisticated credulity and special veneration which is shown toward Moses in certain circles, a letter of encouragement written in 1159–60 by Maimonides' father, Maimon b.

Joseph, to the beleaguered Jewish community of Fez, a community in which he had once lived. Maimon, a competent scholar, had been *dayyan* in Cordoba and was a disciple of the Talmudic master, Joseph ibn Migash; in brief, an accredited member of the intellectual class. North Africa had just been overrun by fervent Muslim Berbers, the Almohades, who zealously persecuted all nonbelievers and used every form of psychological and physical coercion to secure Jewish converts. Maimon's letter was addressed to a Jewish community which was in the eye of the storm.

Maimon writes of the certainty of God's redemption. He reminds his correspondents that Moses continues to serve Israel in Heaven and will continue to do so "until a time shall come when God will be pleased with His world and send Moses back to it to assist the King who is to reign" (*JQR* 11:99–100). He is certain that Moses will play a major role in the messianic drama. Several of the hymns written to memorialize the death of Moses shared this hope. "May God preserve you [Moses] forever/That you may again be our teacher in the latter days/As you were before in the first days/And may [you] soon join [together] the wonderful people and come to them" (Weinberg 222).

Maimon sees no hope of quick relief from Muslin pressures and oppression nor can he promise that the Exile will soon end. But he insists, in traditional fashion, that God has promised to redeem Israel, and patience and loyalty will be rewarded. Israel can have faith in redemption because God Himself promised it and because the promise was transmitted by "our teacher [Moses] who speaks only the truth." Maimon seems almost to suggest that Moses' repetition of God's words added authority to them.

For Maimon, Moses is "the best of creatures, the greatest

of men, the noblest of apostles." Moses was created separately from the rest of mankind, physically perfect and twice again as tall as any other person. Though the angels fear to speak to God for more than a moment, Moses spoke with Him for forty days and forty nights, not once but twice. Moses was not of the same flesh and blood as other mortals; his body was as pure as that of the angels. Moses' hands were so pure that he could take hold of the Throne of Glory, which even the archangels were afraid to touch. His feet were so pure that he could walk on the clouds of holy light. When he laid his hands on Joshua to commission him as his successor, capacity flowed into Joshua so that in a mere six months he was able to understand all the Torah. Even when he was a child divine light played on Moses' face, and as he grew older the light grew in intensity until no one dared look at him unless Moses shrouded his face with a veil. One could not even look at his back without shielding one's eyes. Maimon finds Moses' virtue and power comforting. Through the greatness of the apostle you will understand the greatness of the Power Who sent him.

Maimon insists that Moses' power still protects Israel. Moses' death did not end his power.

When we say 'his death' we must not liken it to the death of mortal men. His corpse remained pure even in death. He was as if in a sleep for God appeared to him as usual. . . . His spirit was taken from him . . . without the bitterness of death and it was at once united with the angels and clothed with the body of angels like Michael and Gabriel. . . . Even when he was among the angels his power was not less than theirs. It was not lost when he was clothed in bodily form; surely, it was not less now that he was clothed in the form of angels [*JQR* 11:99–100].

When told of his impending death, Moses had worried that there would be times when the people would lack a teacher who could instruct them in the certainties of God's promises. To prevent this, Moses foretold the history of Israel and spoke the blessing which guaranteed that the promised redemption will occur (Deut. 32–33). Maimon then picks up a tradition which associated Psalm 90, the one psalm ascribed to Moses, with his valedictory hymn, Deuteronomy 32. Deuteronomy states the promise "the Lord will vindicate His people and take revenge for His servants" (32:36) and Psalm 90 elaborates, "O satisfy us in the morning with Thy mercy; that we may rejoice and be glad all our days" (14).

Maimon concludes with an extended line-by-line commentary on this psalm by "Moses, the man of God," a phrase he interprets to mean that Moses was and is *the* man of God, the only such who ever lived. Then Maimon offers a personal confession, unusual in rabbinic literature. For many years he has recited this psalm every morning as part of his regular devotions. He has done so not simply because he is stimulated and encouraged by its promises, but as a mystical exercise. By restating the prophet's words Maimon believes he is hastening their realization, and he tells his correspondents that if they adopt the same practice their confidence in the future will be strengthened and redemption will be hastened. Change a word here and there and you could easily imagine Maimon asking his correspondents to accept Moses as their savior, just as a minister might ask the unbaptized to accept Christ. Technically, this was not the case, but there is no doubt that he is encouraging the transformation of their essentially passive faith into an ac-

tive one by becoming one with the spirit of "the first apostle." Judaism here approaches as close to Mosaism as it will
ever come.

Parallels are notoriously difficult to establish, but the life
and writing of the philosophically minded Muslim mystic,
Ibnu l'Arabi (1165–1240), come to mind. Ibnu l'Arabi tells
of talking with Mohammed in the World of Ideal Forms
while the prophet was seated on a throne surrounded by
angels, prophets, and saints. He calls Mohammed the Perfect Man and sees him as the Logos, the Mediator, *Khalifat
Allah*, the vice-regent of God, in effect a God-man who has
descended to earth to make manifest God's Glory (Nichol-
son 403). Contemplating the words of Mohammed is one
way of attaching oneself to the Divine Spirit and, by so
doing, adding to the redemptive force of that spirit. The influence of this speculative Sufi teacher, called the Grand
Master, was great, and it is altogether possible that some of
the same Neo-Platonic, Gnostic, Sufi, and mystical ideas
around which Ibnu l'Arabi built his ideas influenced the
way Maimon shaped his. In both cases the Prophet is clearly
someone who has transcended human limitations and who
is or has become one with some manifestation of God's
Presence. The influence of Ibnu l'Arabi on Maimon, Maimonides, and especially Maimon's scholarly grandson,
Abraham Maimonides (1186–1237), whose writings have
long been acknowledged to show the influence of Sufi specu-
lations, requires closer examination.

We noted earlier that the naming practices of the Muslim
world encouraged Jews to break completely with the venerable taboo against naming a son Moses. Many of the names
which became popular among the Jews of Arab lands during

these centuries express the communities' messianic hopes: Sar Shalom (prince of Peace); Mevasser (messenger of good tidings); Semah (sprout [of David, cf. Zech, 6:12]); Sherira (the saved remnant). I believe that Moses' name should be added to the list.

CHAPTER
# VIII

# Moses and
# the Kabbalah

**K**ABBALAH simply means received tradition. The term was used in Talmudic times to describe those teachings which were accepted as Torah but were not included in the written Torah. In the thirteenth century Kabbalah began to be used as a specific label for the esoteric teachings of Judaism and ever since has designated the world of mystic activity, theosophic speculation, and messianic calculation which provided much of the emotional energy and spiritual urgency of Jewish life during the Middle Ages.

The mystic tradition of Judaism has Biblical roots. When the prophet Isaiah visited the Temple in Jerusalem he sensed the numinous, God, reaching out to him from the Holy of Holies and heard angels calling out to each other: "Holy, holy, holy is the Lord of hosts, the whole earth is full of His glory" (Isa. 6:3), words which the medieval mystics often repeated as a mantra in their spiritual exercises. The best-known instance of theosophical vision in the Bible appears in the opening chapters of the book of the prophet

Ezekiel. The Jerusalem Temple had just been destroyed; Ezekiel, who found himself among the exiles in Babylon, had a vision of the Presence of God coming from the north to be with the captives. Later, during the Second Temple period, particularly toward its close, apocalyptics flourished; their knowledge of the future course of history and of messianic matters was based on secrets revealed to them in Heaven, usually by an angel or immortal. A small number of apocalyptic tracts named Moses as the mediator of this secret wisdom. *The Assumption of Moses* (first century C.E.) purports to record the prophet's final instructions to his successor, Joshua. Moses tells Joshua that he is bequeathing to him several volumes of apocalyptic secrets and that, after he has read them, they should be properly wrapped and buried so that they can be taken out on the Day of Redemption and bear witness to God's control of history (Assumption 1:16–18).

During the Talmudic period, many rabbis practiced what came to be called *kabbalah ma'asit*, the use of secret knowledge to heal, curse, and exorcise. We have discussed the Name mysticism on which many of their powers were presumably based. At about this time the so-called *Hechalot*, Palace Literature, began to appear, describing the sights a mystic would see once he had gained entrance to the Palace, as well as the discipline he must practice and protective formulae he must know to gain admission. The esoteric tradition came to include a wide range of subjects: revelations about the Messiah, Judgment Day, Resurrection, and the hidden world and its inhabitants and wonders—angels, evil spirits, the immortals, God's court, and His Throne of Glory. The term *Kavod*, glory, became the general term for the whole field of interest.

# Moses and the Kabbalah

During the Islamic period, Jews, like their neighbors, buried incantation bowls under the thresholds of their homes, paid holy men to conjure up angelic intercessors and to write amulets which could shield the anxious and ill from evil spirits. But during the ninth and tenth centuries, the heyday of the Geonim, the rabbis as a class seem to have distanced themselves from the *ba'alei ha'shem*, the users of The Name. Diviners, exorcisers, and wonder-workers now tended to be found on the fringes of the educated class. This separation of the holy man from the rabbi was in many ways due to Mohammed. Mohammed denied that he was a wonder-worker. Islam's religious authorities followed the pattern he had set; they concentrated on the *shariyah*, the legal tradition, leaving the esoteric and theosophic traditions, the unofficial religious life, to a variety of holy men, fakirs, and Sufis. Jews fell into the same pattern. Religious leadership rested with the masters and disciples of the great schools which trained their graduates to act as jurists and teachers in the communities. Those rabbis of mystic bent, and there must have been a goodly number, kept their interests and activities fairly private. There was now an official religio-political enterprise and an unofficial religio-mystical one— and no measurable diminution of interest among the masses in theosophy or magic.

Rationality and community discipline are important virtues but they are not the virtues which enliven the religious spirit. The rabbis who occupied themselves with "official" Judaism sounded basic themes and doctrines that were ethically noble but held out an elusive promise. God had revealed the way at Sinai. The community had failed in its duties under the Covenant and consequently had been sentenced to exile. The purpose of the religious life was *te-*

*shuvah*, repentance, the full return of the community to the practice of God's Instructions. God had promised that when *teshuvah* was fully accomplished, He would send the Messiah.

Since the rabbinic view of man rules out his transformation into a saint and expects no one to fully transcend the contradictions of his nature, the Jew could not prove—or expect to prove—to God that his *teshuvah* was complete. In essence, the Jew was told, Do your best, be patient and throw yourself on God's mercy. In sermon after sermon the Jew was reminded that at the gates of Heaven he would be asked, "Did you *wait* confidently for deliverance?"

Patience has its limits. When the skies began to darken in the twelfth and thirteenth centuries a growing number of the religious intelligentsia in northern Spain and southern France could not or would not believe that there was nothing they could do to hasten redemption. A religious program based on obedience and patience no longer satisfied them. These were disappointing times. Religious apartheid sought to separate the religious communities and, more, to degrade the Jew; the special dress he was forced to wear was the mark of Cain. Long legislated by the Church, demeaning dress codes were now enforced by the Catholic kings. These were desperate times and places. The Spanish and Albigensian Crusade and the Inquisition were in full cry. The Mozarabs, the Catharii, and Christian heretics were the designated victims, but the Jews, too, felt the heat and power of the Imperial Church. Kabbalah flourished in a deteriorating political situation. One of the early leaders of the Spanish Kabbalists, the Catalan exegete-Talmudist, Nahmanides (1194–1270), was forced by his king into a public debate with an apostate; though he conducted himself with courage and circumspection, the very fact that he had publicly challenged some Christian affirmations led the local clergy to demand and win an edict of permanent exile.

We know more about medieval Kabbalah than about earlier forms of the Jewish theosophic tradition because the medieval mystics tended to be somewhat more open about these matters than earlier sages who had, for the most part, obeyed Talmudic restrictions which sealed off the esoteric tradition from public discussion. The major reason for the change was cultural. Sufi masters and Christian monks were openly teaching the mystic way, and much which had once been secret was no longer. A spate of books devoted to the Kabbalah appeared, none revealing "everything" but all containing broad hints. By the end of the twelfth century one can, for the first time, speak of a widely dispersed Kabbalistic culture.

Throughout the Middle Ages there was, as there had always been, an esoteric tradition concerned primarily with the use of secret knowledge to effect a cure, exorcise a dybbuk, determine the propitious date for a marriage, or protect the home from the ghosts of the dead. What is new is the spread of Kabbalah among the rabbinic class. A learned and speculative Kabbalah began to flourish which combined Talmud, philosophy, and theosophy in a unique blend. Kabbalah came to represent a sophisticated mystical and theosophical culture with special idioms and rituals, animated by the conviction that a master of Kabbalah could do something about Israel's destiny. Kabbalah's original theme is the assertion that an adept can affect God and impel the redemptive enterprise. The Kabbalist was not willing to wait patiently for deliverance.

Kabbalah's appeal derived from its ability to set the tradi-

tional passivity of rabbinic Judaism aside without challeng-
ing familiar patterns of authority or practice. The mystics
were observant and learned Jews; what they rejected was
only the emphasis on patience which lay at the heart of Talmudic theology's teaching that the ultimate virtue was *bittahon*, steadfast confidence, a loyal acceptance of the yoke
of the commandments and calm endurance under the chas-
tenings of God. In the Bible God controls man. In Kabbalah
the special man, he who knows, has some control over God.
Kabbalah presupposes a gnosis, a special and saving wisdom
given, some said to Adam, but most said to Moses, which
had been kept secret and preserved by a select few in each
generation. Presumedly, the security of the community, Israel's redemption and mankind's, depend on those who
have mastered the secret lore. Nahmanides, in explaining
the motivation which had prompted the Israelites to build
and worship the Golden Calf, seriously suggests that the
Calf was built not as an idol but as a replacement for Moses,
the *moreh derech*, the person or object full of magical power
who keeps the community alive and secure. The camp had
miscalculated the time Moses had told them he would remain away; when Moses did not appear when they expected
him, they despaired of his return and could not contemplate
even a day without some power like his among them.

The Kabbalists gave Moses' familiar title, *ish-elohim*,
God's man, a new meaning. In Hebrew law *ish* designates a
husband and rabbinic exegesis uses *elohim* as God's Name,
which refers particularly to His attribute of mercy and is
identified with His Immanent Presence, or the *Shekinah*.
Combining these definitions, *ish-elohim* can be translated
"husband of the *Shekinah*." A sermon preached on the festival of Simhat Torah reads, "Were it not written in the

Torah it would be impossible to say such a thing as this: just as a man gives an order to his wife, so Moses gave orders to the Holy One to have things done" (PRK Sup. 1:13). Basing his sermon on Deuteronomy 33, which contains Moses' blessing of the tribes, the preacher is saying that by speaking this blessing Moses was, in effect, forcing God to abide by the promises that Moses had made.

How Moses—and the masters of Kabbalah—manage to have power over God requires explanation. Kabbalah moves beyond Biblical assumptions that God acts as He wishes whenever He wills and that God's being is simple and singular. It develops a constuct in which God is conceived not as a simple unity but as a complex unity in which divinity flows within and between all the parts. There is a hidden life of God. There is a constant movement of divine energy from the upper world to the lower world, and there is a constant return of divine energy from the lower world into the upper spheres. Everything emerges from God, including the attributes of God, and everything returns to God, including man's thought and speech.

Isaiah had seen God seated on a high throne surrounded by cherubim. *Hechalot* writings had described the Heavens as a city consisting of seven concentric walled areas with God's Palace in the innermost court and God as a presence seated on the Throne of Glory behind a veil in the innermost room of the Palace. Some of the theosophical books of Talmudic times, like the *Shiur Komah*, had even included suggestions about God's majestic size. In Kabbalah a new image emerges, one more appropriate to a tradition which claimed to take seriously the Second Commandment. God is not a majestic presence on the throne, but *Ein Sof,* a dark, impenetrable mystery from which light or speech emerges, forming various *sefirot,* or emanations, each manifesting the flow of divinity. *Ein sof* is the ultimate mystery, formless and unknowable, the mystery of God's transcendence. The *sefirot* are manifestations of God's Immanence, separate yet mysteriously part of God's unity. The Torah's simple imagery—God decides and brings into being—is replaced with an image of a number of emanations revealing themselves and existing permanently outside God's unknowable essence. These manifestations are described as *sefirot,* steps outward or downward toward the familiar world.

The *sefirot* are links between man and the unknowable transcendent God. They participate in God's unity and are described as discrete manifestations of the unity; at the same time, each emanation is assumed to have a particular quality and to affect different areas of earthly life. Something of the flavor of this approach can be illustrated from the kind of commentary on the Torah Kabbalists began to write. The closing paragraph of the second chapter of Exodus indicates that when the king of Egypt died the Israelites cried out because of their misery and that God heard their cry. The actual text reads: "God looked upon the Israelites, and God took notice of them" (2:25). Nahmanides was intrigued by the duplication of phrases in this text, which he explains "by way of the truth" as "a suggestion of one of the great mysteries of the Torah." These two phrases, he insists, indicate two separate actions within God: "the afflictions of the Israelites came up first to the attribute which is closest to man and then were passed along to the attribute which is the closest to the unknowable *Ein sof*" (Nah. to Exod. 2:25).

Conditioned by the idea that light streams down from Heaven, the Greek tradition generally described the flow of divinity as a stream of light and the goal of mystic communion as enlightenment. Many Kabbalists also used light metaphors to define the *shefa,* the divine flow. But there was also an understanding of the *shefa* which defined the primal substance not as light but as speech. God's speech flows through these emanations, slowly taking up recognizable meanings and shapes until it becomes the words/forms by which the world is created and the words/Instructions of which Torah is constituted. Conversely, man's speech, prayer, and meditation, properly directed, ascend through the power of mystic meditation and concentration until they are purified of earthbound meanings and become one again with heavenly speech. *Shefa* seen as speech was a uniquely useful image for Jewish thinkers. A Kabbalist could easily identify the Torah as a manifestation of God's speech. He could also validate most of the peculiarly Jewish mystical exercises through which he and his colleagues expected to prepare themselves for communion with and/or effect on God. Among those exercises was the practice of *kavannah,* a purposeful concentration on certain Torah readings or liturgical recitations, on words, in the expectation of propelling the divine essence of these words, God's speech, into the *sefirot.* By concentrating on the divine within the words of his prayers and on the particular *sefirah* to which the prayer was addressed, the mystic felt that he could send creative speech back toward the source from which it had, unfortunately, been detached. In this way he fills the Heavens again with the *shefa,* the flow of the divine.

*Shekinah* represents the emanation closest to man, the one through which man apprehends divinity. The name is taken from a Hebrew root which means "to dwell" and was used to personify the Presence of God in human life and the principle of divine immanence in creation. Kabbalah reserves the term for the outermost of the circles or for the lowest, depending on the image being used. Generally, most Kabbalists taught that it is through the *Shekinah* that the divine light or speech reaches the earth and that man's prayers and speech reach the *sefirot*.

Kabbalah is not a single theosophic system but a collection of metaphysical constructs developed by speculatively minded scholars who spent time and effort puzzling out the mysterious relationships between God and creation and between God and the Jewish people. Some systems assumed that the divine flow comes to the earth through the lowest and closest of the emanations, others that all the *sefirot* could affect and be affected by human activity. All agreed that whatever happens on high affects life below and whatever happens here below affects what happens on high. The *Zohar*, the "bible" of the Kabbalists, notes that Moses' first reaction when Amalek attacked the tribes was to tell Joshua, "Pick some men for us and go out and do battle" (Exod. 17:8); it then asks rhetorically, "Why did Moses abstain from fighting in this, the first battle which God Himself had commanded?" The *Zohar's* answer is that Moses had divined the true meaning of his master's command; hence, he said 'I will prepare myself for the war above and you, Joshua, prepare yourself for the war below.' This is the meaning of the words 'When Moses lifted up his hand Israel prevailed' (Exod. 17:11). That is, Israel prevailed in the Heavens above." (*Zohar* Exod. 65b). To the author it is clear that Moses did not participate in the war on earth, so that he would not be distracted from the war in Heaven where the issue of victory would be decided.

It was assumed that the proper relationship among the ten *sefirot* and the relationships betweeen the upper and

Moses and the Kabbalah

lower spheres had been disturbed, some said by the evil forces, *sitra ahra*, some said by Adam's sin, and others by Israel's sins. And it was believed that the restoration of these relationships depends largely on man, specifically on the actions of the prayermaster or the mystic adept. The process by which the mystic affected God was called *tikkun*. Through mystic contemplation of God's speech as manifested in the Torah or in the liturgy or through the recitation of other formulae which express the power of God, the adept returns God's words, something of God's essence, to the Heavens, and brings the world closer to redemption.

The upper and lower worlds, some Kabbalists taught, were sometimes close to each other, sometimes far apart. The upper and lower worlds had been close at creation. God had intended for things to remain that way, but Adam had sinned and God's Presence had moved off. It moved further away when Cain murdered Abel and further still during the wicked generations of the flood, the Tower of Babel, and Sodom and Gomorrah. The piety of the patriarchs had drawn the Presence of God closer and the special merit of Moses had brought the Presence of God back to the nearness that the upper and lower spheres had enjoyed at creation. The two worlds touched when Moses ascended to meet God and God's Presence descended to meet Moses; but then the Israelites sinned with the Golden Calf and the Heavens and earth moved apart. When the tribes refused to obey God in the wilderness, the Presence of God moved still further away. Once they entered the Promised Land the sins of Israel grew greater and greater until distance became concretized in the exile. The Kabbalist was confident that he could, through his actions, bring the two worlds closer together and bring nearer Israel's redemption.

Moses had brought the divine speech, the Torah, down from Heaven. Following his pattern and using the secret knowledge which Moses had passed on, the adept could draw some of the divine flow to Israel, thereby strengthening the community. Moses' career suggested this role. The battle with the Amalekites was the famous struggle in which Israel prevailed as long as Moses' hands were lifted heavenward. According to the Kabbalists, by lifting up his ten fingers, Moses drew down strength from each of the ten *sefirot* so that they would fight for Israel (Nah. to Exod. 17:12). The uplifting of the hands during the Priestly Benediction had for centuries been viewed as a protective act. During Second Temple days the community had associated the power of this benediction with the fact that the ineffable Name of God was spoken during the blessing. The medieval Kabbalists lived at a time when the Tetragrammaton was no longer spoken aloud, and they associated the power of this moment with the upraised hands of a priest concentrating on the *kavannah* of the blessing. If he was capable and prepared, he drew down the divine flow to the congregation.

In Talmudic times prayer was understood as petition addressed to God. Kabbalistic prayer was a complicated business. The adept needs to know exactly which of the divine manifestations is to be addressed, which prayer mantra will be most effective, and how to achieve the mental state which will release that prayer's power. Nahmanides' discussion of one of Moses' intercessions illustrates the approach. God's anger ran high when the tribal council refused His command to begin immediately the conquest of Canaan and He announced that He would disown the nation. Moses intercedes. His exact language is: "Let my Lord's forbear-

ance be great" (Num. 14:17). Nahmanides explains that
Moses specifically evokes the *sefirot* of Long Suffering and
Loving Kindness and carefully avoids evoking the *sefirah* of
Truth for, in truth, the people were guilty, and it would
have been disastrous to summon that *sefirah* (Nah. to Num.
14:17). Mystical prayer is so complex and subtle an art that
even armed with knowledge the adept is not always successful; Moses prays effectively for a successor, futilely for
the privilege of entering Canaan.

The famous section, chapter 3 of Exodus, in which Moses
asks God for His Name, is presented by the Torah straight-
forwardly. Moses wants to know how to identify God to the
Hebrews, and God tells him how. In the Talmud the sages
treat this text as the dialogue during which God reveals to
Moses the secrets of His Name. The Kabbalists took the
Talmudic explanation for granted and, further, read the dialogue as a coded discussion through which Moses discovers
the nature of his mission. They were intrigued by Moses'
question: "When I come to the Israelites and say to them,
'The God of your Fathers has sent me' and they ask me
'What is this name?' what shall I say to them?" Moses, they
observed, must have known that a name out of the blue
would have no impact on the Israelites and, never one to
waste time or effort, he must have had something else in
mind when he asked this question. According to their interpretation, Moses was asking God which of the *sefirot* would
control his mission. If his mission would be governed by one
of the lower emanations, he would know that his task was
simply to bring about the Exodus, a purely political act. If
his mission was governed by the highest emanation, it would
involve the creation of something new—the mediation of
the Torah. In effect, Nahmanides says, Moses was told by

the wording of his commission that he was not only to redeem but to reveal (Nah. to Exod. 3:13).

Let us follow this reasoning. If Moses already understood the creative nature of his mission, why did he hesitate? Some early commentators had even suggested that Moses was sent against his will. The Kabbalists understood why Moses had at first tried to avoid God's commission. It is dangerous to meddle with matters divine and no small matter to believe the future of the world depends on your activities. Many Kabbalists really did not want to get into the business of dealing with God, but they were irresistibly drawn.

Though interest in Kabbalah was broadly shared in medieval Jewry and scholars can describe a Kabbalistic culture, mysticism is essentially a solitary enterprise whose procedures and techniques have varied surprisingly little over the centuries. The mystic way is a private way. The Greek term *myein* from which our word *mystic* derives designates the discipline of shutting out the distractions and influences of the outside world. Students of religious experience usually define three separate but consecutive states through which the mystic passes: an unexpected awakening of interest and concern; a period of concentrated preparation and purification; and the liberating sense of having attained illumination or communion.

A unique feature of the Kabbalah, one which distinguishes it from Christian mysticism, is that the Jewish mystic rarely writes of his experience. Anyone who approaches Kabbalist literature hoping for a look into the mystic's inner life will leave disappointed. Most of this literature is highly conceptual and speculative, downright dull. The writer rarely tells us why or how he became interested in the precipitating incident. At most we learn a bit about the period of preparation. Some studied Torah the night long, seeking the manifestation of God which lies within and behind every line and word. Others placed their heads between their knees and recited hymns of esoteric import. Others fasted, bathed in cold rivers, and rose at midnight to meditate on the mysteries and to wrestle with the furies of evil.

As might be expected, in their discussions of the mystical experience, these men often used incidents taken from Moses' life: the unexpected summons at the Burning Bush; the seven days of separation and preparation before the ascent of Mount Sinai; and the time of enlightenment, the forty days and forty nights on the mountain top when Moses spoke face to face with God. The Kabbalists found the Torah's narrative suggestive in many ways. Moses had asked to see God and had learned this was not possible: "You cannot see My Face, for man may not see Me and live" (Exod. 33:20). Kabbalah is a mysticism of limits which promises an experience of God's Presence but not comprehension of God's Essence. The mystic can sense God but not see God. Kabbalist theory assumed that there was an unknowable God, the dark and impenetrable *Ein Sof*, and that what Moses saw, God's back (Exod. 33:23), was the flow of light or speech which at creation went out from the *Ein Sof* and formed itself into *sefirot*.

Kabbalah was remarkable in another aspect; it represents the least institutionally subversive of all major mystical traditions. Mysticism, since it claims direct contact with God and knowledge of divine secrets, by its very nature poses a constant potential challenge to authorized religious ways and traditional leadership groups. But since the Kabbalists were, for the most part, well-trained Talmudists, pious members of the Jewish community, and often part of the leadership, that challenge rarely emerged, at least not in the early years. Three safeguards were established to insure that their speculation did not get out of hand and subvert the revered tradition. Raising Moses to a special rank was one. Separation of the mystic way from the prophetic way was another. A third was to make it appear that all their teaching derived from the accepted Torah.

A little-noticed but important characteristic of the Kabbalah is that these men who found Moses' experience so enlightening never spoke of duplicating the intimacy with God Moses had enjoyed. They lavishly praise Moses. He is *av ha-hochmah* (Nah. to Exod. 3:13), the father of esoteric wisdom; and *gadol b'ma'alat ha-nevuah*, first in prophetic rank (Nah. to Exod. 3:2). Both titles imply singularity, as well as superiority. No mortal can expect to go where Moses had gone or know what Moses had known. The Kabbalists looked on themselves as mystics rather than prophets and sharply distinguished the two phenomena. The prophet receives the Word of God. The initiative is God's and the received words are specific and instructional. The mystic seeks to draw close to God. The initiative is his. Though his experience is exalting, his moment of communion is temporary and he does not expect to come down from the heights armed with new teaching. The Kabbalists' goal was *Gilluy Shekinah*, a sense of God's Presence, rather than specific Instructions from God.

They underscored in many ways the difference between all other moments of communion and Moses' experience with God. Saint Bonaventura defined mysticism as "the reaching out of the soul to God through the yearning of love." Most mystical traditions employ graphic sexual imagery to express the exaltation of mystical attachment. Generally a celibate, the mystic feels urgent expectation and liberating fulfillment that often simulate highly erotic sensations. The Kabbalah does not use love or sex images as metaphors for man's communion with God, *devekut*. There is one exception: Moses' relationship with God is described as a mating. The *Zohar*, the freewheeling esoteric commentary on the Torah, spins out an image based on Moses' activity once he had completed the desert sanctuary. The Torah says: "On the day Moses finished [*kallot*] setting up the Tabernacle, he anointed and consecrated it" (Num. 7:1). Connecting the Hebrew verb *kallot* with the Hebrew noun *kallah*, bride, the *Zohar* states, "This was the day when the bride entered under the wedding canopy, and it was by the hand of Moses [as Moses' bride] that she entered there" (*Zohar* Num. 148a). When a mystic cleaves to God he figuratively takes the *Shekinah* as his bride. In the monogamous European Jewish community, the mystic felt he must first give up his earthly bride. Kabbalists were advocates of ascetic denial, but celibacy posed something of a theological problem for them. On the one hand, withdrawal from all family connections is the usual first step in any program designed to shut out the distractions of the world. On the other hand, the Torah emphasizes the importance of marriage and family. According to the Talmud one of the principal questions which will be asked of every Jew on Judgment Day is: "Did you fulfill your duty with respect to establishing a family" (b. Shab 31a)? The Kabbalists resolved this conflict of obligations by advocating that they be fulfilled sequentially. First, they said, establish a family and fulfill the command to have children and then put family interests aside and concentrate on God. The text continues:

"Someone asks why Moses is praised for putting Zipporah aside. God Himself answers, 'Moses had already fulfilled the command of bearing children, now I want him to espouse the *Shekinah.*"

Reserving this image of a mystic marriage to Moses' relationship with God underscores its uniqueness in human experience. The marriage metaphor not only emphasizes the closeness of Moses and God—at Sinai they were as one—but allows the Kabbalists to say with confidence that the Torah passed between Heaven and earth without being at any time separated from God, thus retaining its divine power on which so much depended.

The *Zohar* applies the same metaphor—images of mystic marriage and intimate love—to the relationships among the *sefirot.* Just as there can be no separation between these dynamic elements of the divine unity, so there was no separation between Moses and God. Only Moses among all men knew this union with God—and we are left with a conception of Moses participating in the divine unity. Where the Bible's Moses is a human prophet summoned to God's service, the Kabbalah's Moses is a unicum, a man like unto no other: "From the place Moses was formed no other man was formed" (*Zohar* Exod. 21b). In the *aggadah* Moses is clothed with light and becomes a heavenly creature on his death; the Kabbalah suggests that divinity was always part of his nature.

Moses is the link between the Heavenly Torah which is God's self-revelation and the Written Torah of the synagogue. He is also the guarantor that the Kabbalists are not conjuring up improbable fancies. Moses had seen the Heavenly Torah which consists only of the Names of God and had been taught the code which unlocks the secrets of the

Torah which had been revealed. To the Kabbalists the familiar Torah of commandments and prohibitions is not the real thing but a manifestation of God's speech appropriate and necessary to the human condition. The author of the *Ra'aya Meheimna* (fourteenth century), a late section of the *Zohar*, identifies these two Torahs with the two tablets of the law: the one Moses broke and the one he brought down after his second forty days and later deposited in the Ark. The first tablet, which had been shattered, had been made of the Tree of Life and consisted entirely of the Names of God. It was a straightforward manifestation of God's being. No earthling but Moses had ever read this Torah. The second tablet had been made of the Tree of Knowledge and included the rules and prohibitions with which all Jews are familiar. The trees, of course, are from the Garden of Eden story and by using these symbols the author makes the point that the tablet made of the Tree of Life was appropriate until men sinned. All that an innocent Adam needed was a manifestation of God which he could ceaselessly contemplate. Once man had sinned and all the contradictions of his nature had come into play, it was necessary to give man the knowledge— commandments and prohibitions, the do's and don'ts—of the received Torah.

Since Moses had seen the Heavenly Torah before it had been given its earthbound shape, he knew that the scroll's text was not only what it appeared to be but also a manifestation of God. If not for Moses' knowledge of the *derech ha'emet*, the way of truth, the Torah's secret wisdom would be inaccessible. The familiar opening of the *Mishnah* tract, "The Sayings of the Fathers," which reads, "Moses received the Torah on Sinai and passed it to Joshua, Joshua passed it to the Elders...," in context meant that the Oral Torah had been communicated through a chain of authorized interpreters and therefore could be trusted. The Kabbalists for whom the Oral Torah was and had been public property gave the text a different meaning. The Torah tradition which Moses had passed on was the secret Torah which contained the substance of their teaching.

Generally, the Kabbalists content themselves with the fact that they had received their secret tradition from a master who stood in the unbroken chain of trusted authorities which reached back to Moses, but a few authors put the chain of authorities aside and imagined that their secrets had come directly from Moses. The *Ra'aya Meheimna*, which means "the trustworthy shepherd," is presented as a dialogue between Moses and the pseudonymous author of the *Zohar*, Simon bar Yohai, on the meaning of the commandments. This work might as well have been titled *The Book of Moses*, since *Ra'aya Meheimna* is a well-known title for Moses which appears frequently in the Talmud and the *Midrash*. It suggests Moses' occupation in Midian as a shepherd for his father-in-law and his forty years in the wilderness as shepherd of the Exodus generation. God, the medieval preachers often remarked, never gives office to a man until he has tested him in little things (Exod. 2:3). Many a sermon was preached on how Moses had followed and found every lost stray; how he had let the lambs into the field before the older sheep so that they could crop the tenderest grass; and how he had carried the lambs too young to walk. Some years later a work called *The Fountain of Wisdom, Ma'ayan ha-Hochma*, presented itself as the list of secrets an angel committed to Moses. A fourteenth-century work, *The Book of Gates, Sefer ha-Shearim*, takes the form of questions and answers between Moses and some students on mystical and esoteric matters.

Though prone to detach Moses from his human endowment, the Kabbalists, like all who preceded them, imposed their ideas and experience on Moses' biography. His life is made to reflect their faith that the adept's activity rather than the time-honored practice of *teshuvah* will ultimately determine the destiny of Israel. Chapter 14 of Exodus describes the departure of the Jews from Egypt and the pursuit of the Egyptians. As the Egyptians drew near the Israelites cried out to God: "Was it for want of graves in Egypt that You brought us to die in the wilderness?" (14:11). Moses responds: "Have no fear! Stand by, and witness the deliverance which the Lord will work for you today" (14:13). The *Zohar* suggests that Israel's deliverance depends upon Moses' presence:

Rabbi Simeon said: "Blessed were the Israelites to have a shepherd like Moses. It is written: Then he remembered the days of old, Moses, his people" (Isa. 63:11). This indicates that God counted Moses of equal importance with the whole people. The people's shepherd does not merely represent them but actually is himself the people. If he is worthy, then the whole people is worthy; if he is not so, then the whole people is punished for his guilt [*Zohar* Exod. 47a].

The *aggadah* had divided Moses' life into three equal parts—Egypt, Midian, and the mission—illustrating the law of symmetry in the life of a righteous man. The life of a mystic followed a different pattern. According to Nahmanides, Moses was a lad between twelve and twenty years old when he left Egypt and an elderly man nearing eighty when he came to Midian. During the intervening sixty or so years he was a wanderer following an itinerary which can no longer be discovered (Nah. to Exod. 2:23). Many of these Kabbalists traveled for years in search of a master who would teach them the secrets of the mystic way, years that must have been dulled by pain and poverty, best forgotten. Even when a master is found and agrees to teach, the time of preparation is lengthy, just as Moses' was. At the Burning Bush Moses sees only an external manifestation of the Immanent Presence of God, "the angel," not the *Shekinah* (Exod. 3:2); Moses' prophetic powers are not as fully developed as they would be later, and for the time being he must keep his distance. When he returns to Sinai the second time he will be prepared to draw closer to the darkness where God is.

Moses is nearly eighty when he enters Midian, meets and marries Zipporah. He lives with her only long enough to sire two sons. Because celibacy and denial are central elements in the mystical life, the *Zohar* praises Moses for staying away from Zipporah after his commission and contrasts his strength of purpose to the changeableness of Joshua, who is able to keep apart from his wife only at certain times (*Zohar* Num. 148a). Family and occupation are peripheral concerns to the Kabbalist. Not only is enlightenment a lonely enterprise but so much depends on his performance of *tikkunim*, acts of cosmic remedy and restoration, that he is consumed with a sense of urgency.

The Kabbalist is a metaphysician, not a magician. Moses' rod is not in evidence and Moses' confrontation with Pharaoh's sorcerers is turned into a struggle between the forces of good and evil in the hidden world. The mystic must always be in a state of purity. Nahmanides explains the incident in which Moses pitches his tent outside the camp as

Moses' desire to separate his dwelling from a camp made impure by the sin of the Golden Calf.

Kabbalah is an erudite credulity, a scholar's passion which reflects the preoccupation and prejudices of the scholar class. Moses is named in the Torah as a member of the tribe of Levi, and Kabbalists like Nahmanides repeat an old *aggadah* that the Levites had not been forced to perform physical labor in Egypt because they had been recognized as "the teachers and counselors of Israel" (Nah. to Exod. 5:4). These mystic-rabbis had their share of genteel pretensions. They claimed that Moses' merit is in part inherited from his parents, that his grandmother and father were "among the righteous of the most high, worthy to be listed among the patriarchs of the world" (Nah. to Exod. 6:14). Both claims reflect the fact that the esoteric tradition, like the office of the rabbi, was often a carefully preserved family tradition. Like the mandarin class in medieval China, only certain privileged families managed to provide advanced education to their sons; ordination was available to anyone who could satisfy his masters, but most families could not provide their sons either opportunity or financial support.

Kabbalah was not for the young. Moses was eighty when he was drawn unexpectedly to the Burning Bush (Nah. to Exod. 2:23). Only the mature—thirty years of age and a proper scholar was the general rule—were taught the secrets. Physical beauty had little meaning in the world of the Kabbalist. "A goodly child" (Exod. 2:2) was not taken to mean that the child was divinely formed but that Moses displayed as an infant exceptional spiritual capacities. Moses is no longer, as he had been to the Hellenist historians, a fit model for Praxiteles. Indeed, there are few physical descriptions of Moses in Kabbalist literature. His speech impediment, however, is real and Aaron is truly his spokesman, but not because Moses lacks oratorical skills. Aaron's support is a sign to the knowing that what happens on earth suggests what happens in Heaven. Moses whispers the words to Aaron and Aaron speaks the words aloud to Pharaoh and the elders, just as the divine flow of speech moves from the silence of the *Ein Sof* and becomes louder and louder as it moves down the *sefirot* until it becomes audible to the six hundred thousand who stood at Sinai (Nah. to Exod. 6:13).

The Torah describes Moses as "very meek" (Num. 12:3). Most commentators identified that meekness with a sovereign's dignified patience with lesser men and their advice. The Kabbalists understood a more saintly virtue: indifference to being badly used, an unwillingness to return abuse for abuse, the ability to face vilification silently (Nah. to Num. 12:3). Though he was in his own mind a man of ultimate importance to God and the world, the adept was after all simply another Jew to be taxed, cursed, fleeced by the Christian lords, and often suspected by many of his Jewish neighbors. The divine Moses of the Kabbalah was an admission of the impotence of his human creators.

CHAPTER

# IX

# Moses in
the Modern Mind

I N 1904 Ahad Ha-Am (1856–1927), the spiritual father of cultural Zionism and the best-known Hebrew essayist of his generation, published a three-volume collection of writings, *At the Parting of the Ways, Al Parashot Derachim*, which included an essay on Moses bearing all the hallmarks of the modern spirit. Ahad Ha-Am argues that the long debate over the influence of great men on history—did the man make the times or did the times make the man?—was pointless. No man transcends himself. Outside the immediate range of a man's activity, his importance is a creation of others. It is the image of a great man which affects history, not the man himself.

There is not a single great man in history of whom the popular fancy has not drawn a picture entirely different from the actual man; and it is this imaginary conception, created by the masses to suit their needs and their inclinations, that is the real great man, exerting an influence which abides in some cases for thousands of years—this, not the concrete original, who lived a short space in the actual world, and was never seen by the masses in his true likeness [Ha-Am 306].

Consequently, according to Ahad Ha-Am, it is no particular benefit "to raise the great men of history from the grave in their true shape," to search for the original Moses (Ha-Am 307). The original Moses is dead. All that remains is an evanescent afterglow. What lives is a particular image of Moses enshrined in the hearts of the Jewish people. This Moses has exerted a powerful force, a historical force. He "has been our leader not only for forty years in the wilderness of Sinai but for thousands of years in all the wildernesses in which we have wandered since the Exodus" (Ha-Am 309).

Ahad Ha-Am went on to argue that this Moses is a creation of the Jewish people, a heroic figure created in their own image. He does not use the psychological term, projection, but it is the mechanism he has in mind: the Jewish people have ascribed to Moses their highest self-image. It is a proud image. According to Ahad-Ha-Am, it is an image of Moses as the ultimate prophet; a man of truth who sees life undistorted by class prejudices or hunger for personal advantage; an idealist committed to absolute righteousness who works without compromise or thought of self, who concentrates his whole heart and mind on his goal and is determined to make the world do service to his ideal. This Moses makes no distinction between men and men, only between right and wrong. When Moses first goes out into the world—when he confronts the brutal Egyptian taskmaster—"he is at once brought face to face with a violation of justice, and, unhesitatingly, he takes the side of the injured." Though he is compelled to flee, "this experience does not make him prudent or cautious" and when he next hears the "cry of outraged justice" he goes immediately to support Zipporah and her sisters whose rights at the local well are being abused by a group of local toughs (Ha-Am 314–15).

Moses becomes a personification of Judaism's commitment to an ethical messianism. "Israel has never lived in the present. We have been inspired with brilliant hopes for the future, and an ineradicable faith in the coming triumph of the good and the right" (Ha-Am 327–28). Moses' life is a sermon on leadership. All his hopes for the newly freed Hebrews are dashed when the tribes dance before the Golden Calf, but Moses does not give up. He realizes slaves cannot be turned overnight into a nation. He recognizes that the sight of God's wonders can arouse a momentary enthusiasm but cannot implant feelings and inclinations of any stability or permanence. Undeterred, Moses summons all his patience to the task of bearing the troublesome burden of his people and training it by slow steps until it is fit for its mission (Ha-Am 323).

The purpose of Ahad Ha-Am's essay-sermon is to challenge the Jewish people to be a prophetic people. His hope is that they will follow the lead of the great prophet who led the tribes out of Egypt toward the Promised Land and will leave the flesh pots of Europe for the difficult, necessary, and compelling effort to build an ideal Zion in Palestine. Using the same Moses metaphor, Ahad Ha-Am two decades earlier had organized a secret society and called it *B'nai Moshe*, the sons of Moses, in the hope that a group of men of high morals and principles could be the catalyst for what he called "the reincarnation of Moses" in the spirit and activities of the Jewish people.

# IMAGES *of* MOSES

As an extended *Midrash* on Moses' life, Ahad Ha-Am's
essay is traditional in form but unmistakably modern in approach. *Midrash* used the Torah narrative freely, sermoni-
cally, and with confidence in its accuracy. Ahad Ha-Am
does not assume the Torah's reliability as a historical document. He has read the works of Julius Wellhausen and other
nineteenth-century Biblical critics and, though not sanguine
about the practical value of these studies, he accepts their
general thesis that the Torah is a composite work drawn together from a variety of sources, most of which can no
longer be traced back to their origin. The past is irretriev-
able, but ideas and artifacts live on as constitutive elements
in civilization. Moses is dead but an ideal of Moses lives.
Ahad Ha-Am says, in effect, Turn away from what cannot
be accomplished. It doesn't matter that Jews can't resurrect
Moses; what matters is that they understand and respond to
the Moses who lives in the hearts of the Jewish people.

The modern spirit is existential. It researches the dead
Moses but cares about the living Moses. History cannot establish meaning—the meaning is in the moment, existen-
tialism insists—but modern thought has used the discipline
of history quite effectively to free itself from the grip of the
past. Medieval thought valued order, assumed a static universe governed by eternal truths, and consecrated the prerogatives of class and status as elemental parts of God's design. Modernists used history to prove that God's design is
dynamic, not static, and that all claims to privilege based on
the authority of the tradition have no foundation in God's
design.

When Jews were allowed to enter the modern world they,
willingly subjected their tradition to historical analysis.

History was the basic discipline of the Haskalah, the Jewish Enlightenment. The early Haskalah concentrated on non-Biblical subjects like the synagogue, the sermon, and the liturgy, issues which were being debated between traditionalists and reformers. But it was not long before the Bible was subjected to similar analyses. The rabbis had tended to treat Judaism as a conclusion, a single tradition since Sinai. Haskalah saw Judaism as process. The more historical research was pursued the more apparent it became that Judaism was and is the organic, therefore ever-changing, religious civilization of the Jewish people.

As long as Jews lived in cultures dominated by the Muslim and Christian traditions, critical theories suggesting that Moses may never have lived received little or no support. However bitter the religious polemic between the religious communities, the existence of Moses or his virtue as a leader never became a controversial issue. The New Testament had used Moses as a witness to Jesus' mission. The Quran had listed Moses among God's apostles. In modern times the emergence of religiously neutral pockets of population in Western society, particularly in the unversities, removed Moses from the list of historic figures whose life and worth scholars could take for granted. The more the Torah texts were analyzed, the more questions were raised about the life and work of the original Moses. In 1905 the German historian Eduard Meyer (1835–1930), who had gained international fame for his work in Pharaonic chronology, lent the weight of his scholarly distinction to those who argued that search for the historical Moses would never be successful because the existing texts do not provide the kind of material a researcher would need to recover a historic figure (*Die*

*Mose Sagen und die Lewiten,* 1905). An equally famed disciple, Martin Noth, took the same position. Pending any unexpected discoveries, studied agnosticism remains today the most creditable scholarly stance.

History brings all certainties into question, including all the certainties which have developed around the Torah. If there was no Moses, how could there be a *Torat Moshe?* One would have expected scholarly agnosticism about Moses to cause an angry defensive reaction throughout the Jewish world. Actually, the reaction was milder than might have been anticipated. The traditionalists simply declared that as the Word of God the Torah was a unique document which could not be subjected to the forms of analysis useful in understanding all other literature; and the modernists simply declared that, however the Torah came into being, it was a new force in the world whose results were far-reaching and culturally seminal, and that no reinterpretation of Moses' role would increase or diminish the Torah's value. Martin Noth put it this way, "The core of the Sinai tradition was a historical occurrence, however little it may be historically grasped in detail. . . . The gradually developing tradition of the Pentateuch, the religious content of which is quite without parallel, becomes a clear token of the particularity and qualitative uniqueness of Israel's position among the nations" (Noth 136–37). The *Midrashic* cast of mind which Jews had developed over the centuries predisposed them to look behind the surface meaning of a text, the so-called facts, to its philosophic or psychological implications and to value these implications as much as the facts. As we have seen, the *Midrash* had for centuries been presenting the Moses who lived in each generation's soul. Since Moses

294

had never died in Jewish consciousness, the exhumation of the original Moses did not seem to be an urgent issue and the academic search for the historical Moses began as and remained an almost entirely non-Jewish enterprise pursued by such scholars as Hugo Gressmann (*Mose und Seine Zeit,* 1913) and Paul Volz (*Mose,* 1907).

That Judaism had not consecrated any formal catechism was also an important factor in easing the readjustment. Jews did not have to deny a litany memorized in childhood when they speculated on Moses' life or accepted the idea that Judaism, like any religion, is a dynamic organism. Though it includes doctrine, it is not a set of abstract ideas but a cluster of ideas, institutions, values, myths, ritual, and hopes through which Jews draw meaning out of experience and define reality, duty, and the future promise. Though modern Jews were contemplating ideas about Moses and the Torah that a medieval Jew would have considered heretical, the absence of a set of dogmas which had to be specifically denied made the change less traumatic.

As the twentieth century began, existentialist attitudes emerged which emphasized the moment, the living Moses, and the living tradition. The German Jewish philosopher-theologian Franz Rosenzweig (1886–1929) expressed ideas not unlike Ahad Ha-Am's but arrived at them from an entirely different philosophic basis.

Even if Wellhausen would turn out to be right in all his theories . . . it would not make the slightest difference to our faith . . . we, too, translate the Torah as one book. For us, too, it is the work of one spirit. We do not know who it was; that it was Moses we need not believe. . . . Among ourselves we call him by the sign which the higher criticism uses to designate the final redactor, assumed by it, "R." We resolve this sign not into redactor but into *Rabbenu* (our teacher) for whoever he was, whatever sources he might have utilized, he is our teacher, and his theology is our teaching [Rosenzweig 351].

Using similar philosophic tools, Martin Buber (1878–1965) expanded on this approach in his book, *Moses* (1944). *Moses* is not, as the title suggests, a biography but, rather, an essay in Biblical appreciation. Buber assumes the existence of an historic Moses and offers as proof the inescapable impression, which he feels any sympathetic reader will come away with, of a sensitive and powerful spirit behind and within various Torah narratives. Buber's approach rests on a postulate he took over from the studies of philologists and students of ancient languages and literatures (particularly the Iranologist, Ernst Herzfeld) who had concluded that the classic sagas were not purely literary inventions but literary elaborations of someone's dramatic personal experience, particularly the radical surprise a writer or singer felt at some unexpected event he had participated in or witnessed.

Buber assumes that the nucleus of the Torah text represents Moses' expression of radical surprise at his various meetings with God. Buber had read carefully the Biblical critics and accepted their conclusion that on the basis of the Torah narrative no one can present a fully articulated biography of Moses.

Such an account as that attempted here must admittedly renounce one thing. It cannot undertake to submit a consecutive record of the course of events; for what is provided in its sole source, the Biblical narrative, deals for the greater part with only two incidents: the Exodus and the campaign at Sinai. To these are added an introductory legend regarding the previous history of

Moses and a number of more or less fragmentary reports of post-Sinaitic events. It is impossible to produce a historical continuity out of these disparate saga complexes [Buber 5–6].

But Buber claims that certain key episodes of the Torah refract the reality of an intense and creative meeting between God and a remarkable man, a meeting whose force and nature are still so strong in the text that an open-minded reader will experience the reality of the encounter.

Buber's Moses is a God-intoxicated man, a mystic, an active leader always conscious of the responsibilities of office, and "an undivided entire person who, as such, receives the message and as such endeavors to establish that message in life" (Buber 200). In this last respect Moses is unique. There are many leaders of men, but few who, like Moses, are possessed of an original vision and able to transform their society according to it. Buber describes Joshua as typical of the ordinary run of leaders, a man of spirit and capacity, but one who has never known the transcending and transforming spiritual experience which had marked Moses' life.

The Burning Bush episode becomes a classic model of the moment of tension when one feels prudence war with commitment in his soul, when "God commands and man resists" (Buber 46). The Torah language captures and refracts the moment of recognition when Moses becomes aware of a compelling mission and aware that he must choose to respond to it. Sinai becomes a collective moment of recognition when the community under Moses' guidance senses its destiny. Buber thought of himself as an analytical scholar, but in reality he was an old-fashioned *Midrashist* who uses throughout the old technique of interpreting the text from within the text; he does so brilliantly and reveals much, but his conclusions are impressionistic, not historical. The Torah text simply does not reveal to every sensitive reader the afterglow of a series of I-Thou meetings between the prophet and God. As indicated in chapter I, I discover little of Moses' personal experience in the Torah. What I discover there is a record of the community's meeting with God and its awe before God's redemptive power. I find it unlikely that a text which consistently diminishes Moses' role would be shaped around Moses' personal experiences.

The similarities in approach between *Midrash* and that most familiar and typical of early modern art forms, Impressionism, is striking. Impressionism represents an attempt to capture colors and shapes as a particular artist sees them at a moment in time rather than to capture the timeless essence of a scene or person. The Impressionists hoped to capture a single instant or a characteristic pose and to fix these on a canvas with rapid strokes. They were less interested in detail than in general effect, less interested in the object than in their response. Buber's Moses tells us more about Buber than Moses.

I was forcibly struck by the tendency of Jews to push aside the historical questions in favor of the *Midrashic* approach when my father, Abba Hillel Silver (1893–1963), published a historical evaluation of Moses, *Moses and the Original Torah.* His arguments apart, what fascinated me at the time and since was the resounding silence which greeted the book's publication (1959). Despite his worldwide fame as a scholar and leader in the Jewish world, the book sold poorly and was rarely reviewed in the Jewish press. I read this silence as a way of saying that the historical question he posed did not merit the effort he had invested in trying to answer it and perhaps should not have been asked at all. I came to believe that most Jews shy away from the search for the historical Moses out of an instinctive feeling that Judaism's credibility does not depend on, and cannot be allowed to appear to depend on, the historical accuracy of the Torah's narrative.

Using the judgments and tools of Biblical criticism, Silver sought to recover the original Moses and the original Torah, the actual teaching of Moses. He argues that Moses' original words dealt with the unity of God and righteousness and are found in the familiar Decalogue (Exod. 20; Deut. 5) and various other parts of the law, specifically those apodictic oracles (*devarim*) which are the "you shall" and "you shall not" commandments. He describes Moses as a religious pioneer who refined the basically monotheistic faith of the patriarchs by adding to it the covenant of righteousness, a thorough-going opposition to idolatry, and a sense of national mission.

According to Silver, the birth stories are legends. Moses was actually born in Egypt, and Egyptian religion and culture were essential parts of his upbringing. Moses, he writes, was affected by the religious ferment of the thirteenth century B.C.E. which centered on Akhenaten, the Pharaoh who destroyed many of Egypt's shrines and made the worship of Aten, the sun god, into a state religion. Moses' religious teachings go beyond Akhenaten's short-lived reformation, far beyond this Pharaoh who sensed a single high God but never abandoned a symbolized god, never denied the divinity of other gods, and never rejected the divinity of the pharaohs and pharaonic claims to absolute power. In many ways Moses' Torah represents a reaction to what he had seen in Egypt. It outlaws incest, a common feature of Egyptian so-

ciety, and put an end to lifelong slavery. It rejects the idea of
kings who claim to be gods incarnate and wield unlimited
power. The God to whom Moses bound himself and his
people is a zealous God intolerant of the worship of other
gods and the making of images, but in relation to His people
a "God merciful and just, slow to anger, and abounding in
steadfast love and faithfulness" (Silver 29). Moses' major
theological insight, which catalyzed a radical shift in religious history, is a vision of God which denies that dread and im-
placability are the essential attributes of His being. In his view
this newfound faith in a dependable and caring God made
possible the study of science and of political philosophies with
some expectation of useful findings about society's future.
The argument is close and scholarly, but it is doubtful that
a dispassionate outside observer would accept the author's
arguments as ineluctable. The more interesting question
is why Silver broke with the general Jewish silence and ex-
plored the historical questions which surround Moses' life. I
have always felt that he did so because he was not really
raising the historical issues. He was convinced in the deepest
recesses of his being that Moses was "the foremost religious
genius of all times," the creator of the Jewish people, and
the effective founder of the faith. Therefore, the problem,
as he saw it, was not whether Moses had lived but what was
the nature of Moses' accomplishment, which is really the
question, In what does Judaism's uniqueness consist?

The twentieth-century Jew has taken his Moses from
novels and sermons, critical *Midrashic* forms, rather than
from manuals of critical Biblical research; and his preachers
and writers have treated Moses just as their predecessors
did, but with greater license and individuality. Leafing
through Theodore Herzl's *Diary*, I discovered that the foun-

der of political Zionism had once thought to write a play with Moses as the central character. The year was 1899. The Zionist movement was launched but the work was not going as he hoped. His well-to-do friends, whom he counted on for financial support, thought his ideas crackpot, if not dangerous; and the movement was rent by bitter ideological and personal rivalries. Herzl pictures Moses as "a tall, vital, superior man with a sense of humor." Herzl was fairly short, sometimes lethargic, known for his sense of humor, not at all bashful about his talents. "The theme of the drama: How he [Moses] is shaken inwardly, yet holds himself upright by his will. He is a leader because he does not want to be. Everything gives way before him because he has no personal desire." Herzl outlines the play. Act I: Moses returns to Egypt, the wretchedness of the Israelites, Moses gives them hope, but they are rebellious. Act II: Korah, the rebellion. Act III: The Golden Calf, the rebellion. Act IV: Miriam, the rebellion. Act V: Moses' death (Herzl 3:267).

Some wrote to justify themselves, others to capture the spirit of a powerful personality. Both Louis Untermeyer (1928) and Sholem Asch (1951) wrote novels titled *Moses*, which drew freely on the *Midrashic* deposit, but to my taste the most sensitive and accessible modern work is the one volume which set out to be a recreation not of Moses but of *Moshe Rabbenu*, Edmund Fleg's *The Life of Moses* (1928). Such novelists depended on the translation of the ocean of *aggadah* and *Midrash* into a European language. A number of anthologies were prepared early in the century—for example, Moses Gaster, *The Example of the Rabbi* (1924); Angelo Rappoport, *Myth and Legend of Ancient Israel* (1928); and the most important, the many-volumed *Legends of the Jews* (1910–13) by Louis Ginsburg. What distinguishes Ginsburg's work is not only his encyclopedic knowledge but the three volumes of notes which he subsequently provided (1925–28), in which he cites the sources of each incident and records variants of the narrative.

All subsequent studies, including this one, depend heavily on Ginsburg's research, ideas, and leads; but more recent studies have abandoned his method. He set out the legends in a continuous narration based on the sequence of the Torah narrative, imposing an arbitrary order on what was originally a disorderly accumulation of discrete *aggadot*, *Midrashic* comments, and folk tales. It leaves a reader without any sense of before and after, only the sense that all these stories, however inconsistent in implication and contradictory of detail, are somehow part of a single consistent entity, Judaism. The same is true of the notes in which he lists variants but makes no attempt to separate materials into their appropriate cultural modalities. We are left with a profound respect for the flexibility of rabbinic Judaism but without much appreciation of the distinctive cultural strands which in fact shaped the Jewish continuum. An erudite scholar, Ginsburg was also a traditional Jew in that he accepted on faith the essential unity and consistency of the Jewish experience. His scholarship admits variations of the Moses theme, or any other theme, but not the substitution of a significantly different set of values for an earlier one. He saw the different ways in which Moses was dressed but not that a different actor sometimes played the part.

Today the great divide between Jewish thinkers lies between those who insist that the revelation, the Torah, stands outside of time and cannot be judged by the usual analyses and those who do not exempt the Torah from critical analysis. Both groups describe Judaism as a dynamic tradition;

but the traditionalists insist that the historical process must be governed by and limited to God's original Instructions and the nonorthodox hold various views as to what these Instructions were and the degree to which modern life must conform to them. The traditionalists argue that the Torah comes from God and is unique, that it was not written by a man who was taught by other men and whose values were conditioned by his environment, and, therefore, that it cannot be subjected to the same forms of criticism which scholars use with all other classic texts. The uniqueness of Torah is an article of faith which is often supplemented by criticism of Biblical critics. The traditionalists make much of the existence of conflicting views, claiming such conflicts demonstrate that the ideas are nothing more than theories and, given the degree of scholarly disagreement, not persuasive theories at that. To those who are eager to believe, the most persuasive traditionalist argument is a pragmatic one. Like archeological field work, Biblical criticism cuts away and destroys in order to uncover. And when the work is over the results are meager and uncertain and, in any case, irrelevant to the questions of value and purpose which the seeker must address.

Isaac Abarbanel (1437–1508), who is best known for various messianic works and Biblical commentaries, was one of the few grandees of Spanish Jewry who accepted exile rather than baptism when King Ferdinand and Queen Isabella issued in 1492 the draconian order which required this entire community to convert or be summarily expelled. In exile he wrote, among many other works, a commentary on *The Sayings of the Fathers,* in which he provides a classic statement of this rabbinic position. Interpreting a sentence we have often quoted—"Moses received the Torah from Sinai and gave it to Joshua, Joshua gave it to the elders" (M. Avot 1:1)—Abarbanel ponders the prepositional phrase "from Sinai." Moses received the Torah from God *on* Sinai; why then "from Sinai"? He answers his rhetorical question by observing that "from Sinai" is a causative phrase which suggests that Moses acquired his wisdom during his lonely preparatory sojourn on Sinai. People normally learn from teachers. Moses was not taught by any man. Moses was taught by God. The revelation is outside of time and is outside all human categories (Abarbanel to M. Avot 1:3).

Many caught in the contradictory push and pull of ideologies, philosophies, and mores which clamor for attention are comforted by the thought that there are answers beyond question. But for others the existence of such truths is not beyond question. For everyone the historical questions still hang in the air. The orthodox response has been either to ignore them or to blunt their challenge by changing traditional vocabulary sufficiently to remove any umbilical connection between revelation and Moses. Where the older Judaism generally used the label, *Torat Moshe*, the Torah of Moses, modern traditionalists tend to substitute the phrase, *Torah min ha-shamayim*, the Torah which comes from Heaven, revelation. It is a subtle shift—no orthodox Jew, however modern, would deny Mosaic authorship—but nevertheless it puts the emphasis on the mystery of revelation, which many find captivating, rather than on the fact of Sinai, which many find troubling. In this way modern orthodoxy emphasizes the message, the mystery, and the miracle of the teaching rather than the man tradition calls its prophet.

Abraham Isaac Hacohen Kook (1865–1935) was the chief rabbi of Palestine during the 1920s and early 1930s. A scholar as well as a theologian, inclined to mysticism, Kook was that rare orthodox leader of his time who did not turn his back on the young pioneers of the first Aliyah. In 1914, just before World War I, while he was a rabbi in Jaffa, Kook published an anthology of his work, *Zironim, a Row of Planets.* It included an essay, "The Sage Is More Important than the Prophet," in which he examined the role of these two traditional types as sources of instruction for the Jewish community. He likened prophecy to poetry, "with its ability to portray the nobler sides of life, its beauty, its dynamism and vitality" (Kook 253). He defines the prophet as a man of righteousness who knows how to "portray the evils of life and protest against them vigorously," agreeing with, though he does not cite, Ahad Ha-Am's description of the prophet (Kook 254). For all his vision, or perhaps because of it, the prophet lacks the particular cast of mind able to devise structures which will help ordinary people organize their lives around a grand ideal. The sages, on the other hand, are men of practical wisdom who can create institutions necessary for everyday life. They can structure the prophet's accomplishments into the social order.

Biblical prophecy eliminated idolatry. Once that struggle was won, the sages took over and labored to create a society which would reflect the achievements and concerns of the prophet. Unfortunately, as time passed, the sages lost sight of the larger prophetic purposes of Judaism and became increasingly involved with minutiae. Kook had in mind those rabbinic colleagues so involved with ritual and medieval attitudes that they fought against all that hints of modernism, and particularly those who hurled bans of excommunication against the young pioneers who were resettling the Promised Land. Kook felt that his fellow rabbis who fixed on the reli-

gious doubts and uninhibited social attitudes of the young
settlers failed to appreciate their many good values and their
real accomplishments; he believed the way to win them
back to Jewish observance was to work with, not against,
them.

Kook closes his essay with the hope that at the end of the
present epoch the spirit of prophecy will revive and "the
soul of Moses will reappear in the world" (Kook 255).
Kook's *Midrash* is not far removed from Buber's, though the
two men certainly held diametrically opposed views on the
centrality of *halacha* in the prophet's teaching and in the life
of the emerging Zion—proof, if proof be needed, that
*Midrash* can be used to suit any philosopher's purposes.

Almost a century and a half ago, the Gibbon of Jewish
historians, Heinrich Graetz (1817–91), published an essay,
"An Introduction to History," in which he analyzed three
recently published manuals on Judaism. The authors, Samson Raphael Hirsch, Zacharias Frankel, and Samuel Hirsch,
were all scholars, but each presented a different Judaism.
Graetz demonstrates that each had read into the Torah tradition exactly what he was prepared to find there. Samuel
Hirsch, the convinced liberal, described Judaism as open
minded, non-dogmatic, this-worldly, committed to civic re-
form. Samson Raphael Hirsch, whose major accomplishment was to provide a philosophic basis for a modern orthodoxy, described Judaism as an all-embracing and ennobling
rule which enabled men to lead good and responsible lives
by delineating God's Will for them. Frankel tried to balance
these opposing views by suggesting the role of community
consensus in establishing the meaning of Torah. Each said
some interesting things about the nature of Torah tradition,
but as Graetz pointed out, an outsider reading the three vol-

umes would have wondered if they described the same religion. Each saw what he was prepared to see, and none succeeded in defining any objective criteria which would enable another researcher to arrive at his conclusions. Graetz described the three works as impressionistic studies, essentially the work of connoisseurs with individual tastes. Their descriptions were provocative, contradictory, and personal.

Orthodox believers may not be pleased to recognize—indeed, may refuse to—that in every religion successive generations of the faithful have drawn significantly different pictures of the founder and of the founder's faith. That fact ought not surprise anyone else. Religions are not catechisms of abstract ideas which float somewhere beyond mankind, but ideas taken into the soul of an individual and into the collective soul of a community and, inevitably, reshaped by each person's perceptions and by all the changes which affect every living community. So long as it commands a following, a religion is always and ever dynamic, reshaping and recreating the past for its own purposes. Religious traditions are living entities. All that lives undergoes an unceasing process of transformation. The adult is not an elongated child. He has lost the child's innocent amazement at the world and mythic approach to life. He thinks conceptually. His bones have hardened and his musculature has changed. New glands and new drives have come into play. To be sure, as Freud taught us, the past has not been abandoned, it lives, buried but powerful; the child is in the adult, but the adult is quite different from the child. As times change, as people change, that is, as they are differently conditioned, their needs and visions change, and their religious understandings change. Over time religions tend to retain their calendar, holiday worship patterns and scripture, but each

generation reads its perceptions and values into those familiar forms. Ahad Ha-Am named passionate civil morality as
the dominant characteristic of the living Moses. Biblical
man would have named patient obedience, Philo enlightened reason, and the sages of the Talmud his competence as
teacher and exemplar of the law. To the editor of Deuteronomy, Moses was a contemporary of Joshua's, the first among
the prophets, a holy man. To a Jew conditioned by Hellenistic cultural norms Moses was a lawgiver who founded the
civil religion of Jerusalem, not unlike Solon or Lycurgus,
who had founded the respected civil religions of Athens and
Sparta. To the Talmudic sages Moses was *Moshe Rabbenu*,
the first among their colleagues, a master of Torah study, a
holy man and faith healer. To generations of ordinary Jews
suffering the pains of an outrageous fortune Moses was an
intercessor who sat beside God in Heaven and spent his days
presenting their needs to the Almighty. To modern Zionists
Moses was the original liberator of the Promised Land, a
leader determined to change his people's fate. To know a
community's Moses is to know something of its soul.

Modernity has struck a serious blow against all confident
apologetes and their confident descriptions of the unvarying
essence of their religious tradition. The continuities in Jewish life tend to be formal and institutional rather than theological and doctrinal. A dynamic religious community is always at work pouring new wine into old bottles. Once a
society has consecrated a holiday or a founder or an idea and
surrounded its symbol with an aura of deep spiritual significance, the society tends to hold onto that symbol. A religious symbol—and a great religious figure of the past is precisely that, a symbol—has a life of its own, born out of the
universal human need to find certainty amid life's flux.

The power of a religious message is its ability to convey the sense that it conforms to and expresses the fundamental nature of reality. A religion is most encouraging to its believers when it exudes the confidence that it is built on solid rock. Religious ritual focuses its worshippers' eyes, ears, and mind on symbols and signals of permanence. In a Buddhist temple the statue of the founder is always before the worshippers' eyes. A Christian church presents the cross. Moses is not present in the synagogue, but his Torah is.

Conservative theologians accept the idea of change in religious practice, but they limit it to matters of form. They often cite European painting galleries filled with pictures of Biblical and New Testament scenes in which the protagonists are dressed in the costume of sixteenth-century France or fifteenth-century Italy and argue that such anachronistic costuming is understandable and essentially innocent; the scene, they insist, has not lost its associations or traditional meaning. That is not quite true. The painter of a Sienese Madonna and his patron knew the lady through the Mariolatry of the medieval Church in ways Athanasius or Augustine did not. The Greek-speaking Jew who approved Moses' generous and scrupulous support of the nation's rites, his strong leadership, and his brilliance as a lawgiver led a life governed by a different set of values than the medieval Kabbalist who knew Moses as the ultimate mystic and prophet, God's man who lived as much with God as with man.

Medieval philosophers often used the image of a tree as a metaphor to describe the development of Jewish life. The seedling was planted at Sinai; over the centuries the trunk thickened as each generation added its understanding of Torah; in time the tree's main branches lengthened and thickened as commentary added detail to the basic themes:

God's unity, free will, providence, reward and punishment, the messianic promise. Each spring the tree came to leaf and each fall shed its leaves as the communities developed customs appropriate to their circumstances and then, under new circumstances, changed or abandoned them. As long as it survives the tree retains its original shape, so the metaphor is attractive to Jews who believe that their religion's basic doctrine never changed. I question this metaphor's usefulness as a definition of what actually occurred.

Studies like this one of Moses have led me to replace it with a river metaphor. I look on Judaism, as indeed I look on all major religious traditions, as a mighty river, say the Mississippi. The Mississippi begins as a small stream feeding a clear Minnesota lake and flows several thousand miles to the Gulf of Mexico. The Torah begins in an event, the revelation at Sinai, whose substance cannot be fully recovered, and flows down three thousand years to today. I doubt that many molecules of the water which emerge at the Mississippi's source actually reach the Gulf. Some are taken away by evaporation. Farmers pipe water for irrigation and cities draw water to support their populations. Other waters flow into the stream. Tributaries mingle with the original waters. Much of what existed in Moses' days is no longer, but the mighty stream flows on.

One can locate the Mississippi on the map and bathe in its waters, but no one can deny its changeful nature. The Mississippi is a single river, but as it flows it changes its aspect. Sometimes it runs calmly for miles, other times it races through white water rapids. In Jewish life there have been quiet and uneventful centuries and times of dramatic change. The Mississippi flows in a single direction, drawn on by the fall of the land and the spin of the earth, by God's hand. Jewish experience flows into history, drawn on by changing times, by the changing needs of Jewish life, by the changing education of Jews, or, as a theologian might put it, by God's creative purpose.

The discipline of history has precipitated theological divisions among Jews, between those who accept Sinai on faith and those who look on Sinai as a beginning rather than a conclusion. But thinkers in both camps spend little time searching for the man who once lived, preferring to think in *Midrashic* terms about the Biblical stories or the *aggadot*. Moses exists for all Jews because he is in the Torah and because the Torah stories play a large role in Jewish worship and study. When a rabbi speaks, he speaks on the Torah text. When a child is in religious school, his texts speak of Moses and Torah. These stories provide many of the ideas and illustrations which fill Jewish memories and conversations. What is left of the original Moses may be only an afterglow; but as Ahad Ha-Am wrote, Moses is inextricably embedded in the Jewish way and spirit. Moses and the stories about Moses reach out to us. They are certainly irresistible to the preacher.

My own favorite sermon on Moses examines the four choices Moses faced. Its thesis: we are tested by life, must wrestle through each challenge, and can expect each, if we are successful, to strengthen our character and personality.

Moses' first choice was between personal advantage and a life of privilege or loyalty to his people who suffered in slave pens. A happy accident had given Moses a place in the palace while his brethren endured the forced labor camps of Egypt. Their destiny was bleak, his was assured and full of promise. But Moses knew he was of the slave people, and as he matured he had to confront a problem which would not let him go: Should he cast his lot with the powerful or with the impoverished? With the princes or with the prisoners? Should he accept privilege, or take a desperate plunge into an unknown future? Moses kept faith with his people. How many of us would choose obligation rather than opportunity?

Moses' second choice was between ease and mission. After Moses struck down the taskmaster and fled Egypt, he made his way to the security of Jethro's tent, where he found happiness, love, and marriage. Yet something in his soul continued to trouble him. His conscience would give him no rest. Memories of his kinsmen and their suffering kept recurring. How was it with them? Ought he return to his people? Worry and concern led to a sense of revelation—the bush that burned and was not consumed—a call to return to Egypt, a mission to deliver his enslaved brethren. Moses found himself once again in the dread valley of decision and tried to escape it: "Please, O Lord, make someone else Your agent" (Exod. 4:13). In the end duty overpowered him. Between personal comfort and unsettling duty Moses chose the service of his fellowman. How many of us would put aside family and security when God calls?

Moses' third choice was between love of self and love of his people. After the Reed Sea had been crossed, Moses struggled with his people and brought them to Sinai. He left the camp to go up the mountain to receive God's Instruction, but his people proved inconstant. Moses had labored and suffered so much for them, yet they had forsaken him and his instructions at the first opportunity, abandoned the discipline he had set for them, made for themselves the Golden Calf, and ecstatically danced around its image. Descending with the law, Moses was crushed by the knowledge of failure, a sense of terrifying futility. His high hopes for his people were shattered and at that moment he heard the voice of God offering him release from the burdens of leadership. I will destroy this stiff-necked people "and make of you a great nation" (Exod. 32:9). Here was an opportunity to abandon an ungrateful and inconstant people, yet Moses would not take it. Between hurt pride and abiding love Moses chose love, concern, and steadfast loyalty. Moses went back to the Lord and said: "Alas, this people is guilty of a great sin. . . . Now if You will forgive their sin well and good; but, if not, erase me from the record which You have written" (Exod. 33:32). How many can accept such abuse and fickleness and retain their idealism and love of mankind?

The final choice that Moses made was between defiance to God and submission. He was an old man. He had brought the people within sight of the Promised Land. For forty years he had endured the heat and thirst of the desert, rebellion, the grumblings, and the complaints of his people. He had been attacked by ambitious tribal chiefs and by enemies without. Now his dreams were about to come true. He would be repaid for all the heartache and hardship of these years. At this very moment of high expectancy the voice of God came to him: "Moses, look well over the Promised Land—with thine eyes shall thou see it, but into it thou shalt not come." How could it be? What crueler destiny can confront man than to be denied victory at the threshold of accomplishment? We would expect a cry of outrage and frustration. Moses' first words after this unexpected sentence were not words of anguish or denunciation or complaint. He began to intone a blessing, his last sweet blessing to his people. "May Reuben live and not die" (Deut. 33:6).

Let Israel live and not die. Between rebellion and submission Moses chose submission. How many of us can express sweetness and generosity in the face of bitter disappointment? Would you?

Though it is a compelling sermon, it clearly indicates how far Jewish life has flowed since the Torah narrative was constructed, for it is a thoroughly modern sermon that would have puzzled Moses himself. Where the preacher knows a heroic Moses, a hero who always chooses what is right and courageous over the self-serving and prudent, the Torah knows a Moses who, once he is commissioned, has few choices. It reports his murder of the Egyptian taskmaster as an impulsive act. At the Burning Bush Moses balks at his assignment. Nowhere does the Torah indicate that Moses ever thought to challenge the decision that he may not enter the Promised Land. The Torah's Moses is not created in the image of a hero but in the image of God's ever-faithful servant. In subsequent periods of Jewish life, the preacher and the congregation lived in a world in which choices must be made, and they imagined Moses living as they lived.

The real choice a modern must make is whether he will accept the consensus of his time as a statement of what is necessarily true for all times or whether he will appreciate the dynamic quality of all thought, including the ideas of the religion he professes, and not try to freeze history to suit his preconceptions. It is not an easy task, but then neither did Moses have an easy task.

Whenever I reread the *aggadah* which describes Moses' visit to Akiba's classroom I wonder what might have happened if instead Akiba had visited the Heavenly Academy where, according to the rabbis, Moses carries on his studies. Would Akiba have understood Moses' interpretation of Torah? I think not. Each generation is confident it possesses the truth. What it possesses, if it is fortunate and wise, is the truth appropriate to its time and place—a humbling thought which, I would submit, is the beginning of wisdom.

# List of Abbreviations

| | |
|---|---|
| Abarbanel | Isaac Abarbanel, *Nahalot Avot* (Commentary on Avot) |
| Adam | *Adam: A Religious Play of the Twelfth Century*, trans. E. N. Stone |
| Aelian | *On the Characteristics of Animals*, trans. A. S. Schoenfield |
| al-Bukhari | Abu Abd Allah, *Al Sahih*, ILM |
| al-Ghazzali | Abu Hamid al-Ghazzali, *Fatihat Al-Ulum*, trans. A. S. Schoenfield |
| al-Harizi | Judah al-Harizi, *The Tahkemon*, trans. V. E. Reichert (Jerusalem, 1965) |
| Ant. | Josephus, *Jewish Antiquities*, trans. H. St. J. Thackery |
| ARN | *Avot d'Rabbi Nathan* |
| Avicenna | *The Persian Commentary on the Recital of Hayy ibn Yaqzan*, trans. W. Trask (London, 1960) |
| | |
| b. | Babylonian Talmud |
| B. B. | Baba Bathra |
| Ber. | Berakoth |
| B. M. | Baba Metzia |
| Git. | Gittin |
| Kid. | Kiddushin |
| Meg. | Megillah |
| Pes. | Pesahim |
| Shab. | Shabbath |
| Sotah | |
| Zeb. | Zebahim |

# List of Abbreviations

| | |
|---|---|
| Buber | M. Buber, *Moses* (Oxford, 1946) |
| Cant R. | *Midrash, Song of Songs Rabbati* |
| CM San. | Maimonides, *Commentary on the Mishnati*, Sanhedrin |
| *Contra Celsum* | Origen |
| DVM | Philo, *De Vita Moyesis*, trans. F. H. Coulson (Harvard, 1935) |
| Deut. R. | *Midrash, Deuteronomy Rabbah* |
| Eusebius | *Preparatio Evangelica* |
| Esther R. | *Midrash, Esther Rabbah* |
| Exod. R. | *Midrash, Exodus Rabbah* |
| *Gates* | *Gates of Prayer*, The New Union Prayer Book (New York, 1975) |
| Ginsberg | L. Ginsberg, *Legends of the Jews* (Philadelphia, 1966) |
| *Guide* | Maimonides, *The Guide of the Perplexed*, trans. S. Pines (Chicago, 1963) |
| Ha-Am | *Selected Essays of Ahad Ha-Am*, trans. L. Simon (New York, 1962) |
| Hai Gaon | *Otzar Ha-Geonim, Hagigah u'mashkim* |
| Ha Levi | Judah Ha Levi, *The Kuzari*, trans. H. Hirschfeld (London, 1905) |
| Herzl | *The Complete Diaries of Theodor Herzl*, trans. H. Zohn (New York, 1960) |
| Hertz | *Daily Prayer Book* |
| ibn Ezra | *Commentary on Tanakh*, ed. I. J. Hertz (New York, 1948) |
| ibn Kammuna | *ibn Kammuna's Examination of the Inquiries into the True Faith*, trans. M. Perlmann (New York, 1967) |
| j. | *Palestinian (Jerusalem) Talmud* |
| Ber. | *Berakoth* |
| Horayot | |
| Kil. | *Kilayim* |
| Peah | |

# List of Abbreviations

| | |
|---|---|
| JQR | *Jewish Quarterly Review* |
| Jubilees | *Pseudepigrapha of the Old Testament*, trans. R. H. Charles (Oxford, 1913) |
| | |
| Kittel | Rudolf Kittel, *Great Men and Movements in Israel*, trans. C. Knoch and C. Wright (New York, 1968) |
| Kook | *The Lights of Penitence (Zironim)*, trans. B. Z. Bokser (New York, 1978) |
| | |
| Lec. on Deut. | Martin Luther, *Lectures on Deuteronomy* |
| Lev. R. | *Midrash Leviticus Rabbah* |
| | |
| M. | Mishnah |
| Avot | Pirke Avot |
| Ber. | Berakoth |
| Men. | Menahot |
| Peah | Peah |
| Markah | *Memar Markah*, trans. J. MacDonald (Berlin, 1963) |
| Mek. | *Mekhilta de Rabbi Ishmael* |
| Mid. Teh. | Midrash Tehillim |
| | |
| Nah. | Moses b. Nahman (Nahmanides), *Commentary on the Torah* |
| Nicholson | R. A. Nicholson, *Literary History of the Arabs* (Cambridge, 1930) |
| Noth | M. Noth, *The History of Israel* (London, 1960) |
| | |
| Onkelos to Deut. | Targum Onkelos to Deuteronomy |
| | |
| PM | *Midrash Petirat Moshe* |
| PRE | *Midrash Pirkei de-Rabbi Eliezer* |
| PRK Sup. | *Midrash Pesikta de-Rav Kahana, Supplement* |
| Prob. | Philo, *Quod Omnis Probus Liber Sit*, trans. F. H. Coulson (Harvard, 1935) |
| *Pseudo Jonathan* | Targum *Pseudo Jonathan* |

# List of Abbreviations

Quran

| | |
|---|---|
| Rashi | Solomon b. Isaac, *Commentary on the Torah* |
| Rosenzweig | F. Rosenzweig, *Briefe* (Letters) (Berlin, 1935) |
| Saadiah | Saadiah b. Joseph, *The Book of Beliefs and Opinions*, trans. S. Rosenblatt (New Haven, 1948) |
| Sifre Deut. | *Midrash Sifre on Deuteronomy* |
| Sifre Num. | *Midrash Sifre on Numbers* |
| Silver | A. H. Silver, *Moses and the Original Torah* (New York, 1961) |
| *Som.* | Philo, *De Somniis*, trans, F. H. Coulson (Harvard, 1935) |
| Stern | M. Stern, *Greek and Latin Authors on Jews and Judiasm*, vol. 1 (Jerusalem, 1971) |
| Tan. | *Midrash Tanhumma* |
| *Vir.* | Philo, *De Virtutibus* (On virtue) |
| Weinberg | L. Weinberg, "The Death of Moses in the Synagogue Liturgy" (Ph.D. diss., 1963) |
| *Zohar* | *The Zohar* |

# Index

Aaron, 8; priestly interpolations enhancing rank of, 10–11; priests claim descent from, 19; on Sinai, 164; spokesman for Moses, 103, 286; wife of, 239–40

Abarbanel, Isaac, 303–4

Abihu, 164

Abiram, 20, 204, 209, 219

Abisha scroll (Samaritan Torah), 149

Abraham, 126, 127, 231, 242

Absalom, rebellion of, 23

Acts, book of, 138

Adam, 231, 273

*Aegyptiaca* (Hecateus), 54–55

Aelian (Roman zoologist), 80

*aggadah*, 127; Artapanus, 76–77; creation of, 61–62; desacralization of, 199–200; on Hebrew education of Moses, 145; as imaginative literature, 196–97; Josephus', 75–76; in *Midrash*, 202; on *Moshe Rabbenu*, 197; on secret tradition, 188; in Talmud, 202

agnosticism, scholarly, 294

Akhenaten, reformation of, 299

Akiba, 186, 314–15

Akkad, 6

Alexander the Great, 49

Alexandria: anti-Jewish riots in, 58; construction of, 49; priests in, 109; racial prejudice in, 65; success of, 50

alphabet, 67

Amalekites, 274

Amarna, 47

Amaziah, 35

Amenophis (nineteenth dynasty pharaoh), 52, 57, 59

Amos, 103

Amram, 8; remarriage of, 203, 205–6

Angel of Death, 148, 212, 214–15, 250–51

Angel of the Presence (Metatron), 175; as Moses' Virgil, 179–80

angels, 127; role in Sinai revelation, 175–76; treason of, 128

Apion, 59–60

apocalypse, 172; Moses as mediator of, 264

# Index

# Index

# Index

esoteric tradition, 264; public revelation of, 267
ethical standards of Hellenized Jews, 63–65
etymology of Moses' name, 12
Eupolemus, 66, 68, 83; *On the Kings of Judah*, 67
Eusebius of Caesarea, 67–69
Excalibur, 207
Exodus, 15, 37; "accurate" version of, 60; dating of, 47; lack of contemporary reference to, 3; Manetho's version of, 56–58; polemic around, 56; retelling of, 52–59, 153
Exodus, book of, 9, 17, 21, 28, 41; God's attributes listed in, 63; legal sections of, 174
Exodus generation, 145
Ezekiel, book of: opening chapters, 215; vision in, 264
Ezekiel (playwright), 53; disencumbering Moses of black wife, 65–66; *Esagoge* (Exodus), 67–68; on Moses' wizardry, 70
Ezra, 243; and Targum, 200

faith, 36–37
*famalia shel ma'alah* (celestial family), 128
Fast, Howard, 92
Fleg, Edmund, *The Life of Moses*, 301
*Fountain of Wisdom, The*, 282
Frankel, Zacharias, 306
Freud, Sigmund, *Moses and Monotheism*, 63, 142
fundamentalism, *viii*

*galut*, 222
Gaon Saadiah b. Joseph, 97
Garden of Eden, 281
Gaster, Moses: *The Exempla of the Rabbis*, 301; on *Revelation of Moses*, 180–81
Gautama, 178
*Gedulat Moshe* (Midrash), 180
*Gemara*, 201
geneology, 8–9
Genesis, 17
Geonim, 199
Gerizim, Mount, 149
Gershon, 20
Gilgal, 170
*Gilluy Shekinah*, 181, 278
Ginsberg, Louis, 146, 161, 172, 174, 177, 180; *Legends of the Jews*, *viii*, 301–2
God: choosing Moses as prophet, 9–10; communion with, 178, 215; crowded court of, 127–28; dependable and caring, 300; direction of Moses by, 22–27; Hellenized Jews' conception of, 63; as hero, 14; Immanence of, 181; Instructions of, 129, 170; man's control over, 268–69, 271, 273; Moses' ascent to, 117; Moses' intercession with, 38–40, 274–75; Moses' relationship with as mating, 279–80; name(s) of, 71, 72, 211–13, 274–75; palace of, 174; presence of (*Shiur Komah*), 215; protective power of, 35; redeeming power of, 27–32, 41–43; return to instructions of, 94; on Sinai, 166–67; speech of, 271; taboo against using name

324

# Index

of, 171; Throne of, 177–78; transcendent, 112, 175

Golden Calf, 8, 35, 226, 273; explanations of, 225; as replacement for Moses, 268

Goliath, 6

Gospel: of John, 140; of Matthew, 137

Graetz, Heinrich, "An introduction to History," 306–7

*Great Men and Moments in Israel* (Kittel), 4–5

Gregory of Nyssa, *Life of Moses*, 117–18

Gressman, Hugo, *Mose und Seine Zeit*, 295

*Guide of the Perplexed, The,* (Maimonides), 95; translated into Hebrew, 252

Ha-Am, Ahad, 311; *At the Parting of the Ways*, 289–92

*Hag* (festival), 161

*Haggadah*, 42

*halacha*, 195

Ha Levi, Judah, 245–46

Haman, 216

Hardaniel (angel), 177

Harizi, al-, Judah, *The Tahkemoni*, 252

Haskalah, 293

*Haskamah*, 96

Heaven: gates of, 214; Moses' ascent to, 174–75; Moses' second ascent to, 241–15; Moses' tours of, 179–81; war in, 272

Heber, 124, 252–53

Hebrew: in Greco-Roman era, 200; Maimonides translated into, 252

Hecateus of Abdera, *Aegyptiaca*, 54–55

*Hechalot* (Palace Literature), 181, 264, 269

Heliopolis: Imhotep-Asklepios' shrine at, 82; Onias' temple in, 85–87; Osiris worshipped at, 57–58

Hell, 180

Hellenistic world, 50–51

Hermes-Thoth, *see* Thoth-Hermes

Hermes-Trismegistus, 84

hero: community leader (*sophos*) as, 51; conventional, 23; diminished, 3–43; God as, 14; Hellenistic attitude toward, 50–52; and hero worship, *ix*; imagined, 5; as intercessor, 40; magical and esoteric, 72; natural desire for, 163; praise of, 101; without name, 13; *see also* religious heroes

Herod, 137

Herzfeld, Ernst, 296

Herzl, Theodore, *Diary*, 300–1

*hesed* (covenant loyalty), 40

Hezekiah, 196

Hillel, 186

Hirsch, Samson Raphael, 306

Hirsch, Samuel, 306

historical reconstructions, 15–16

historical writing, 40–41

history: great men and, 289–90; and the Haskalah, 293

Holmes, Sherlock, 74

holy man: courage of, 34–36, 39–40; Moses as, 37–40,

# Index

# Index

Joshua, 4, 223; changeableness of, 284; investiture of, 172, 249–50, 256, 264; Name of God imparted to, 213; scroll of, 169; on Sinai, 164; as a soldier, 272; transformation of, 185

Joshua b. Korha, 241–42

*Journal of Jewish Law, The, xii*

*Jubilees* (Palestinian text), 62, 63, 173–76; as Torah, 173–74

Judaism, 18–19; absence of dogmas in, 295; adaptation of, 129; asceticism in, 219–20; attempts to separate Moses from, 141–42; commitment to monotheism, 217, 237; emergence of, 165–66; mystical tradition of, 163–65; and myth of all-encompassing revelation, 168; orthodox (*see* orthodox Judaism); Pharisees' reshaping of, 184–85; postexilic, 132; as process, 293; and prophecy, 131–32; rabbinic (*see* rabbinic tradition); river metaphor for, 310–11; stand against idolatry, 81, 87; tree metaphor for, 309–10; varied descriptions of, 306–7; worth of questioned, 63

Judean rebellion, 189

Judges, 20, 41

Kabbalah: dispersal of, 267; least subversive of mystical traditions, 277–78; Moses and, 263–86; and redemption, 267–68; Torah commentary of, 270–72

*kabbalah ma'asit*, 264

Kanisat Musa (synagogue), 248

Karaites, 183; Oral Torah rejected by, 199

*kavannah*, 271, 274

*Kavod* (Glory), 264

Kenuel (angel), 176–77

Khadir, al-, 235–36

Khrushchev, Nikita, 27

Kings, 41

Kittel, Rudolf, 13–14; *Great Men and Movements in Israel*, 4–5

Kohath, 8

Kook, Abraham Isaac Hacohen, 304–6; *Zironim*, 305

Korah, 8; rebellion of, 23

Lagash, 6

l' Arabi, Ibnu, 258

law: early scroll of, 169; Islamic, 236–37; Moses', 143–44; oral, 182–89; Torah's origin in, 165; universal value of Moses', 68

*Legends of the Jews* (Ginsberg), *viii*

Leo Baeck College, *xii*

Leontopolis, 85–87

Levi, 8

Levi (tribe of), 8, 285; rebellious members of, 9

Leviticus, 17, 28, 41, 111

libido, 111

*Life of Moses, The* (Fleg), 301

*Life of Moses* (Gregory of Nyssa), 117–18

*Life of Moses* (Philo Judaeus), 99–117

limbo (*galut*), 222

# Index

literature: apocalyptic, 172; at core of rabbinic education, 200; Jewish (see Jewish literature); Palace, 181; rabbinic (see rabbinic tradition); rabbinic suspicion of, 94

liturgy, 147; early, 28–32; Torah's origin in, 165

Long March (Mao Zedong), 16

Lourdes, 82

Luther, Martin, 143

Lycurgus, 56

Lysimachus, 52, 58–59

Ma'aseh Bereshit, 187, 215

Ma'aseh Merkavah, 187, 215

Ma'at, 84

magical powers, 195–96, 210–13; and miracles, 224

Maimon b. Joseph, 254–58

Maimonides, Moses, 121, 243; Commentary on the Mishna, 252; The Guide of the Perplexed, 95, 252; on Moses' prophecy, 244, 247

Making of the President, The (White), x

malach (angel), 127

Malachi, scroll of, 153

Manetho, 52, 66; attacks on Jews, 56, 78; Egyptian History, 56–58

manna, 218

Mao Zedong, 16

Mariolarity, 309

Markah, 150–51

Mattan Torah, 165, 181

Matthew, 137, 140

Mazdaism, 127, 199, 229

mazzal (sign), 123

Meir, R., 115–16

Memphis: necropolis of, 82–83; ruins of, 248

Mercenaries, Jewish, 48

Merlin, 209, 223

Meroe, 76–77

Mesah b. Arzi, 122

messianism: Christian, 142–44; and Moses, 255–58, 291; rabbinic, 152–55; Samaritan, 148–52

Meyer, Eduard, Die Mose Sagen und die Lewiten, 293–94

Michelangelo, 140

Midian: battle against, 244; Moses in, 104

Midrash, 96, 180; aggadot in, 202; biography absent from, 92; Ha-Am's essay as, 292; and Impressionism, 298; and Moses of each generation, 294; uses of, 306

Midrash Petirat Moshe, 249

miracles, 237–38; and magic, 224

Miriam, 8, 203; leprosy of, 39, 84

Mishnah, 201, 281–82

Mohammed, 97, 122, 265; Balaam as stand-in for, 245; as caliph-prophet, 231, 239; death of, 249; miraculous tales about, 238–39; Moses and, 229–59

monotheism, 170; Judaism's commitment to, 217, 237; popularity of, 78

morality: Biblical, 110–11; and censorship, 96; Hellenistic, 111–12; and magical powers, 195

Mordecai, 216

# Index

Moses: Aaron as spokesman for, 103, 286; absent from *Haggadah*, 42; at academy of Akiba, 186; accepted biography of, 188; accomplishments of, 32–33; adopted into Jethro's tribe, 7; and Angel of Death, 148, 212, 214–15; apocalyptic wisdom of, 264; asking God's name, 275; assassination plot against, 77–78; at the battlefield, 34, 274; Bible reports of, 4–5; as biographical subject, 91–92; birth story of, 24; burial of, 20; career reshaped by Hellenized Jews, 60–61; Chaeremon's attacks on, 59; chant of, 29; and circumcision, 78; as commander-in-chief of Egypt's armed forces, x, 75–77, 79, 208; of communities through history, 308; created in image of Jewish people, 290; death of, 11, 169–70, 215, 248–52; as "divine man," 114–15; dream of, 67–68; earliest description of, 53; editorial treatment of, 19–43; education of, 62–63, 145; Egyptian perspective on, 47; Egyptian taskmaster killed by, 11, 25, 26, 103–4, 195–96, 204, 219, 233, 290; and Elijah, 153–55; entering Heaven, 176–77; entry into public life, 25–27; as ethical model, 63–65; eulogy of, 34, 149; existentialist attitudes toward, 295; faith of, 36–37; familiarity of, xi; as father of civilization, 66–69; fig leaf descriptions of 66; as foun-der and lawmaker of Jerusalem, 54–55; four choices of, 311–14; frescoes depicting, 53–54; geneology of, 8–9; as God's servant, 15, 21–22, 27–28; in heaven, 127; Hellenized portrayal of, 50–55; as high priest, 109–10; historical, 295; as holy man, 37–40; ideal of, 292; identification with Torah, 17–18; intercessions of, 38–40, 274–75; interpretation of Torah by, 315; Jewish heritage denied, 141–42; Josephus's eulogy of, 51–52; and Kabbalah, 263–86; as king, 239–42; lack of physical images of, 6, 9; law of (*see* Torah); Lysimachus's attacks on, 58–59; major accomplishment of, 16; marriage of, 25; married to black wife, 65–66, 79–80; messianic role of, 152–55, 255–58, 291; of Michelangelo, 140; in Midian, 104, 284; in the modern mind, 289–315; and Mohammed, 229–59; multiple names of, 124; and Musaeus, 83; name of shortened, 11–13; passing prophetic authority to Jesus, 140; Philo's biography of, 99–117; oratory of, 10, 32–34; as philosopher-king, 116; power over God, 269; praised in Kabbalah, 278; predictive oracles of, 172; promise of second, 133–36; Quran's biography of, 232–35; reincarnation of, 291; relationship with God as mating, 279–80; as religious pioneer, 299–300; rod of, 27, 204;

# Index

Moses (*continued*)
212–13; role in the Torah, *x, xii*; as *Safrah Rabbah b'Yisroel*, 97; scribal activities of, 242–43; second, 133–47; sex life of, 23; shrine of, 73–74, 81, 85–87; on Sinai, 107–8, 165; sin of, 37; as sole prophet, 150–52; sons of, 20; as spiritual master, 181; submission of, 313–14; taboo against naming after, 121–28; and Thoth-Hermes, 83–84; tongue-tied image of, 9–10, 285–86; transcending experience of, 297; transformation into *Moshe Rabbenu*, 216–17; unique position of, 131–33; valedictory speeches of, 146, 172; various lives of, *viii, x–xi*; as vital, dynamic leader, 13–14; as wizard, 70–72

*Moses* (Asch), 91, 301

*Moses* (Buber), 296

*Moses and Monotheism* (Freud), 63, 142

*Moshe Rabbenu*, 97, 193–226, 301; *aggadah's* approach to, 197; as aristocrat, 220; ascents to Heaven, 214–15; celibacy of, 220; death of, 215, 226; early life of, 203–5; failings of, 225; as holy man, 209–10; magical powers of, 195–96, 210–13; 223–24; as role model, 226; as scholar, 220–21: semi-divine nature of, 216, 222–23

Musaeus, 83

*Mystere D'Adam, Le*, 142–43

mystical tradition, 215, 239; Biblical roots of, 263–64; celibacy

and denial in, 284; Kabbalah least subversive of, 277–78; light metaphors of, 270–71; privacy and, 276–77; sexual imagery in, 278–80

myth: of all-encompassing revelation, 168, 193; of personal salvation, 216; West Asian, 160

Nadav, 164

Nahman, Samuel b., 186

Nahmanides, 134, 243, 266, 270, 283, 284–85; on Golden Calf, 268; on Moses' intercession, 274–75

name(s) of God, 71–72, 211–13, 275; spoken during blessing, 274

naming, 121–24, 258–59

*Natural History* (Pliny the Elder), 71

*Neofiti* (Targum), 201

New Testament, 229; Moses in, 136–37, 293

Noah, 231

Noth, Martin, 294

Nubia, Moses' campaign in, 75–80

Numbers, Book of, 17, 21, 28, 41, 65

Onias IV, 85–87

*On the Jews* (Artapanus), 53

oral tradition: fidelity of, 3; *see also* Torah, oral

oratory, Moses', 10, 32–34

# Index

# Index

rabbi: role in Talmudic times, 194–95; separation from holy men, 265

rabbinic literature, 93–94; and censorship, 96; on immutability of Torah, 128

rabbinic tradition, 87; biography lacking in, 92–93; constancy prized in, 130; esoteric knowledge of, 187; flexibility of, 302; and hero worship, *ix*; human development in, 92–93; learning in, 116; messianic drama in, 152–55; naming in, 126; and rabbinism, 197–98; study limited by, 94–95, 97

rabbinism, 197–98

racial prejudice: in Alexandria, 65–66; of early Church, 141

Ramesses II, 4, 47

Rappoport, Angelo, *Myth and Legend of Ancient Israel*, 301

Rashi (medieval Talmudist), 218–26

Rav (Babylonian Talmudist), 200

redemption, 27–32, 41–43; Kabbalah and, 266–68, 273; Moses' role in, 179

religion: and need for order, *viii*; purpose of, 40 shift in interest in, 216

religious heroes, *ix*

religious tradition: continuities within, *vii–viii*; as living entity, 307–8; river metaphor for, 310–11

revelation: all-encompassing, 168, 230; angels' role in, 176–77; mechanics of, 175

*Revelation of Moses*, 180–81

Rosenzweig, Franz, 295–96

Saadiah b. Joseph, *The Book of Beliefs and Opinions*, 237

Sadducees, 183

saga(s): of David, 22–24; embellishment of, 19; as literary elaboration, 296

sage(s), 132, 305; and Joshua's forgetfulness, 185; Moses called *Rabbenu* by, 194

Saint Catherine's Monastery, 159–60

Sakkara North (necropolis of Memphis), 82–83

salvation, 216

Samaritans, 148–52; origin of, 149

Sandalfon (angel), 177

Sanoah, 124

Sargon, 19

Satan, 216; autonomy of, 127; temptation of Moses by, 233–34; treason of, 128

Schechem, 170

Scripture: importance of geneology in, 9; lack of physical description in, 6; and prophecy, 131–32; values read into, *vii–viii*

Second Commandment, 125

Second Temple Period: apocalyptics in, 264; blessing during, 274

*seder*, 42

*sefarim hitzonim*, 96

*Sefer ha-Shearim* (Book of Gates), 282

*sefirot* (emanations), 270, 272

# Index

Serapis, 70

Sermon on the Mount, 137

Sesostoris, 69

Seth (devil god), 56, 60

*Shariyah* (Islamic law), 236–37

*shefa* (divine speech), 271

Shekinah (Immanent Presence), 268, 271–72; as bride, 279–80

Shelomit, 219

Shiloh, 162

*Shiur Komah*, 269

shrine(s): at Elephantine, 49, 81–82; of Moses, 73–74, 81, 85–87; unification of, 170

Silver, Abba Hillel, *Moses and the Original Torah*, 298–300

Simeon, 170

Simhat Torah, 248–51

Simlai (Talmudist), 148

Simon bar Yohai, 282

Simon Magus, 152

Sinai, Mount: angels' role on, 175–76; location of, 159–62; Moses' ascents of, 107–8; Moses' ascent to Heaven from, 174–75; Moses' authority transferred on, 140; oral Torah received on, 182–83; and promethean drama, 178–79; reliability of revelation on, 166; Torah vague on details of, 163–65

Socho, 124

Solomon, and Queen of Sheba, 65

Solon, 56

*Song of Songs*, 65

soul: ascension of, 177–78; of communities, 308; divine, 175; of the generations, 294; transmigration of, 125

speech: Moses' impediment, 9–10, 285–86; as primal substance, 271

staff: Moses', 27; as sign of the wizard, 70

Stalin, Josef, 27

Stephen, 138–40

Stern, Menahem, 57–58, 71

Stoicism, 100–1

study: as discipline of piety, 95; limitation of, 94

Sufis, 239, 258

Sumer, 6

superstition, 70

synagogue practice, 309; in Talmudic period, 217

Syrus, Saint Ephraem, 142

tablets: inscription of, 166; of sapphire crystal, 168; in *Zohar*, 281

taboo: against using God's name, 171; against using Moses' name, 121–28

*Taheb* (Samaritan messiah), 152

Talmud, 96; Babylonian, 98, 202; biography absent from, 92; on celestial family, 128; *Gemara*, 201; *Mishnah*, 201; Palestinian, 202

Talmudic period, 95; idolatry in, 203; synagogue practice and popular prayer during, 217

*Talmud Torah* (Torah learning), 94–95

Targum (translation): development of, 201; origin of, 200–1

*Targum Onkelos*, 201

*Targum Yerushlami I* (Pseudo Jonathan), 201, 211, 240

# Index

# Index

*Torat Moshe* (Torah of Moses), 171, 294

transcendence, 111–12, 215; need for, 166; of Original Sin, 144

transfiguration: Matthew's vision of, 140; Paul's rewriting of, 144

translation: of Maimonides, 252; of Torah, 60, 62–63, 112; *see also* Targum

transmigration of souls, 125

Tree of Knowledge, 281

Tree of Life, 281

truth: appropriate to time and place, 315; keepers of, 148; way of, 281

Tutenkhamen, 47

Untermeyer, Louis, 92, 301

veil, Moses', 144

Versailles, 5

Vespasian, 85

virtue: absolute standard of, 112–13; Moses', 102, 104–5; sermons on, 63–65

Volz, Paul, *Mose*, 295

Wagner, Richard, 13

Weimar Republic, 5, 13

Weinberg, L., 251, 255

White, Theodore, *xi*; *The Making of the President*, *x*

Work of the Chariot, 215

YHVH (Tetragrammaton), 212; taboo against use of, 171; translation of, 62

*Yigdal*, 129

Yohanan, R., 185

Zagzagel (angel), 205

Zionism: cultural, 289; political, 301

Zipporah, 8–9, 204–5, 291; on stage, 66

*Zohar* ("bible" of Kabbalists), 272, 281, 284; on Israel's deliverance, 283; pseudonymous author of, 282; sexual imagery in, 279–80

Zoroastrianism, *see* Mazdaism

Zoser (early pharaoh), 69, 82

**Temple Israel**
Minneapolis, Minnesota

IN MEMORY OF
SAMUEL & JEANNETTE PADDEN
FROM
MARK LUTHER